T0347153

WORKING EQUAL

RoutledgeFalmer Studies in Higher Education
Volume 25

ROUTLEDGEFALMER STUDIES IN HIGHER EDUCATION
This series is published in cooperation with the Program in Higher Education,
School of Education, Boston College, Chestnut Hill, Massachusetts.
Philip G. Altbach, *Series Editor*

Working Equal

Academic Couples as Collaborators

ELIZABETH G. CREAMER AND ASSOCIATES

ROUTLEDGEFALMER
NEW YORK   LONDON

Published in 2001 by
RoutledgeFalmer
29 West 35th Street
New York, NY 10001

Published in Great Britain by
RoutledgeFalmer
11 New Fetter Lane
London EC4P 4EE

RoutledgeFalmer is an imprint of the Taylor & Francis Group.

10 9 8 7 6 5 4 3 2 1

Library of Congress Cataloging-in-Publication Data

Creamer, Elizabeth G.
  Working equal : academic couples as collaborators / Elizabeth G. Creamer and associates.
    p. cm. – (RoutledgeFalmer studies in higher education)
  Includes bibliographical references and index.
  ISBN 0-8153-3544-X (alk. paper) – ISBN 0-8153-3545-8 (pbk. : alk. paper)
    1. Academic couples–Professional relationships –United States. 2. College
  teachers–Research–United States. I. Title. II. Series.

LB1778.45 .C74 2001
378.1'2–dc21

CONTENTS

Preface

I begin this book at the same place I began my first book about faculty publishing productivity. That is, with the confession that I have always been fascinated with writers—the desks they use, the schedules they keep, their habits of mind, how they organize their lives to make time for writing, how exactly it is they do it.

This book, too, is about how faculty today craft lives in the service of scholarship. In particular, it is about what I believe is a new generation of faculty who have joined forces to work collaboratively with a spouse or partner who is also an academic. They illustrate the many ways academic couples work together. Now reaching seniority in American colleges and universities, this is a group of people who entered adulthood in the 1970s, just as attitudes toward women, work, and families were undergoing revolutionary changes. It is a group of people who have created lives with little division between their personal and professional lives or between the personal and professional aspects of their relationships.

I have a spouse who is also an academic and who, like me, is deeply engaged in both our relationship and his work. Our own collaborative efforts during the early days of our marriage in the mid-1980s produced some scholarship that is still recognized, but the collaboration ended when battles over authorial voice began to threaten our personal relationship. Over time I have come to realize that my admiration for the couples I describe in this book has much to do with my own struggle to craft a mutually enriching working and personal life with my husband. It is a struggle that, I am confident, is shared by many couples in many settings and occupations.

A whole spectrum of events intervene between the conception of a project such as this and its completion. Chapter authors become engaged in other projects. Family members become critically ill. Careers and jobs change. The couple I presented in one of the cases separated between when I interviewed them and the publication of the manuscript. Such events add to the magnitude of the task any writer undertakes when he or she sets out to write a book and to the awe that one feels on its completion.

It is customary to sprinkle a preface with acknowledgments of the many people who helped to make this work possible. Above all, I am deeply indebted to the generosity of my case participants, both in the time they gave me and in their willingness to share their stories with an unfamiliar audience. Their trust and confidence in me to represent them authentically is something I treasure.

WORKING EQUAL

Introduction

I think that it is not so much quantity. That isn't the case. I probably would have published just as much. I think it has made me more innovative. It has made it easier for me to continue to grow and to step outside a conventional data analysis paradigm that I would use from my discipline. *–Woman, Professor, Sociologist*

Parallel to the dramatic growth in the presence of dual-career couples in most sectors of employment in the United States is the emergence of dual-career academic couples in higher education since the 1970s. Academic partners are a subset of dual-career couples who are in the same profession, if not necessarily in the same type of position, in the same academic field or working at the same institution. Although among faculty women are less likely than men to be married,[1] a significant number of both men and women faculty have a spouse or partner who is also an academic. In 1988, more than one-third of men and 40 percent women faculty and administrators had a spouse or partner who is also in higher education.[2] Marianne Ferber's and Jane Loeb's *Academic Couples: Problems and Promises* (1997) is the first book to mark this growing trend.[3]

Faculty productivity is a term that encompasses teaching, service, and outreach. Scholarly or research productivity refers to a wide range of activities that advance knowledge and contribute to the arts.[4] Scholarly publications, particularly those that appear in prestigious outlets such as refereed journals and university presses, are central to the faculty reward structure. Kathryn Ward and Linda Grant reflect on the centrality of publications in the academic reward structure when they observe:

> Given current social relationships and American universities, publication not only makes or breaks individual academic careers, but

3

it also creates and re-creates the content of academic disciplines. The study of academic publication processes therefore belongs at the center, rather than the periphery of contemporary scholarly research, particularly research aimed at illuminating equity issues.[5]

Studying the lives of academic couples makes clear that personal relationships and the social and material conditions in the domestic setting also impact scholarly productivity.[6]

Working Equal is about academic couples who have collaborated together in the production of scholarship.[7] My interest in the topic emerged from interviews I conducted between 1992 and 1996 with highly productive women scholars. During these interviews, I was surprised by how often faculty women introduced the role of a spouse, including as a collaborator, as one of the factors that contributed to their ability to be productive as a scholar.

As the book's title suggests, I grew to consider many of these contemporary partnerships to be egalitarian in character. The egalitarianism was evident in the interchangeable, non-sex-based[8] roles assumed in collaborative projects, in expressions of mutuality, and in comparable priority awarded to each member's professional goals. It was often articulated in a shared worldview. These couples challenge the assumption that family responsibilities interfere with career achievement.

The information presented in *Working Equal* came from a number of sources. Each of the women in the partnerships presented in the case narratives responded to a national survey about collaboration, including with a spouse or partner, that I conducted in 1996. They were among a carefully selected matched sample of 750 senior faculty at research universities targeted to identify prolific scholarly writers. I conducted individual interviews with 14 of the 28 prolific survey respondents who had coauthored with a spouse, with the spouse or partner of seven of them, as well as with twelve additional faculty who were identified through a snowball sampling technique. From this sample of 33 academics, I wrote case narratives for four couples, selecting three to present in this book. A description of how the case narratives were constructed is presented in the next chapter.

A detailed description of the characteristics of the survey respondents and interview participants is presented in Appendices A, B, and C. The data presented in the appendices support a central point reiterated throughout this volume: that point is that while the faculty members presented in the case narratives may in some ways be exceptional, they are not isolated examples. It is my argument that scholarly collaboration is not unusual among academic couples. I believe that as the number of women receiving advanced degrees continues to expand, even in academic areas where they have been historically absent, the familial arrangements I depict in the case narratives will become even more prevalent than they are now.

At least one member of each of the academic pairs I studied qualified as a prolific scholarly writer by virtue of the number of publications produced over the course of a career.[9] Prolific scholars are a small group of senior scholars, generally located at research universities, who have sustained an interest in research and publication over decades. Because they produce a disproportionate percentage of the publications in a field,[10] they are major actors in shaping the dominant theoretical and methodological paradigms in an academic field. Historically, women have been woefully underrepresented among the ranks of the prolific.[11] Examining the daily lives of highly productive and prolific women writers provides an opportunity to scrutinize the material and social conditions that have historically blocked women from entry to this elite group.

A by-product of any study of prolific scholars is that the publication level required serves to delineate a population that is both elite and relatively homogenous.[12] For decades, this population has been almost exclusively white men in the senior ranks of faculty at research universities, whose experiences are not representative of faculty as a whole. The painfully small numbers of nonwhites among senior faculty at research universities and the criterion I used for publication level severely limited the number of minority faculty members who qualified to participate in the study. Although only heterosexual pairs who are domestic partners are presented in the case narratives, it not my intention to reify heterosexual relationships or to suggest that there is anything sacrosanct about the heterosexual bond in terms of productivity or creativity. Findings that same-sex couples are more likely than heterosexual couples to have egalitarian relationships[13] suggests, on the contrary, that relationships with mutual career benefit are even more likely among this population.

An unanticipated consequence of studying academic couples who have collaborated together is that it shifts the focus of study from conventional work settings to the household. Rather than professional conferences or campus offices, laboratories, or conference rooms, these couples described the work-related activities they accomplished in their home. One of the ways members of the faculty couples who participated in this research project accommodated a strong commitment to a personal relationship and a demanding career was by relocating the setting of some of their work to the home and by collaborating with a partner on scholarly projects. Advances in technology are part of the changing nature of workplace that have offered some faculty more freedom to accomplish their work away from the traditional work setting.[14]

Analysis of how members of these couples manage to sustain productivity suggests, as did Arlie Hochschild in her book *The Time Bind*,[15] that social change is not necessarily occurring because the workplace is being fundamentally redesigned to accommodate the needs of dual-career couples. The experiences of faculty couples in this study suggest that the more profound social change that is occurring is reengineering the nature of family life to accommodate the demands of two members with a comparable commitment to career success.

Contribution to the Literature

Coauthorship is the most frequent topic of research about collaboration.[16] Dickens and Sagaria (1997) identified intimate collaborators as one of four relationship patterns among coauthors, observing that this collaborative pattern "has been invisible and undocumented in published work."[17] These relationships are characterized by both emotional and intellectual intimacy.[18] When the family is analyzed as a collaborative unit, married couples are only one of many possible configurations. Studying the personal element of collaborative relationships adds consideration of the affective dimension that has been inaccessible by traditional quantitative research methods.[19]

The literature about couples crosses a number of disciplines, including family studies, sociology, the history of science, and humanities. Historical biographies of couples use personal papers, diaries, correspondence, and the recollections of friends and relatives to re-create the contribution of personal, familial, and collegial relationships to the creative process. Authors of these works generally present them as a challenge to cultural Western myths about singular achievement, heroic individualism, and solitary genius and the implicit assumption that these are largely male qualities. Individual accomplishments are contextualized to recognize the social nature of creativity and achievement and the support supplied by significant others and a community of colleagues.

Intimate domestic partners are sometimes part of the social and material conditions that enable or constrain the creative or intellectual life. Varying by personality and context, partners have played a wide range of roles that contribute to productivity: muse, patron, audience, publicist or promoter, protector, foil, editor, archivist, coproducer, and nurturer or enabler. An influential spouse can provide access to intellectual circles not historically open to women, particularly unmarried women.[20] A spouse or partner can provide a readily accessible source of community for academics who are otherwise isolated from like-minded colleagues because of their race, sexual orientation, gender, or the marginalization of their scholarly interests.

Several portraits in the literature explore the relationships of visual artists, such as the painters Diego River and Frida Kahlo[21] or Georgia O'Keeffe and Alfred Stieglitz,[22] or of writers, such as George Eliot and George Henry Lewes.[23] Couples are more likely to be studied for their reciprocal influence on the content of each other's work than for actually coproducing work. Scientists, such as academics in a variety of fields in the social sciences and the physical and biological sciences, offer the opportunity to explore examples of couples who have jointly produced work.

The benefits of heterosexual life partnerships are most frequently presented in the literature as one-sided rather than reciprocal. Paralleling the implicit assumption of a hierarchical arrangement within heterosexual relationships, one spouse is usually cast in a supporting role as the nurturer or enabler who helps to create an environment that is conducive to the partner's work. This is the case, for example, in the narrative portraits of the relationship of five Victorian couples presented in Phyllis Rose's 1984 work, *Parallel Lives*. Most typically, it is the male who is portrayed as benefiting from the invisible labor of a spouse or partner and the woman who is cast in the role of invisible "other."[24] Less frequently, a woman might be the beneficiary of collaboration with a partner through role reversal. Rose illustrates this pattern through a description of the relationship between the poet Elizabeth Barrett and her husband Robert Browning. This pattern is also manifested, according to Rose, in some same-sex relationships among historically prominent figures, such as the wifelike role assumed by Alice B. Toklas in relation to Gertrude Stein.[25]

Marriage among scientists has been of interest to feminist historians of science because it has been a vehicle some women have employed to gain access to scientific careers.[26] Perhaps to compensate for the social stigma of deviating from conventional norms of femininity, a very high proportion of women scientists in such fields as physics and biochemistry have a spouse who is also a scientist.[27] Pnina Abir-Am and Dorinda

Outram argue that while the exclusion of women from science is not an intentional strategy, it is a by-product of exclusion of the domestic arena. They note that the literature has: "totally overlooked the possibility that the gender structure of modern science, with its massive underrepresentation of women, comes not so much from the exclusion of women from science, but rather from the exclusion of the domestic realm from science, and the incidental concomitant exclusion of women."[28]

Through the early 1900s, most scientific work was done at home and often involved family members.[29] This continues to be the case with many other kinds of workers, including writers, visual and material artists, and others who work from offices and studios in their homes. Overlooking the domestic setting contributes to the erasure of women's contribution to science. It reduces the work women accomplish in that realm to that which is domestic, sexual, or reproductive, and minimizes work that contributes to production.

While most authors have focused on the constraints of intimate relationships, others have celebrated the diversity within these relationships and pointed to the potential for mutuality. Relatively egalitarian relationships are one of four patterns identified in a historical study of creative couples in the sciences.[30] Without necessarily transgressing socially acceptable masculine and feminine roles, some couples have managed to reshape the traditional terms of these partnerships.[31] What is instructive is not how people, particularly women, have been victimized by such relationships, but how members of some couples have been able to negotiate creative alternatives to traditional configurations and to present new models of creative partnerships.[32] bell hooks calls for the importance of alternative models for personal relationships:

> Feminist activists need to affirm the importance of family as a kinship structure that can sustain and nourish people; to graphically address links between sexist oppression and family disintegration; and to give examples, both actual and visionary, of the way family life is and can be when unjust authoritarian rule is replaced by an ethic of communalism, shared responsibility and mutuality.[33]

The literature about couples in the sciences and the arts underscores a number of important points that are central to this book. One is that for people whose work is central to their identity, the demarcation between the private and public spheres not only is artificial but also may serve to reinforce the marginalization of women's contributions. Shifting the focus from individual academics to collaborative accomplishments among academics also relocates the settings where that work might be accomplished. Second, that while historically, social conventions about sex-appropriate male and female roles, as well as the traditional, patriarchal ideology of marriage, have presented most intimate relationships as being largely one-sided in their benefits, the academic couples presented suggest that these relationships can be characterized by mutuality. Because of sensitivity to power relationships and the potential for exploitation, women may be especially drawn to working and personal relationships that are nonhierarchical.[34]

Audience

The book addresses the interests of a cross-disciplinary audience. A primary audience is policymakers at colleges and universities who are weighing the advantages and disadvantages of partner-preference hiring policies. It is also of relevance to academic administrators sensitive to the forethought required to design a work environment that nourishes sustained scholarly productivity among academics. Administrators who oversee faculty tenure and promotion practices will find the work invites dialogue about the traditional injunctions that persist in many academic fields against coauthorship and long-term collaborative partnerships.

Faculty and members of academic couples are a second major audience for the book. Academics and aspiring academics with a spouse or partner in the same profession will find insight on how highly productive scholars lead their daily lives as well as a realistic appraisal of the challenges they face. Others who are not involved in long-term intimate relationships will discover strategies scholars utilize to collaborate. Readers who have a partner who is in an entirely different occupation will learn how some faculty have found a way to accommodate a steadfast commitment to research and publication within a personal relationship and a lifestyle. How successful collaboration is accomplished is equally instructive to single faculty and to those who balance their energies between teaching and research.

Additional audiences for the book include scholars in several related academic fields. These include students of contemporary faculty life as well as those who study scholarly productivity, particularly those who focus on gender differences in the correlates of publishing productivity. They also include scholars who study collaboration and teamwork. Scholars in family studies and sociology who examine the interplay of work and family life will find the book presents an interpretation of egalitarianism among couples that is defined by occupational rather than domestic roles.

Organization of the Book

The nature of the topic and qualitative research methodology utilized demanded a somewhat original approach to the organization of *Working Equal*. The book is organized in three major parts that differ substantially from each other. The first part of the book centers on case narratives of three academic couples in different academic fields (geography, psychology, and creative writing and anthropology) who have coauthored scholarly publications. Each case narrative traces the evolution of a long-term collaborative relationship and is preceded by an introduction that sketches revealing elements of the work setting and identifies key factors associated with productivity. The case narrative is followed by a response from another academic who shares the experience of having a partner who is also an academic. The purpose of the case response is not only to illustrate further the diversity of these relationships but to add to evidence that these types of personal and intellectual partnerships are not restricted to a small scattering of idiosyncratic pairs. Case replies written by Yvonna Lincoln, Peter Magolda, and Stacey Floyd-Thomas suggest the many ways that collaboration can be manifested among couples who share overlapping interests.

The first part of the book and the phenomenological approach of the case narratives mirror a fundamental commitment of qualitative research, which is to capture the viewpoints and perspectives presented by participants as accurately and authentically as possible. The quote that introduces each narrative highlights a key theme that it embodies. The quote that opens the other chapters underscores additional themes and adds the voices of academics who participated in the research project but are not presented in the case narratives.

The second part of the book moves beyond the participants' viewpoints to add some additional voices to the conversation. The chapters tackle several controversial issues that participants were understandably guarded about pursuing, especially those related to the reception to their jointly authored work during the process of promotion. Because I wanted to offer the reader more than one analysis of the issues presented, I invited a number of other academics who have published on related topics to contribute chapters to the second part of the book. Ann Austin, Jane Loeb (coeditor with Marianne Ferber of the 1997 book *Academic Couples: Problems and Promises*), and Jeffrey Milem, Joe Sherlin, and

Laura Irwin contribute chapters that explore how collaborative relationships among life partners contribute to our understanding about how collaboration, collegial networks, and the academic reward structure impact faculty productivity. The invited chapters serve the additional purpose of offering future researchers access to a review of literature that introduces discussion of intimate partnership to the existing research literature.

The concluding chapter provides background for the argument that egalitarianism among dual-career academic couples has the potential to provide reciprocal benefits for the productivity of its members. Evidence that these relationships are not based on a hierarchical, sex-based division of labor challenges the dismissal of these relationships as insignificant to productivity as well as the assumption of the division of private and public domains so central to capitalism. It also invites questions about the duality in faculty cultures that valorize collegiality but save their most prestigious awards for individual accomplishment.

In her reply to the first case narrative in the first section of the book, Yvonna Lincoln proposes that the successful long-term collaborative relationships modeled by the academic couples may provide an archetype for other types of cross-sex collaborative relationships in which the personal component is not such a central fixture. While at first reading Lincoln's suggestion may seem innocuous, a shift from the current situation of largely same-sex writing and research partnerships and teams among scientists to a growing number of cross-sex collegial pairings has unexpectedly widespread implications for the organization of knowledge systems. The pattern of same-sex collegial working relationships is mirrored in same-sex citing patterns. These also reflect patterns of intellectual exchange and collegial networks that are sex-segregated.[35] These practices ultimately reinforce sex segregation in academic fields or topics, as well as traditional disciplinary boundaries.

Cross-sex collaborative pairings can bridge what have historically been sex-segregated areas of expertise.[36] They also foster the type of interdisciplinary teamwork that requires the integration of knowledge from multiple academic fields that is increasingly demanded of scientists today. As the quote that opens the chapter suggests, it may reflect a way of thinking and constructing knowledge that is fundamentally different from that which is done by faculty entrenched in the theoretical and methodological paradigms of a single discipline. Whether cross-sex collaborative teams advance interdisciplinary research is a promising area for future research.

Conclusion

The study of academic couples who have coauthored together shifts to the foreground the contribution of collaboration to innovation and productivity. The examples of long-term collaborative working partnerships among couples described in *Working Equal* share many qualities with long-term partnerships among colleagues who may or may not share a personal relationship. These partnerships can provide the opportunity for innovation through the interdisciplinary integration of knowledge from more than one intellectual domain or tradition. Trust, overlapping interests, and intellectual intimacy developed over time create the potential for "full collaboration" that requires consensus on all aspects of the production.[37] The relationships embodied in the case narratives challenge the academic reward structure to find new ways to reward and recognize innovation produced by teams or other types of collaborative configurations.

PART 1

The Case Narratives

2

Introduction to the Case Narratives

You just weave your work into your sense of your life together. There
is no point at which it stops. —*Woman, Professor, Higher Education*

The introductory chapter provides the context necessary to recognize
how the narratives of the personal and intellectual partnerships
among academic couples presented in *Working Equal* depart from those
previously presented in the literature. One revolutionary aspect of these
relationships is that both partners place work at the center of their lives.
Their lifestyles and, often, worldviews are shaped by a commitment to an
intermingling of their private and public lives. Focusing on the collaborative aspects of these long-term partnerships affords the opportunity to
study how overlapping interests, a strong commitment to a personal relationship, and the advantage of ongoing proximity contribute to knowledge production. The depiction of these cross-sex relationships as
egalitarian and mutually beneficial undoubtedly will be controversial,
particularly among feminist researchers.

The purpose of this chapter is to describe the research method I utilized and to explain critical decisions I made about how to present the
research findings. This explanation may be helpful to researchers search-
ing for ways to present findings about collaborative pairs, including couples. The description of the research method includes an explanation of
how the couples presented in the case narratives were selected, as well as
the rationale for how I chose to present my own voice and the voices of
the participants in the case narratives. Key characteristics of the partnerships related to publishing productivity that cross cases are listed at the
end of the chapter.

The first part of the book is organized around three case narratives.
Each narrative presents members of an academic couple who have collaborated together in their scholarly work for time periods ranging from

15

10 to 30 years. The primary purpose of the case narrative is not to trace personal biography but to investigate the phenomena of scholarly collaboration among academic couples. The case narrative traces the evolution of the couple's collaborative relationship over time and describes how its members report the experience of writing and collaborating together. It captures the rhythm of the couple's daily lives and how a ferocious intensity and a long-lived commitment to writing shape its habits and schedules. The cases embody the point that daily lives and personal relationships are a necessary context for understanding career achievement.

The cases illustrate how material and social conditions of faculty lives are associated with high, if not necessarily extraordinary, levels of productivity.[1] Social conditions are aspects of knowledge production that involve interaction with colleagues. Material conditions are resources required for knowledge production. The case narratives are not an analysis of the dynamics of the personal relationship, as has generally been the focus of the literature about couples. Nor do they serve as an intellectual biography by delineating the interactive impact of a partner on the other's theoretical or conceptual orientation. The cases provide a description of the work setting and enough details about the collaborative process to allow the reader to reach his or her own conclusions about the validity of the arguments I present about highly productive academic couples.

Although it is not sufficient to prove a theory, a case study can be used to invalidate a theory or hypothesis.[2] The case narratives provide evidence that contradicts unspoken prejudices that often confront members of an academic couple. These may be the very prejudices that explain the curious absence in the research literature in the social sciences of consideration of this particular type of collaborative configuration. These stereotypes include that one member, assumed typically to be the woman, provide lower-order tasks in collaborative work; that members of a couple are inevitably of "one mind"; and that the career success, ambitions, and identity of one member of a pair generally take a backseat to promoting or advancing the interests of the more dominant one.[3]

The three couples I present in the case narratives share several characteristics. Members of two of the three couples are in the same academic field (one pair in geography; one in psychology), while the members of the third couple are in two fields with entirely different rhetorical traditions (English and anthropology). The training and interests of the members of each of the three couples overlap in substantive ways. All of the participants presented in the cases have held faculty appointments in academic settings imbued with a "publish or perish" mentality. Two of the couples are employed in universities in the Midwest: one couple is located in the Southeast. None of the participants presented in the narratives lives in an urban area. There are no substantial differences in age among any of the pairs presented. Each of the women elected to maintain her birth names. Notably absent from the cases presented are examples of couples who are engaged or have been engaged in a long-term commuting relationship. Also absent are couples who share a faculty appointment.

Organization of the Case Narratives

Each narrative presented in the first part of the book consists of three chapters: an introduction, the narrative, and a response. The introduction to the case narrative is where I place my voice in the forefront. In it I describe what I discovered about the couple's working relationship by observing them together, seeing where they do their writing, and watching how they interacted with each other during the joint interview. The details in the setting that I chose to describe in the introduction are those that foreshadow important aspects of the case. Although I am not an ethnographer, it was my goal to use observation to understand better the dynamics of the couple's working relationship, including the distribution of power.[4] I also sought confirmation for the hypothesis of the role of egalitarianism in faculty productivity that emerged from the interview data. This topic is explored in fuller detail in the concluding chapter of this book.

The third part of each case is a case response. Each case response is written by another academic whom I invited to contribute a chapter because he or she shares the experience of collaborating with a spouse or partner who is also an academic. The case respondents are not necessarily prolific scholarly writers. The purpose of the case responses is to extend the number of examples of academic couples presented and to reveal further the diversity in these partnerships. They add insight into some configurations missing from the case narratives, including the experiences of young couples just embarking in careers as junior faculty. I asked the authors of the case responses to share their personal stories as well as to explore how their own personal experiences were similar to or differed from that presented in the case. The response attests to the verisimilitude or authenticity of the case.

Each of the case narratives pinpoints different issues that are central to illustrating the relationship between a partner in the same profession and publishing productivity. The first case narrative clearly illustrates the opportunity for long-term collaboration that can occur at the interstices of two overlapping areas of expertise. The second case narrative enlarges on the difficulty academics who collaborate, particularly with an intimate partner, face in faculty cultures that retain the highest premiums for independently produced scholarship. The third and final case describes the collaborative experience of two faculty members in different academic fields. Because the couple has children, the case also illustrates how some academics craft a lifestyle that combines a heavy investment in both work and the family.

Selecting the Cases

I interviewed 33 academics who have coauthored with a spouse and where at least one of the pair satisfied my definition of being a prolific author.[5] From these, I completed four detailed case studies and selected three to present in this book. The fourth case provided an example of a couple in the physical sciences who came of age in the 1970s and who essentially functioned as a team on all dimensions of the faculty role, including teaching, research, and outreach. I chose not to include this case because this intermingling of identities was not a common one. A fuller description of the demographics of the interview sample is presented in Appendix C.

I weighed several factors before I decided which pairs to present in the case narratives. First, I wanted to find examples that represented the experiences of couples in different academic fields so that I might explore disciplinary differences and reach a cross-disciplinary audience. In addition, I selected only couples where I felt strong rapport with both members of the couple and where both members were expansive and reflective about the collaborative experience. I interpreted the latter to reflect that this aspect of their relationship was important to both of them, rather than to only one of them. In each of the cases I selected, after completing the individual interviews, I still felt there was a great deal more to learn about their collaborative relationship. A final selection criteria was that I chose cases that each illustrated different but central issues that emerged from my study of collaborative academic couples.

The relatively high criteria for publication level that I established to qualify to participate in the study served to eliminate couples in which one or both members is just embarking on a career at a research-oriented faculty. It also removed from the sample faculty members who are in the visual or performing arts where scholarship is communicated through performances and exhibits rather than publications. The picture of these couples would be more complete with the addition of cases of same-sex collaborative partnerships. Some aspects of the experiences of minority faculty couples are discussed in the reply to the third case written by Stacey Floyd-Thomas, an African-American woman ethicist and religious scholar.

A few of the characteristics of the academic couples profiled in the case narratives are not entirely representative of the population of highly productive academics I interviewed who had coauthored with a partner in scholarly writing. For example, the couples presented in the case narratives have all been involved in very long-term collaborative partnerships. Among the participants in the study, an equal number took advantage of the unique skill supplied by a partner to collaborate in a single or relatively short-term project.[6] I did not pursue this type of collaborative relationship in a case narrative because the participants often described them in a very perfunctory manner and their contribution to innovation and career productivity is relatively straightforward.

The couples presented in the case narratives differ from the full interview sample in two additional ways. The degree of career symmetry among the couples presented in the cases is unusual for faculty couples. Only one of the couples presented in the case narratives has children, which is a smaller proportion than would be expected in the population of academic couples in the United States.

Sources of Information for the Case Narratives

I used multiple sources of information to construct the case narratives. The primary source of information came from the 8 to 10 hours I spent interviewing the members of these couples. I first interviewed each member by telephone. I subsequently interviewed them together. The two one-on-one interviews and the face-to-face joint interview resulted in a hundred or more pages of verbatim transcripts for each couple. I prepared the transcripts from a tape recording of each session.

For purposes of triangulation, the information from the interviews was supplemented by material from a number of other sources. This includes the curriculum vitae supplied by each participant, field notes I took during and after each interview and visit, informal comments participants made during my visit with them, and their comments when we met to review the transcript from the initial telephone interview. In some cases, when I thought I might gain some insight to the couple's working relationship, I read articles and/or books that one or both of them had written. All of the participants reviewed an early and final draft of the case narrative for accuracy. I incorporated their feedback in revisions. Each ultimately gave me permission to publish the narrative.

Presentation of the Case Narratives

A commitment to present the cases from the participants' viewpoints, an essential characteristic of qualitative research, is what drove the way I ultimately decided to organize the case narratives. I chose not to present the cases as the script of a three-way conversation because I found that the narrative could be understood without inserting my questions and comments. The format I chose allowed me to organize the case by topic, merging comments a participant made about a particular topic on different occasions. It did not prove necessary to divide each narrative into separate sections containing her story, his story, and their story, because topics where there were dramatic differences in interpretation among a couple were relatively rare. The reasons they offered for collaborating and how they explained the process were generally quite consistent. I believe that this unanticipated consistency between most of the partners is a by-product of the "endless conversations" Yvonna Lincoln refers to in her response to the first case, rather than an indication that one member's voice had been subsumed by the other's.

I employ several conventions in presenting the narratives. To keep the participants' voices distinct, I acknowledge who said something I quote and, if it is relevant, refer to the setting where the comment was made. Quotation marks or block quotes indicate that what a participant said is being reproduced verbatim. In writing the narratives, I attempted to use each participant's voice in proportion to how much and at what length he or she spoke during the joint interview. Minimal editing was required. Almost all of the words in the narratives are from the participants. In other words, while I merge comments the participants made on a topic on different occasions, the words, nevertheless, are almost entirely theirs. My motive in doing this is to be as true as possible to what they told me.

My Voice

Some students of qualitative research, as well as feminist readers, may wonder why I chose to present my voice in a chapter separate from the case narratives. It is not to feign positivism. I found that inserting my comments jarred the narrative and seemed both intrusive and unnecessary. What I chose to ask during the interviews, the comments I opted to follow-up, and those I left without probing, while perhaps invisible to the reader, shaped the content of the interviews as well as of the case narratives. My interpretation is presented in the introduction and in other chapters of the text. Neither the introduction nor the reply to the case narrative was available to the participants prior to publication.

Anonymity

Unlike historical research conducted after both members of a couple are no longer living, anonymity is a complex issue when presenting the stories of contemporary couples. I decided to use pseudonyms not only because it is a convention in social science research, but also because my purpose is to focus on the phenomenon of long-term collaborative relationships among academics rather than on personality or personal biography.

I broached the issue of anonymity on more than one occasion with the couples presented in the case narratives. I told participants during the first interview that it was my intention to present case narratives in a book. I advised the participants who are featured in the case narratives that I planned to use pseudonyms and to blur the names of places but not to change the fundamental elements of their story such as the topic of their research in order to try to conceal their identities. I asked them if they were comfortable with the possibility that some readers might recognize them. Participants signed an informed-consent form and said that they were willing to accept this risk. One participant requested that I further conceal their identities by changing their academic field. Although I believe that the participants' motivation to participate in the project largely reflects their commitment to research in general, it has to be assumed that what they chose to reveal is partly a reflection of a clear understanding that it was my intent to publish the case narratives.

Despite the intimacy that is sometimes temporarily experienced while an interview that is going well is in progress, research interviewing is fundamentally a public exchange. This is particularly true for the participants in the case narratives presented in the first part of the book, because they were aware that it was my intention to publish information about their collaborative relationship in a case study. This may be one explanation for why on first reading, despite my probing and direct questions about the negative dimensions of these relationships, the case narratives may seem to present largely positive examples of these partnerships. This was also largely true of the other academics who participated in the one-on-one telephone interviews. The invited case respondents and chapter authors address some of the more negative dimensions of these relationships.

Changes in contemporary attitudes about intimate partnerships that involve a work-related component may explain the absence of some traditional collaborative configurations from the cases presented. Patterns that we have come to expect from the literature cited in the first chapter are not evident in the cases presented here. These include the relationship that began between a protégé and mentor or where one partner serves as the "enabler"[7] for the other by subsuming other interests to mold an environment conducive to creativity and scholarship. Also missing, not only from the cases but from the interview sample as well, are many examples in which collaboration with a domestic partner led to rancor and divorce. I have certainly heard many anecdotal accounts of couples whose relationship ended acrimoniously because of intellectual differences, competition, or ill-timed intrusions into each other's work space. I conclude that these people are unlikely to volunteer to participate in a research project about couples, particularly one in which the author is affiliated with women's studies and, by inference, a feminist.

In analyzing interview and observational data, there is as much to be learned from what is not said as what is said—what is implied as much as what is actually said—and from gauging importance by what is emphasized through repetition or expansiveness. Even though participants rarely placed them in the foreground, a careful reading of the subtexts of the narratives reveals that members of these partnerships are confronted with substantial challenges. For example, the struggle to find comparably satisfying employment that allows cohabitation weaves clearly across the three cases. A substantial portion of each case narrative is devoted to a discussion of how the members negotiated differences in working and writing style. In one way or another, most participants described acrimonious encounters with departmental politics, including the suspicion such intimate partnerships seem frequently to inspire. Professional recognition for work jointly produced with a spouse proved problematic for most of the couples, particularly for the women. These and other topics are pursued in greater detail in the chapters in Part 2.

Key Factors Identified by Participants

Throughout each case study, I have identified in bold key factors participants identified about how an academic partner can impact publishing productivity. In another publication I have traced the basis in the research literature for each of these factors.[8] Secondary factors are identified in italics. They generally cross more than one factor and are not of themselves the key issue, but reflect a key issue. For example, work space in the household is identified as a secondary factor because the real issue is not the space itself but that it mirrors aspects of lifestyle and proximity. Readers interested in participants' observations about the role of a specific factor, such as recognition, can pursue it by using the index and/or by following the trail of a single concept across each of three cases. Although a multitude of factors have been identified in the voluminous research literature about the correlates of faculty publishing productivity,[9] only those consistently identified by participants as ways that a partner in the same profession impacts research productivity are highlighted.[10]

Ongoing access to **feedback** about ideas is the single factor most frequently identified by participants as a way that a partner in the same profession influences productivity. This includes informal feedback about ideas in the formative stages of development, as well as a more formal feedback offered by reviewing and making suggestions for revisions about manuscripts. Feedback about ideas is facilitated by the proximity afforded by shared *space* and by overlapping **private and public lives**. Lifestyle and the amount of time a couple spends together also influence it.

The value, usefulness, or instrumentality of the feedback provided by a partner to productivity is influenced by a number of factors. These include overlap in **training and interest** and the extent they share a **worldview**; how the partners manage a **division of labor** in collaborative tasks (affected by **career symmetry** and **egalitarianism**); **intellectual intimacy**; access to other collaborators through **collegial networks**; time available for work (related to both work assignment and **lifestyle**); success in negotiating differences in **working and writing styles** (influenced by **personal relationship**); the institutional **reward** structure; and **recognition** from colleagues.

Sixteen factors emerged from an analysis of the findings using a constant comparative approach. Most of these factors are not idiosyncratic to partners but characterize other types of effective collaborative pairs as well. The label I have given to each of these factors and a definition are listed in the following section. The relationship of the factor to publication productivity is also summarized.

Career Symmetry

Career symmetry refers to a correspondence or equivalence in career position and career stage. The extent of career symmetry between members of a couple influences recognition from colleagues. Career-symmetrical faculty couples are more likely than asymmetrical couples to bring to a project, highly specialized skills and expertise that are of comparable value. Collaboration among two academics is most likely to be mutually beneficial among partners whose careers and skills are symmetrical.

Collegial Networks
Collegial networks refer to community of like-minded colleagues who share an interest in a topic and a commitment to research, writing, and the communication of ideas. They contribute to productivity by providing visibility or recognition, feedback, and the *opportunity to collaborate with others.* An academic partner can positively impact productivity by expanding access to collegial networks, including in some cases to faculty in different fields, and to cross-sex collaborators.

Discipline or Topic
Discipline or topic refers to characteristics of the academic discipline that facilitate or inhibit collaboration, including research methods and faculty culture. Interdisciplinary topics that require knowledge from multiple disciplines invite collaboration. A partner may provide ongoing exposure to a colleague trained in an entirely different field or methodology. This is not necessarily something readily available to faculty, whose on-campus offices are most commonly located to afford proximity largely to other faculty in the same discipline.

Division of Labor
Division of labor refers to the distribution of tasks, both work-related and household, between partners. Partners are most likely to be on equal footing when each brings unique skills and specialized expertise to a collaborative project. An academic partner can serve as a resource by contributing specialized labor to a project. The contribution to productivity is most likely to be mutually beneficial among members of a couple when the division of labor is not sex-based, meaning that who performs what task is not determined on the basis of sex.

Egalitarianism
Egalitarianism is traditionally defined in the research literature by a relatively comparable division of labor and decision-making authority in the household. A non-sex-based division of labor facilitates the develop-

ment of comparable skills. Egalitarianism is defined for the purposes of this study as comparable priority awarded by members of a couple to their own and their partner's career and personal goals. Egalitarianism is instrumental to productivity when it includes a comparable commitment to the careers of both members and extends to a non-sex-based division of labor in collaborative, scholarly projects.

Feedback

Feedback refers to interpersonal exchanges that center on scholarship, whether face-to-face, in writing, or through electronic, digital, or other forms of communication. It includes informal exchanges such as input about ideas, critiques of manuscripts, and comments that reinforce the importance of allocating effort to scholarly work. It also includes *information exchange* about work-related information. Feedback is related to productivity because it improves the quality of scholarship and contributes to the motivation to sustain productivity over time.

Geographic Mobility

Geographic mobility refers to the opportunity to relocate in order to improve employment conditions. This shapes work assignment, which is directly related to publishing productivity because of its impact on the amount of time available for research and writing. An academic partner with comparable career interests generally substantially reduces geographic mobility. However, restricted geographic mobility may actually enhance the motivation to collaborate with a partner, particularly when the restriction includes limited access to like-minded colleagues.

Intellectual intimacy

Intellectual intimacy refers to the knowledge or familiarity partners share about each other's work, particularly their scholarship. It is influenced by the amount of time collaborators spend talking with each other about their work and the extent that they function in overlapping public or professional spheres. Intimacy with a partner's work promotes collaboration.

Lifestyle

Lifestyle refers to the way a couple chooses to allocate effort, including *quality and control of time* available for scholarship. These are also strongly influenced by work assignment. Lifestyle includes the *space* allocated in their household to work-related activities, such as to private or shared studies. It also includes family *resources* that are committed to work and work-related activities, such as professional travel. Lifestyle influences productivity because it reflects the priority a couple awards to work and work-related activities and the amount of time and resources available to devote to it.

Personal Relationship

Personal relationship refers to aspects of the emotional bond among collaborators that impact productivity. This includes commitment to the relationship as a motivation to collaborate and to succeed as collaborators.

Private and Public Lives

Private and public lives refer to the extent that private (that is, personal and family relationships) and public (that is, work-related) spheres overlap. It is influenced by the amount of time partners spend together (proximity). Overlapping private and public spheres affect *information exchange.* Partners who share overlapping spheres of power are more likely than those who occupy entirely separate personal and professional spheres to have an egalitarian relationship.[11]

Recognition

Recognition is the visibility for scholarship received from colleagues. It is a central measure of quality in the traditional academic reward structure at research universities. Affiliation with a partner can enhance or diminish how successful a scholar is in achieving recognition from colleagues as an independent scholar.

Reward

Reward refers to incentives from the institution for scholarship, including salary, tenure, promotion, resources, and favorable work assignment. Traditionally, the academic reward structure at research universities has discouraged long-term collaborative relationships because it makes the process of judging an individual's credentials more complicated.

Training and Interests

Training and interests refer to areas where collaborators' areas of interest, training, knowledge, and expertise overlap. Partners with overlapping training and interests are the most likely candidates for collaborative research projects.

Working and Writing Styles

Differences in working style include differences in how each partner prefers to approach his or her work and the work rhythms that are natural to each. Differences in writing style include differences in how each person writes and the extent they revise, as well as how each approaches critiquing and editing the other's work. The effectiveness of the strategies partners employ to negotiate conflict about differences in working and writing influences their effectiveness as collaborators and the impact of the relationship on productivity.

Worldview

Worldview refers to theoretical orientation, philosophy, or outlook on life-shaping beliefs and attitudes that a couple shares or holds in common, including ideology about marriage, family, and work, and sometimes a commitment to social change. It is often reflected in lifestyle. A shared worldview and theoretical or philosophical orientation facilitates collaboration.

3

Introduction to the First Case: "Intellectual Homesteading": Disciplinary Crossover among Geographers

The first case narrative of two geographers with expertise grounded in two different hemispheres introduces virtually all of the elements that characterize long-term collaborative working partnerships among the contemporary academic couples I studied. Like other types of collegial pairings, collaboration is stimulated by proximity (physical and increasingly virtual); **overlap in interests** and generally **training; shared worldview**, theoretical orientation, or agenda for social change; and **personal relationship**. Similarly, the process Martha and Greg use to collaborate shares many qualities with other types of collaborative pairs and teams: a negotiated **division of labor**; **feedback** about ideas, and the necessity to negotiate differences in **working and writing styles**.

Key Elements of the Case
Pushing Disciplinary Boundaries
One of the ways the first case distinguishes itself from the other two presented in this section of *Working Equal* is that it raises issues related to conducting interdisciplinary research that is collaborative by nature. Martha Hanson and Greg Barrow characterize their work as interdisciplinary because they have well-defined and distinct areas of expertise even though it is within the same discipline. The interdisciplinary character of their work is manifested in several ways. It is evident in their interests and academic training, which they characterize as cross-disciplinary. They see the nature of their discipline as inherently interdisciplinary. It is also embodied in a worldview they share about the interdependence of people and what they view as impending ecological disaster. This is the agenda for social change that they act upon in their joint writing.

As the quote that introduces the case narrative in the next chapter suggests, the type of collaboration that this couple illustrates may embody a form of thinking and constructing knowledge that is fundamentally different in some ways from that accomplished by scholars who are entrenched in a single discipline. Like the couple presented in the third case narrative, the focus of this couple's efforts is to invent a form of writing that reaches audiences in more than one discipline. As Lincoln points out in her response to the case narrative, this is a form of knowledge construction that allows its creators to borrow foundational concepts from other disciplines. Unusual metaphors are part of this type of thinking and writing, which integrates knowledge from multiple disciplines. "It is all about seeing connections and thinking about things in many ways," Martha says in the case narrative that follows. Lincoln illustrates a similar use of metaphors when she borrows from her partner's discipline in the physical sciences to use an analogy about the interaction of molecules to explain an impact of collaboration. It is also evident in other innovative comparisons that pepper the narrative, such as the comparison of interdisciplinary collaboration to intellectual homesteading that provides the title to the chapter.

The interdisciplinary nature of their joint work is also what Martha and Greg recognize as the primary source of criticism for their work. This is the case for the third couple presented in the case narratives as well. It is difficult to get credibility or recognition for scholarship, Greg argues, unless it is grounded in a discipline. This is the way publishing conventions work and, as Kathryn Ward and Linda Grant[1] argue in a quote that is presented in the first chapter, is one of the mechanisms that reinforce disciplinary boundaries. Greg described the disciplines as gatekeepers and as "keeping your feet in the disciplines" as essential for credibility and recognition for your ideas.

A Strategic Division of Labor

The **division of labor** Martha and Greg typically utilize for preparing jointly authored manuscripts is similar to the one presented in the second case narrative, but quite different from the process utilized by the couple in the third narrative. It is clear that they are quite strategic about the division of labor they negotiate, and alert about ways best to capitalize on their respective strengths and time they have available.[2] Their customary approach is that one of them "takes the lead" in writing the first draft of a manuscript, while the other provides feedback and revisions of subsequent drafts. Who assumes the lead in drafting the article generally requires little negotiation because it is tied to who is recognized as the expert or authority on the topic, and that is something that is clearly defined between them. This is a process that is probably quite similar to that used by other collaborative pairs.

The case respondent, Yvonna Lincoln, describes a second way of dividing up the labor as well as the intellectual authority for a text. She describes a process whereby after she and her partner negotiate an outline, they divide up responsibility for writing different parts of the manuscript so that the division of labor is approximately equal. Many rounds of revisions account for how the text comes to present a seamless voice to the reader.

The participants in the third case narrative describe a third approach to the division of labor for the text whereby they maintain distinct voices but essentially reach consensus about every word and sentence that appears in the final publication. This is a form of collaboration that Ann Austin and Roger Baldwin characterize as full collaboration.[3] This is when intellectual authority for the text is fully shared.

Observations from My Visit

My visit with Martha Hanson and Greg Barrow began with a tour of the house they share. It is a house imprinted by the character of the people who live there and by the nature of their work. It is a place arranged to be functional rather than one kept in pristine conditions for public functions or entertaining. The house is organized around two separate studies; one on the first floor and one on the second floor. Probably because of his habit of working in the hours past midnight, Greg has a large study on the first floor at a point that is as far as possible from the bedroom. His desk, barely visible under piles of papers and two computer terminals, faces a sliding glass door overlooking a deck and a wooded backyard. A floor-to-ceiling, wall-to-wall bookcase, filled to overflowing with books, is within arm's reach of his desk. A printer and a facsimile machine are nearby.

Martha's study is on the second floor near the bedroom. A large, wooden, rolltop desk devoted to finances (which she manages) sits in an adjacent room. Her study has a large, open counter where her computer sits facing a window that opens to the front yard. Her study is smaller and noticeably tidier than Greg's. Differences in levels of tolerance for messiness as well as differences in work schedules emerge during my research as two main reasons that lead couples to maintain separate offices.

During a tour of the house, Martha pointed to several places set aside for informal conversation. These include a couch in each of the two studies as well as a small balcony off the front of the house that is barely large enough to accommodate two chairs. The placement and intimacy of these alcoves reminded me of artists' retreats that I have toured. The functionality of the numerous alcoves and couches is to facilitate the primary site of their collaboration, which is constant conversations about ideas.

After listening to people who do a great deal of writing describe how they collaborate with a spouse or domestic partner, I have found that the organization of their work space reflects both individual working styles and how they accomplish the work they do jointly. I interpret the way that Martha and Greg have organized the space in their home as revealing a number of things about the process they utilize to accomplish their work. The amount of space devoted to their work areas demonstrates its centrality to their **lifestyle**. The lack of demarcation between their work spaces and their private spaces embodies their refusal to compartmentalize their private and professional lives. That their studies are on different floors of the house suggests that Martha and Greg write at different times of the day.

Several observations occurred to me about Martha and Greg's relationship during the interview I conducted with them together. They were easy to interview, being both thoughtful and verbally agile in their replies. They laughed a lot. They both seemed extremely respectful of each other's words, listening intently and adding to each other's thoughts but rarely interrupting or contradicting each other. It was not uncommon for either one of them to speak the equivalent of several paragraphs without interruption. Both spoke for an equivalent amount of time.

Greg has a particularly thoughtful quality to his speaking. No matter how trivial or straightforward the question I asked, he seemed to give it his utmost attention. Even after the conversation had moved forward in response to another question, Greg would sometimes return to a prior question to provide an even more expansive answer. At these points, Martha carried the conversational thread forward with me, while Greg seemed to disappear mentally for a few moments to pursue a thought. The thoughtfulness the participants gave my interview questions and the attention they gave to crafting replies carefully were qualities I discovered to be characteristic of many of my participants.

Martha spoke in detail about each of their working and writing styles and how they differed. Being self-reflexive is probably part of her training as an ethnographer. Martha can itemize her own as well as Greg's strengths. It is clear that she has given this aspect of their relationship a good deal of thought. These are not things that Greg talked at length about.

The Case Response

Yvonna Lincoln's reply to the first case narrative brings us squarely into facing an issue many of us would like to think is a remnant of the 1950s. That is the sexist assumption, most often shared with me as something women in early faculty cohorts experienced, that the husband often served as the "ghostwriter" for work carrying a woman's name or that married women often benefited from a ride on the "coattails" of a more famous spouse. It is a charge that Lincoln recognizes she was attuned to because of differences in age and career status between her and her partner.

While Martha and Greg both noted that alliances among academic couples, particularly those in the same academic unit, can provoke jealousy and tension from colleagues who are threatened by it, issues of **reward** and **recognition** are not topics either lingered on. They struggled more with issues of how to gain credibility for their joint work because it is interdisciplinary rather than because they are an academic couple. The couple presented in the third case narrative voiced a similar perspective.

There are several elements in this case that may help to explain why issues of reward and recognition were less prominent than they are in other cases. One is that Martha and Greg do not hold positions in the same department. In fact, at present Greg works outside academia in a setting that does not even reward publication. Another reason that maintaining distinct identities as scholars may be less of a battle for this couple than it has been for other academic couples is that they began collaborating together only after both were well established in their careers. That they collaborate with a wider circle of colleagues contributes to the vitality of their own collaboration as well as to maintaining distinct identities. Finally, even though they are in the same academic discipline, their expertise being in geographical regions in different parts of the world provides a clear marker for colleagues to distinguish and evaluate their contributions.

An additional political issue about academic couples that Lincoln makes visible in her case response may cause some unease for administrators. She argues that the habit of secrecy surrounding knowledge about colleagues' salaries is unlikely to be maintained among couples, making long-standing practices of paying women lower salaries less tenable. Similarly, she suggests that comparisons about such institutional practices as work assignment and resources are inevitable among couples. This type of **information exchange** differs from that which occurs in sex-segregated workplaces and which Barbara Reskin argues is fundamental to the devaluation of women's work.[4]

4

The First Case: "Intellectual Homesteading": Disciplinary Crossover among Geographers

I am from the West and a lot of my outlook comes out of that. My grandmother and grandfather were homesteaders. There was a lot of male-female dependence in those situations: an extraordinary mutual reliance on each other and designing a way of life that would work under peculiar constraints. That brings me to the idea that the relationship can be used to stake out new positions in a somewhat hostile environment. That would be the problem that we are working on, which is how to cross-fertilize the physical and social sciences. That was our pioneer habit, somewhat unoccupied territory at the time. –*Greg Barrow, May 1997*

Martha Hanson and Greg Barrow are both self-described geographers with expertise grounded in different regions of the world. They came together as a couple and began collaborating after both achieved recognition as independent scholars and were well established in their careers and in the habit of writing. Their relationship reflects a **lifestyle** and a shared **worldview** or philosophy about interdependence. It also deeply embedded in an agenda about environmental degradation and social change.

Background
Martha and Greg are within one year of each other in age. Martha studied English, geography, and anthropology as an undergraduate student; Greg's undergraduate degree is in history. Martha earned a doctorate in geography with a minor in environmental science from a large research university in the early 1970s; Greg earned his doctorate in geography a few years later. Martha's area of expertise is a region in Western Europe; Greg's is climatology. Both travel frequently for their work. Martha has done fieldwork almost every summer for 21 years, generally supported by both the univer-

34

sity and external agencies such as the National Science Foundation and the National Endowment for the Humanities. Greg identifies himself as an academic but at present is employed by a private consulting company.

Their Personal Relationship

Martha and Greg did not attend graduate school together. However, as part of their graduate work they both did fieldwork at the same location. Although they were never there at the same time, when Greg visited the site a few years after Martha did, he was captivated by the elegance of a map she had drawn of it.

Martha's and Greg's personal lives went in separate directions as both established themselves in faculty careers. Each earned tenure at a research university in a different part of the country. Greg married. Martha was involved in a long-term personal and collaborative relationship with a male colleague in the same academic department where she had her first permanent faculty appointment. They coauthored a book together. Partly because of the controversy generated by this relationship, Martha relocated to another tenure-track faculty position at a research university in the Southeast in the mid-1970s. Her partner at the time tried unsuccessfully for several years to relocate to a faculty position within commuting distance of her.

Martha's and Greg's **personal relationship** first began to unfold during a social gathering at a professional conference after she had moved to the Southeast. Greg eventually resigned from his faculty position to relocate to live with her. To make this kind of couple-based collaboration work, he basically gave up an academic job, Martha said (**geographic mobility**). Greg said that he was relieved to escape departmental politics and to be freed of undergraduate teaching, which he had grown to feel was holding back his scholarship. Greg observed that he now has the advantage of working in a place that shares many similarities to a graduate department, except that the people he trains work for him for years, rather than graduating and leaving after a few years. Through his connections with Martha, he has an appointment as an adjunct faculty member at the university where Martha is now a full professor. Greg has children, but Martha does not.

Their Collaborative Relationship

Martha and Greg had been writing together for about 10 years when I interviewed them. They have coauthored several of the articles among Martha's steady output of two or three publications a year. They are now focused on writing a book together while they both keep pace with serving as contributors and editors to other volumes as well.

Martha and Greg enumerated several reasons for their decision to collaborate together. These included their training, the nature of their academic field, and the nature of their overlapping research interests.

Training

Both Martha and Greg described themselves as having similar educational **training,** which they identified by the label of "crossover training." By this they mean that their undergraduate and graduate work spans several disciplines. Martha described her own background in these words: "One of the things that certainly I feel is different about my own training is that from an early age I have been equivalently attracted to humanities, natural sciences, and social sciences. I have a strong interest in all three of those major areas. . . . That is an essential characteristic of my intellectual work."

The Nature of the Discipline

A second reason Martha and Greg pointed to for their long-term collaboration is the nature of their academic **discipline,** which is now called human or cultural geography. This is a field that studies a range of social, cultural, economic, and political aspects of a place, locality, or region. Martha observed: "I think that people in our field self-select for collaboration. You just don't last very long if you are not someone who can get along with other people in the field and figure out how to fold in your part of the work with somebody else's part of the work."

Topic

A third thing that propels Martha and Greg's scholarly collaboration is an **overlap in interests.** In response to my opening question during the telephone interview about the reasons he and Martha collaborate, Greg used the phrase "intellectual homesteading." When I asked him what he meant by it, I discovered that a number of ideas were embedded in this rich metaphor. As reflected in the quote that opens the case, he situated his outlook in his Midwestern roots while highlighting the extraordinary mutual interdependence that marks couples who homestead the land. In a remark that opened our interview Greg said:

> I look at it from the perspective of human evolution and how human evolution has set us up for intellectual homesteading.

There are a lot of species where males and females never associate with each other except when they are breeding. For humans, there is a theme of males and females associating year-round. I am of the opinion that the design is nearly to the point of symbiosis. That doesn't mean that the individual people can't do perfectly well alone, but there is a great functionality that accrues when these two codesigned parts are put together.

When Greg referred to the pioneer habit in the quote that introduces this chapter, he meant the interdisciplinary challenge of how to cross-fertilize the physical and social sciences. He and Martha also call it the crossover problem or third-culture writing. Martha said: "I am really interested, and Greg is too, in what basically is called the two-cultures problem. That is that science writing and humanities writing are very different kinds of writing. Both of us are trying to cross over and to communicate with the two audiences." They are inventing a form of writing that is intentionally interdisciplinary.

Both Martha and Greg expressed the keen sensitivity that often characterizes writers about how to communicate effectively with diverse audiences and how to get their work into a form other people can understand and use. Ever alert to the nuances of words, Martha said: "The critical thing is asking ourselves how can we provide enough science for the scientists and enough sensibility and appreciation for life for the historian."

Pointing to the complexity of the problem they are struggling to present, Greg said: "Life and society are just too complicated for one person to grasp and come up with useful insights. We are past the days of the lone scout out there trying to plumb the depths of society and philosophy." Referring again to the idea of symbiosis, Greg observed that two people conferring frequently over a substantial period of time "offer a set of powers that are just much greater than the two people acting apart." Voicing a conviction that this type of collaboration is associated with enhanced quality, he said: "The sum is greater than the whole of the parts."

How They Accomplish Their Work Together

Their individual and joint scholarly work is central to Martha and Greg's lifestyle and worldview. Elements of their lifestyle associated with their scholarly work are: (a) the habit of writing, (b) feedback about ideas facilitated by physical proximity, (c) engagement with a community of like-minded people, and (d) allocation of resources.

Worldview

Martha and Greg's decision to collaborate is not just a matter of an occasional project afforded by convenient access to each other. It is an element of a shared **worldview**. For them, it reflects both a philosophy and outlook on life and a lifestyle. Preoccupation with ideas is an element of this worldview. Martha said:

> Both of us are driven by ideas. Both of us are very content and have been all of our lives, with the excitement of the life of the mind. It makes us very compatible because it is something that we can really understand about each other. Many other people do not understand it very much—either about us or, maybe in some circumstances, other relationships we have been in. It is a philosophy about what life is about. It is about seeing connections and thinking about things in many different ways and figuring out how to express that.

Speaking when they were together in the joint interview, Martha acknowledged the integration of **private and public lives** inherent in her description of their lifestyle. She admitted that even as a teenager she fantasized about a life where she and a partner might sit down at the breakfast table together and have an animated conversation about their work. "Some people expect that you can have a day life and a night life. Or a weekday life and a weekend life. We just do not operate that way," she said.

Lifestyle

The expression "life of the mind" captures the idea that Martha and Greg organize their day-to-day lives or their **lifestyle** around their work. A habit of writing is something both brought into the relationship. "What we have in common that keeps us working in the same direction is that we both have worked under the heavy hand of 'publish or perish.' It is habituated," Martha said.

Information exchange afforded by physical proximity is a second element of Martha and Greg's lifestyle. When I first interviewed him by telephone, Greg compared the efficiency afforded by proximity to the design of supercomputers. He said: "When they build supercomputers, they study how much information flows between different components so they can arrange the components with the most information flowing closest together in design. . . . Having a working spouse is clearly part of that supercomputer design that greatly reduces the amount of effort required for information flow."

Martha expressed a view very similar to Greg's when she spoke of the advantages of living with someone you collaborate with. In speaking of a life where conversations about ideas are central, she said:

> The advantage of living in the same house together or spending a month together somewhere is that we can take up those conversations at any time. Greg is as likely to be standing in the shower and me standing outside of the shower door talking to him about some idea as we are to be doing that in some sort of proper circumstance where we are sitting down at a table or at a desk writing. The fact that these conversations can go on anywhere, anytime, day or night is the thing that makes it so much fun.

Timely and informal **feedback** about ideas is an advantage of shared physical space that they both described. "You get a lot of guidance about what is going to work, and you get it pretty quickly," Martha observed. Rather than giving each other written feedback by handing drafts of a publication back and forth, Martha and Greg utilize iterative rounds of ongoing informal conversation to develop a conceptual argument.

Martha and Greg admitted to false starts in many of their joint projects. Greg labeled an aspect of the feedback they gave each other as "corrective jogs." This is one way they avoid spending a lot of time on a project only to find that it does not reflect their mutual thinking. Similarly, Martha described their informal exchanges as a way to correct each other's course. "If it sounds silly when you say it, or if the other person says, 'well, I don't know if that is going to work because of this or that,' then you know pretty quickly that you need to take another tack. So you don't waste much time."

A third element of Martha and Greg's lifestyle associated with their writing is their engagement in **collegial networks** consisting of a community of friends and colleagues who share their interests. When I asked them during the joint interview if they were connected to a group of people who do the same kind of work or if they live day to day feeling perpetually odd, Martha replied that they have a number of friends whose partners are in the same field. Martha added, however, that "Most of our friends consider us slightly more fanatical than anyone they know." Greg replied to this comment, saying, "We do have this mission. There is a role and scope to our activities that most people do not have. Most other couples are operating at a survival level." Martha agreed: "The means by which we have chosen to fulfill our mission is our writing."

The *opportunity to collaborate with others* is one aspect of their engagement in a community of scholars. Martha and Greg are involved individually and as a team in writing with other people. Some of these partnerships are with current and former graduate students as well as with male and female colleagues. Collaborating with others is something that helps them maintain intellectual autonomy and keeps their store of ideas and information fresh.

A fourth element of lifestyle and how it is shaped by their commitment to their own as well as to a mutual research agenda reverberates in their willingness to commit their personal *resources* to their scholarship. This aspect of their relationship and lifestyle was voiced more clearly by this pair than by the other couples. It is embodied, for example, in the amount of space in their home dedicated to their work. It is also evident in their modest home, low-maintenance landscaping, and well-traveled cars. They made the decision to forego a month of Greg's income so that he could accompany Martha out of the country on a research-teaching assignment. Reflecting a carefully calculated approach to the decision, Martha said:

> We just decided that it was worthwhile to figure out how we could financially afford for Greg to come too for a month. We had to really think about that and whether or not that was really a worthwhile thing for us to be doing. We had to think about whether it was a good expenditure of our money. I thought that a month of his time was probably more valuable than a month of nearly anyone else I could think of because he is so much better at that than a lot of other people who might have stared into space for two weeks and written for two weeks. He was so eager to have that time that I knew that he would put it to good use.

She admitted that many people might find that decision incomprehensible unless it was associated with profit or book sales. She also observed that anyone who is an academic would know that economic incentives are not a primary source of the motivation to write.

Division of Labor

In addition to sharing a philosophy of life and a lifestyle, a second way that Martha and Greg accomplish their work together is through a carefully negotiated **division of labor**. Through trial and error, they have developed strategies to work effectively together despite differences in personality and working style. They divide the tasks required to accomplish their work together in a way that reflects personality, their respective strengths, and the amount and type of time each has available at any given moment. Martha takes the leadership in the political aspect of the shared elements of their agendas. She has been appointed to key positions on some committees where their agenda about the environment might be enacted. "I am better at insinuating myself onto the right committees and being invited to the right conferences," she said. These are opportunities where they can get their agenda about the environment on the table for public policy change.

On the other hand, Greg is the one responsible for keeping up with the literature related to the book they are doing together. He is writing much of the first draft of their jointly authored book. Martha described Greg as the one who has added to their theoretical approach in terms of concepts. Of him she said: "He is amazingly prolific. He just manages to work all of the time on lots of different projects and get them all done in a timely manner."

When I asked if over time their respective strengths grew more similar or more distinct, Martha replied that she saw it as fundamentally an issue of personality. Pointing to Greg's habit of doing most of his scholarly work between 3 and 7 o'clock in the morning, she said: "You cannot buttonhole people at a conference at 3:30 in the morning." On the other hand, she said, "I sleep peacefully, jump into the shower, put on a pair of heels and a suit and go out and negotiate. That is the kind of the thing that is pretty basic to our personalities."

In addition to reflecting differences in other areas, the division of labor that Martha and Greg have negotiated also reflects the intense time demands of their respective careers. With Martha often away from home for months, time pressures are like a third dimension of their relationship. Both Martha and Greg made multiple references to the intense pressure of time constraints and to the efficiency they gained by working jointly. Each spoke of exactly how many pages of text they could produce in a given period of time. Decisions about allocation of time and use of different types of units of time is another dimension of the lifestyle choices they have made to produce their scholarship.

Awareness that different types of scholarly work require different *quality of time* reflects the interconnectedness between work, time, and lifestyle. For example, Greg explained that a month in another country afforded him the kind of time that he needed to pull together ideas and to see the big picture. "While you can use a two-hour block of time to edit a paper and tinker with how something sounds," he said, "this type of quality time afforded me the opportunity to establish the whole super-structure of the book." Greg described his unpaid leave of absence as one of the best times he ever had. He described a typical working day during that time period in these words:

> I would get up in the morning and have a nice strong cup of local coffee. I would work on the book for five or six hours. At that point, the sun came into the room where I was working so brightly that I could no longer see the computer screen. Then I would go down and get a glass of wine and listen to music for the rest of the day.
>
> There are only so many hours a day that you can work at that level. It is not the kind of writing that you can just grind out. My limit on that is four to six hours at a time. It was thirty days of prime time. Uninterrupted. No telephone. Plenty of time between sessions to think through problems. This is the sort of circum-stance that makes for synthesis. You can get enough ideas in your head that you can start making cross-references.

Martha returned each night, after a day of dealing with bureaucrats, appreciative of the opportunity to speak English again and available to read problematic passages and to give feedback about ideas that Greg might then use to start writing the next day.

Negotiating Differences

In the trial and error required for their collaborative relationship to flour-ish, Martha and Greg continually navigate differences in writing style and opinion. It took a number of years to negotiate differences in **writing and working style.** Being of the two more expansive on the topic, Martha said of her writing style: "I write prose the same way that I write poetry, which is that I craft every sentence, word by word, sentence by sentence, paragraph by paragraph. I do it like Tinkertoys. I put all of the pieces together as I go along." She attributed her writing style to her training in English and said that one advantage was that she did little rewriting.

Martha used the word "journalistic" to describe Greg's writing style. He is the faster writer of the two, but his writing style requires much more extensive rewriting. "He gets it down and worries later about what the bits are and if the bits are where they need to be." Responding, Greg said: "It has to be in some sense journalistic in that it allows people from both sides to at least read what is going on." He writes quickly, he said, to station his ideas in a written form before he forgets them.

Martha acknowledged that reconciling the differences in their writing styles has been a struggle but that they had found a way to convert those differences into an advantage. Speaking both to me and to Greg during the joint interview, she referred to her first long-term writing partner, with whom she still writes from time to time:

> I have written with someone who wrote very much like me and that was effortless but also was not taking on the level of complexity that we are dealing with. It was easy and pleasant but not particularly useful in this context. It is really good that we do not have exactly the same writing styles. I have learned over the last decade that our differences in styles are an advantage in our work together, rather than a disadvantage. We have learned how to make that a useful characteristic of our writing. The fact that we do not write exactly the same means that we end up talking about nuances of words, the cast of the sentence, and the organization of an article in a completely different way than if we wrote the same way.

When I asked how they resolved differences of opinion, Martha and Greg pointed to two different strategies. Martha said the first strategy they use to negotiate differences of opinion is to give it some time. She said: "The way I see us working a lot is that we will state something to one another and then go away and think about it. At a later date, we reexplore it. Generally, by then we have moved closer to each other's opinion." She described the experience of each preparing an outline to submit to a publisher for the book they are writing. Acknowledging that there were things that neither of them liked about each other's outlines, they set them aside for awhile and let them "cook." "Instead of getting right down to it and falling into a scrap about it, we backed off and let it cook a bit," Martha said. "The next time we got back to it, maybe six months later, there was not much disagreement. It had fixed itself."

Part of the explanation for how a difference of opinion "fixes itself" is that over the course of a decade Martha and Greg have schooled each other on their respective areas of expertise. "One of the things that we had to do over the last ten years," Martha said, "is to teach each other. He has taught me a lot about climatology, and I think that I have taught him the things you can get out of my area of expertise. We have exchanged some important pieces of information with each other. Now we are in a position to be able to be a lot more useful to each other in terms of how well our individual contributions are understood or how useful they are going to be." Pointing to the efficiency gained from a shared knowledge base, Martha commented:

> If I were to say what the most useful aspect of this kind of collaboration is, I would say that it is that you don't have to explain your every step. You may have to explain every step when you write about it, but you don't have to spend a lot of time laying the background like you would with an uninitiated colleague. You do not have to explain very much. That is a great advantage.

Writing the book would have been a lot more contentious a decade ago than it is now, Martha admitted. At different points during the interviews, each referred to the other as being "theoretically of the same mind." This is part of the evolution of a shared worldview mentioned earlier. "Now we are very much working on the same page," Martha said. By that she means that they are now clearly focused on a shared goal or mission rather than a single project or piece of work. A publication is secondary to the goal of communicating their perspective to a wide audience.

Which one of the two of them takes the lead on a project is related to who has time and who is considered to have the greater expertise. Martha's and Greg's areas of expertise are grounded in different hemispheres. They work with a third colleague whose fieldwork and expertise are situated in yet a third continent. Who takes the lead on the project and who is "subordinate" in a project is defined largely by which part of the world they are writing about.

Issues of Credibility and Recognition

During our initial one-on-one telephone interview, I asked Martha if she had encountered any difficulty about the **recognition** she received for the work she had coauthored with her first partner and later in her career with Greg. She made no references in our telephone conversation to feeling pressured by the reward structure to avoid collaboration with a male partner. She observed that both of the men had established fine reputations before they met her and that those reputations were reasonably secure. She downplayed the suggestion that her contribution might be questioned. She said:

There was never a moment, which I could imagine in certain other contexts and with other people, where someone might say that I was riding on one of their coattails. Anyone who knew one of us would probably know the other, just because it is not that big of a discipline and they would know enough about us to know that both of us brought strengths to the collaboration.

Martha and Greg report mixed feedback from colleagues in their fields about their work together. Both agreed that colleagues can perceive the powerful combination presented by such a relationship as threatening their self-interests. Greg articulated this viewpoint when he said: "The white, male, post–World War II structure is definitely afraid of male-female alliances, especially in situations where it makes a lot of difference, such as in academic departments where people are trying to establish fiefdoms."

The interdisciplinary nature of their collaborative work rather than their personal relationship generates the most criticism from colleagues. With an example that illustrates that they are not exceptions in terms of receiving mixed reviews from editors, Martha described how they share feedback from journal editors. She said that when she reads editorial feedback about an article, she thinks about what she has learned and how she might recast it. Then she and Greg typically talk about what happened, even though it is very likely that he had not read the article before she had sent it off. "Because both of us are writing a lot and in different contexts, any time one of us gets a set of reviews back, that adds to the projects we do together because we have more information."

Their ambition is to overcome disciplinary compartmentalization and to publish in the interdisciplinary domain they alternately refer to as the third culture or crossover culture. Greg said:

> The big question is the third culture, is how do you get credibility. The nature of what is going on there precludes standards, so that the way you get credibility is that you publish in the two cultures or disciplines. Until there is some other method figured out, the disciplines are the gatekeepers of who gets to play. Once you can get past the disciplinary gate, then you can try to play in the third culture.

Both were in agreement when they responded to my question about how they established credibility. Greg replied: "We have to keep our feet in our disciplines." In other words, they established their legitimacy by keeping their feet firmly planted in their respective areas of expertise. "It is little bit like Picasso," Greg said: "First he did sort of nice, realistic paintings early in his career and then, once he established himself . . ." Martha went on to finish his sentence: "Then he could go on and put ladies' eyes in their knees and that kind of thing."

5

Collaboration as a Way of Being, a Way of Living:
A Response to the First Case

Yvonna S. Lincoln

Greg and Martha seem very familiar. While I don't know them, I can make a lot of guesses about the lives they lead; there is something about those lives that seems both intimate and familiar to me. But there are also questions unresolved. Such questions inevitably revolve about those aspects of partner and spouse collaborations that are not the focus of this book, nor the focus of the chapter, nor even the appropriate focus of institutions that may consider hiring and supporting such academic spousal research teams. Consequently, I will take up those aspects of "intellectual homesteading" that may be similar to other academic/ spousal collaborative efforts and that may be both conceptually heuristic and institutionally interesting first, and will then make my final comments about what is unresolved or unaddressed.

Similarities and Differences
The case revolves about individuals who "are . . . geographers with expertise grounded in different regions of the world." If spouse/partner collaborations are to work, and work well, I believe this description points to a critical aspect of such work, which is that they are cross-disciplinary. One might equally say, "they are both," for example, "educationists with expertise grounded in different subdisciplines," as in my own case. Critical to their success, I believe the description of this couple is that both their graduate and undergraduate training spanned more than one discipline. In many ways, such graduate and undergraduate experiences aid and abet the kinds of "cross-fertilization" challenges they face. In my own life, I have found the partnership enriched by having a spouse-collaborator with undergraduate and graduate preparation in the physical sciences (engineering and physics) while my own preparation

has been in history, art history, and sociology. Doctoral studies may create in students the awareness that their undergraduate work was far less inquiry-focused than they might have wished it to be. Nevertheless it is the case that students bring with them to inquiry and research problems later in their academic careers certain inquiry habits, certain ways of looking at the world, certain "habits of the heart," certain characteristics that may be traced back to the unconscious socialization experiences of the undergraduate major. Those unconscious socialization experiences and ways of seeing the world provide a part of the intellectual fodder that fuels the collaborative experience (**training and interests**). Just as Greg and Martha work to "cross-fertilize the physical and social sciences," cross-fertilization occurs with or without deliberation if an academic partnership includes individuals trained in different disciplines with different socialization experiences. In my own case, my spouse's engineering and science training made available to me much more readily the foundational concepts of science, statistics, and experimental inquiry, while my own work in sociology, history, and art history drew me to interpretive stances long before I could fully articulate the bases of such intuitive stances.

Intellectual homesteaders are also similar in that the partnership is "driven [largely] by ideas." A long time ago, I heard Jessica Tandy and Hume Cronyn (a 50-year stage, theater, and film collaboration of acting spouses) comment that their marriage was "one long conversation." The extent to which spousal collaborators are interested in and challenged by the different perspectives that each brings marks the boundaries between good academic spouses and strong academic partnerships that also happen to be spousal. The comment about "one long conversation" characterizes equally well a good marriage or partnership, but also the most fruitful collaborations.

Personal and Conceptual Responses

It is particularly striking that partners often work on different schedules (one does fieldwork while the other writes), in different places (they maintain their own studies and work spaces), with different tolerances for order, disorder, and the disarray of long-term writing projects, often at different times during the day or week, and in different styles (**working and writing styles**). Collaborations between spousal partners nevertheless have to take account of sometimes radically different circadian biorhythms, so that while one partner rises early to hit the keyboard, another might work late into the night after spouse and children have gone to bed, when the house falls silent. Likewise, while one partner might spend some time each day on writing—whether or not he or she feels the writing "went well"—another might save large blocks of time during a special time in the week. Some faculty routinely stay away from the office one or more days each week specifically to write.

How You Write, How I Write

In much the same way, spouses often cannot write in each other's "space" (although I know couples who find great pleasure in sharing a large space devoted to a study). One will read then write, only stopping every once in awhile to check on a specific reference; the other will write amid stacks of books carefully marked with sticky note slips, photocopied journal articles folded back to pages with specific quotations highlighted, and notepads with various notations about what discussions go into what sections. Together, somehow, they manage to work through a book, a chapter, or an article.

Another intensely personal way of working may be how the writing is apportioned (**division of labor**). In some collaborative partnerships, the individual partners may write different pieces and parts, depending on their own interests, expertise, and how the manuscript is organized. In both my own collaborative marriage and in other collaborations with individuals at distant institutions, typically an outline is generated in tandem as a joint project.

The two of us (husband *or* collaborator) determine first what needs to go into the piece we are writing. Then we determine an order for the discussion—a logic to the arguments we wish to make. While this may seem intuitive, it is often not so intuitive, since I am most often engaged in qualitative research work, which has fewer structural conventions attached to it with regard to how the piece may be organized. There is no "set" flow: introduction, problem statement, methods, data, conclusions, results, and implications. Rather, qualitative work, especially some of the newer, experimental or "messy text" work, can follow many different forms for reporting, some of which are even borrowed from literary genres. Consequently, the logic or order to a given presentation will be the subject of some negotiation.

When the work has been outlined, we often—as I suspect other collaborative partnerships do—decide about how much space should be given to each section. Once that is done, we (as likely others do) determine what is "half." "Half" is important if partners write "the front half" and the "back half." All this means is that individuals take one half or the other and write that piece. When the writing is done, the collaborating partners exchange halves and comment upon each other's work. If the pieces seem fairly complete, then the next step will be to incorporate revisions and to merge the two voices so that there is some sense of continuity throughout the work.

If collaborating partners see gaps or problems with each other's work, then other kinds of conversations ensue while the two of them work to a place where they are closer together. Over time, this working-through of competing or noncomplementary viewpoints is a source of great richness and personal and professional elaboration. Working as it does in both spheres, it creates a sense of seamlessness to the lives of the partners; it becomes a *way of being* with each other as well as a way of being in the world.

Writing styles—by which I mean rhetorical styles—vary tremendously, even in the sciences. As a consequence, writing styles sometimes pose a problem for collaborating spouses or partners. My spouse has a direct, forceful way of writing that is a legacy from his more "scientific" years; my other major collaborators have somewhat more relaxed, less terse writing styles or "voices." Working with three different "voices" has its problems, but the major issue is always making a given work seem to proceed either from one voice or from a well-matched duo. Shifting styles jar readers and create a certain level of schizophrenia in the written word. Consequently, writing together may be problematic for collaborators with dramatically different writing styles.

Separate Identities, Same Breakfast Table

While this was not perceived to be an issue by the couple presented in the first case, it is especially striking that some of the couples presented in the first part of the book refer to a problem that is both personal and institutional: the ongoing suspicion that if a piece is coauthored by a spouse, the "real" work has necessarily been done by the male partner (**recognition**). It is hard to know why this prejudice lingers, related as it is to the nineteenth-century conception of women as unfit for scholarly or intellectual work, the practice of which would surely make women unable to conceive or at least vulnerable to hysteria and derangement! But the issue is not a dead one; "back then" is also now, and women continue to be subject to the suspicion that a male partner who is a collaborator is doing the vast majority of the "real" work.

The necessity of either "divorcing" oneself from collaborative efforts early on in one's career or pursuing different lines of research for some period of time—or even of concealing one's marital arrangements, all in the interests of creating an independent identity for the woman—seems as benighted to us now as medieval chastity belts. The couple that does not take measures to create separate and somewhat independent identities is compelled to make strenuous efforts to defend the female partner's contributions to scholarly productivity. Without somewhat artificially creating separations, usually by independently authored publications, women are distinctly disadvantaged by virtue of being married to men in the same or closely related academic specialties. It is especially telling that academic couples feel far more confident about their spousal collaborations when each finally has tenure or when one works in another site or organization.

The problem of separate identities is exacerbated, I believe, when one of the partners is quite senior to the other, as in my own case. It has taken many years to achieve the sense of a separate identity, and this probably would not have been accomplished except by a fortunate circumstance: we had separate subspecialties. This meant that I was able to publish in a field unrelated to my spouse-collaborator's specialty area and do much of that publishing alone or with others, men and women. The different fields of specialization created a wedge that afforded some leverage in establishing that I was able to work creatively independently of my spouse-collaborator.

Collaboration as a Disciplinary Mandate

Martha and Greg speak to the necessity in their disciplines of collaborating (nature of the **discipline**). In this instance, multiple perspectives are desirable. In other settings, such as the "hard" sciences, few scholars are able to assimilate all of the data themselves and so find it imperative to engage in work with at least one other individual and more usually with a team composed of individuals with different sets of expertise. In most contemporary federal funding initiatives, including education, programmatic or team-oriented approaches to research are seen as increasingly desirable. Funding arrangements and requests-for-proposals (RFPs) encourage such multi- and interdisciplinary collaborative teams. It is not just the "hard" sciences but the social sciences likewise that are seen as enhanced when multiple perspectives are brought to bear on research problems. This structural stimulus toward collaboration may portend a loosening of the prejudices that linger regarding husband-wife or partners collaborative teams. Additionally, institutions may ultimately discover that it is more in their self-interests to encourage such collaborations—especially those that are able to attract outside funding for research—than it is to maintain old and worn prejudices about women's contributions to scholarly productivity.

Collaborators as Negotiators

One of the strong themes running through all of the case narratives is the obligation, at least early on in the collaboration, to negotiate. It goes without saying that good collaborations—whether or not cohabiting—always involve negotiating findings, results, meanings, implications, conclusions, certainty and uncertainty about research outcomes, and individual responsibilities for writing and analytic tasks and dates. But before the first project is begun, other kinds of negotiations have been under way.

By other kinds of negotiations, I generally mean professional issues such as the establishment of separate identities (on which account collaborating spouses often have to be quite fleet of mental foot) and professional recognition, such as being hired into a position that represents what one wants to do. I also mean personal issues, such as: Where do we work (home or office)? How do we decide what to write? Who writes what? What sorts of criticism may we level at each other's work? When do we work? What constitutes "collaboration" for us? How do we decide whose name is listed as first author? How do we decide when to include others in a writing project? While such issues may seem mundane, they nevertheless represent issues that can demolish a budding collaboration.

Nearly every individual who has been involved in two or more collaborative relationships has a mental list of the individuals with whom they will never work again simply because the *negotiations*—whether around authorship, interpretations, or personalities—failed or some faith was broken. In the same way, individuals will seek out those with whom their collaborative research relationships have been healthy, stable, productive, and creative. I believe this centers directly on negotiation skills. Clearly, long-term partnership collaborators have skillfully managed the long series of negotiations and agreements that lead to the trust and confidence that characterize the best collaborations. Even when partners and spouses describe their discussions of their work as "arguments," they have clearly negotiated the problem of arguing about ideas without involving personalities. They have discovered via trial and error what constitutes a meaningful argument about ideas, and they routinely practice this form of collaborative creativity. Some collaborations that initially seem promising cannot manage this, and disagreements about findings, how to present arguments, authorship, or even outlets for the work end in the instability of mutual doubts about the collaborators' intentions.

It may well be that spousal collaboration works well because some couples have already been successful in negotiating with each other in many other arenas. Their success at negotiating the circumstances of their marriage contributes to their success at negotiating academic and scholarly collaboration. Marriage and scholarly work, when it is done in related fields, may be mutually reinforcing simply because many of the interpersonal tasks of marriage are the same as those for successful scholarly partnerships.

Working the Hyphens[1]

My spouse-collaborator has often joked about himself having been born with a hyphen in his side. He says the hyphen causes him to look for collaborators constantly—people who share his ideas and who are perfectly willing to "share the hyphen" in creating ideas. He has also used the metaphor (from physics) of free molecules. Researchers acting and writing alone, he suggests, are like free molecules. They have enormous degrees of freedom but are sometimes characterized as moving in Brownian motion—a random pattern of movement determined largely by electrical charges on the molecules. Sometimes molecules with attractors manage to attract other molecules and become more stable as the attractor links them and they move in tandem. While molecules lose a degree of freedom in such attraction, new forms of movement and new linkages are created.

Both of these metaphors are useful when thinking about collaboration because, indeed, collaborations represent self-Other relationships that are unique, shape-shifting entities. Even individuals who collaborate within and outside marital partnerships find that collaborations take different forms. In spousal collaborations, the partners may talk about "ideas," manuscripts, the interior logic of a piece (which ideas should go where), or new research avenues over breakfast, lunch, dinner, drinks, on long car trips, even in bed.

Collaborations where the academics do not share a bed-and-breakfast arrangement may look very different (although no less productive). In these instances, conversations about ideas, manuscripts, work that needs to be done, and schedules may be more structured: phone calls, conference calls with editors, e-mails, facsimiles, conferences attended more for the opportunity to find large blocks of time to work together than for the sessions on the conference program. Arrangements may be more formal and structured, since the collaborating authors do not have access to each other on a daily schedule and cannot know when household emergencies or pressing academic requests may interrupt or divert attention from joint scholarly pursuits.

Despite differences, long-term collaborations that are not spousal share at least several common characteristics. First, they exist not only because individuals find them productive, but also because the individuals like each other as people. They often exist because individuals share each other's values and outlooks, or at least enjoy a healthy respect for those values. They, too, are part of a "long conversation," often about a wide-ranging set of interests, not merely about the work in common. They often come into being because of shared professional and even social action agendas;[2] issues such as the creation of academic community and the nature of professional life are often critical.

Intrapsychic and psychological rewards often play a part also.[3] For individuals who enjoy having a certain seamlessness to their lives, the idea of having close to them other individuals whose idea of fun and an interesting life is to play with ideas is a compelling attraction. The sharing of a life, complete with home, possibly children, and an endless flow of ideas to engage the mind, exerts a pull that only enhances normal attraction between partners who would, even without ideas, find each other attractive. But psychological rewards are not limited to spousal collaborations. The best collaborative teams often find that in addition to the good ideas and thoughtful critiques, there is a developing friendship that enriches, extends, and enhances the quality of life for each.

The Contributions of Such Partnerships to Productivity

The contributions of academic/spousal collaborative teams frequently go beyond those of collaborative teams that are not life partnerships. Although often not a part of the bargain, such partnerships typically contribute more because they are working on joint problems more often. Their work lives do not end at 5 o'clock each day, when they return to their separate homes (**private and public lives**). Returning to the same domicile often means that such partners merely move the conversation to a different venue. The "work" of scholarly productivity goes on long after other collaborative arrangements have been abandoned in favor of home life, lawn mowing, or other concerns. The work of collaborators who are also life partners is melded into other ongoing issues and so is pursued together virtually every day.

Another bonus for research productivity is both a personal and an institutional gift. Couples who collaborate often define collaboration in much more subtly nuanced ways than institutions do. So, for instance, several couples presented in the narrative cases define collaboration as providing good commentary and criticism on each other's work even though the work might not be jointly authored (**feedback**). For individuals who find it difficult—if not impossible—to round up colleagues who know their work and who will read in a critical but constructive way, having a live-in "intimate critic"[4] means that there is always someone who can constructively give advice, provide editorial commentary, suggest new usages, and provide ideas for reorganization. When institutions consider spousal collaborators, they might often consider that the institution gets more work from such academic couples if only because work goes on even when the individuals are not at their desks on campus.

Another contribution that spousal collaboration makes to higher education institutions is that in a time when "productivity" is often defined as the number of research articles, monographs, and books produced (and perhaps, too, the number of funded research and development proposals), having a couple share in the work of producing an article or book halves the time it takes to produce such a manuscript. Thus productivity is, in effect, doubled. In the scramble for resources, departments have to consider the overall productivity of two separate individuals working alone or two individuals working together. Typically, collaborators, particularly those whose work goes on after working hours, are simply more productive in terms of actual publication rates. Sharing writing tasks not only creates an economy of scale about what can be produced, but it also contributes readily to overall efficiency in scholarly writing and manuscript production.

Problems for Academic Institutions

Problems with academic spousal collaborators are predominantly structural. They revolve about nepotism rules, where spouses may not supervise one another nor have control over rewards (such as merit pay) nor disciplinary action. This might mean, for instance, that when individuals take positions in the same department, they might have to agree not to become department chairpersons. In some instances this issue could become critical, especially if one spouse or the other exhibits strong administrative leadership and is increasingly viewed by his or her colleagues as "department chairperson material."

Yet a second problem for institutions is the issue of what happens in the event of a separation or divorce for the collaborating couple. Many readers will be familiar with the situation; it occurs often enough that experienced professionals will have been witness to at least one "academic divorce." What happens is, of course, largely dependent on whether the separation is amicable or messy. In amicable separations, frequently both members of the couple go on to pursue their separate careers in the same department in a primarily tension-free manner. When the situation is somewhat messier or when the divorce is less than amicable, colleagues often find themselves in the midst of personal matters to which they would rather not be a party, and indeed, some of the time the personal matters actually interfere with the orderly functioning of administration, classes being taught, and student advising. Doctoral dissertation committees are disrupted and reconstituted; governance committees find their work is put on hold; and routine department meetings take on a hostile flavor. No doubt this situation is a risk, although again, many readers will know of situations where divorces impeded academic functioning even though parties to the divorce were not in the same department.

A third issue for institutions is the merit pay issue. When both partners are publishing roughly equally, handling the same teaching load, and otherwise performing at comparable levels, there is no legal or fiscal reason why both partners should not be paid the same. Nevertheless, it is often the case—well documented in federal labor and manpower statistics—that women receive for comparable work roughly 70 cents on the dollar that men are paid. Such discriminatory compensation policies are likely to cause serious legal difficulties for institutions when spousal collaborators are hired in the same unit (*information sharing*). (Clearly, universities can justify such policies more readily when spouses are *not* in the same unit, arguing "labor market," "demand," or "comparable workload" factors as explanations for lower pay for women.)

For institutions, hiring a couple into the same department or specialty will mean abandoning pay policies that typically reward men more dollars for work that is comparable to what women are doing. Institutions may also need to do some campuswide training regarding the less overt forms of discrimination that arise when husbands and wives work in the same field, to wit, the prejudice that the husband must be "ghostwriting" for the wife. This lingering disrespect for the work of women in intellectual careers continues to plague higher education. Replacing this prejudice with positive affirmations of women's contributions to intellectual and scholarly work will be neither easy nor pleasant. Even men whose public attitudes are welcoming to women in academic careers often harbor suspicions that when husbands and wives are in the same field, she is "riding his coattails" or he is "carrying her." The solution may be, if possible, that spousal partners take assignments in separate but related departments. The option of "job-sharing"—two individuals hired into the same position for a much larger salary than one, but smaller than two separate salaries—is one possibility that is being explored. This is a particularly fruitful option if the partners have young children and wish to share child-care responsibilities during the early years of their academic careers.

On the whole, academic spousal collaborations have much more to offer higher education than institutions have considered. It is not merely that institutions often get more concentrated effort from some partnerships. It is also the case that increasingly, the world on which institutions of higher education relies so heavily—the world of sponsored research and external funding—invites such collaboration and is often unwilling to fund without programmatic intellectual support.

6

Introduction to the Second Case:
Different Chapters, Same Textbook:
Collaboration between Psychologists in the Same Department

The second case narrative describes the collaborative relationship of two cognitive psychologists, Anna Ranero and Roger Strohm, who were both hired, tenured, and promoted as faculty in the same academic department in a highly competitive research university (**career symmetry**). This particular couple speaks clearly to the clash between the academic **reward** structure of research-oriented universities and collaboration, and how it shapes the agenda of faculty. The case also speaks in some detail to the challenge faced by many members of academic couples with overlapping **training and interests** to differentiate themselves (**recognition**).

Because they have both spent their entire careers under "the heavy hand of publish or perish" neither Roger nor Anna felt that their collaborative relationship had a significant impact on the quantity of the publications. Both felt strongly, however, that it had impacted the quality of their scholarship. One unique aspect of this case is the detail with which it presents how this couple negotiated intellectual differences of opinion and the connection they felt that process had to expanding their thinking and improving the quality of their research and publications.

One additional aspect that this case highlights is the role a collaborative relationship can play in sustaining a commitment to research and publication. While adding to the motivation to publish is a benefit offered by many types of collaborative relationships, the faculty members in this case are at a point in their careers where they are grappling with the issue of whether they should go on and shape a life that is more balanced or continue to pour their energies in to research despite the dissipation of external incentives to do so (**private and public lives**). Roger suggested that the importance of the **personal relationship** and satisfac-

58

tion that he and Anna have found from working through substantive conceptual differences with an intellectual equal is what is now most likely to sustain their scholarship.

The Case Response

Peter Magolda's response to the Ranero-Strohm case offers a frank analysis of some of the issues that underlie the suspicion and unease from colleagues that often greet dual-career couples, particularly those working at the same institution and department. Like Anna and Roger, Peter and his spouse, Marcia, have faculty appointments in the same department. They do not however, share the same degree of career symmetry and have very different research interests. Neither couple has children.

Magolda's chapter is organized by a series of vignettes he presents of experiences he has had as the member of an academic couple, which he then follows with analysis and discussion. In the first vignette, Magolda confronts two sensitive issues members of dual-career academic couples face during the interview process: first, the pressure to find a suitable job within reasonable distance of a spouse (**geographic mobility**); second, the dilemma academic couples face during the interview process about whether or not to reveal their personal relationship. He contrasts his own decision to invite discussion about it during a job interview with the decision made by Anna and Roger to refrain from mentioning it.

In the second vignette, Magolda describes the gains from jointly authoring with his spouse despite differences in writing and working style and how this can conflict with the traditional academic reward structure and the priority it awards to individual accomplishments. Similarly, Anna and Roger's case shows how the long process of negotiating differences can result in what they consider to be a far superior product, or a "sum that is greater than the parts."

Magolda's remaining vignettes provide real-life examples of voiced and unvoiced political issues facing academic couples: how they are seen by some students and colleagues as being of one mind, the anticipation that they will collude with each other and operate as a "voting block," and how administrators' attempts to be proactive in hiring well-qualified couples can be viewed by faculty as an infringement on departmental autonomy. His analysis suggests that it is faculty culture rather than lack of initiative on the part of administrators that hobbles institutions from hiring all but the most extraordinarily qualified faculty couple.

Magolda's chapter concludes with a critical look at the debate about "balance" as it applies to faculty lives. He gives examples from his own life about how trying to draw a line between what is labeled as work and what is labeled as personal or family-related has little meaning for academic couples in some settings. He points to the advantage couples have when the care they have for each other is manifested in an extensive investment in a partner's career success and satisfaction. This is at the heart of the argument presented in *Working Equal* about how a partner in the same profession can have reciprocal benefits for some faculty couples.

A Visit to the Heartland

Negotiating the multiple modes of transportation required to reach America's heartland from the East Coast underscored for me the challenges colleges and universities in this part of the country face in recruiting talented faculty members and the challenges faculty must face to stay connected to their colleagues. It made it clearer to me why despite my sampling method, which drew from universities across the country, so many of the members of academic couples I interviewed seemed clustered at several large research universities in the Midwest.

My visit occurred on a Friday in April 1997, more than a year after I interviewed Anna by telephone and about eight months after I talked with Roger. With the directions Anna had supplied, I had no trouble locating their contemporary home on the top of a hill in a wooded subdivision just a few miles from campus. Anna's and Roger's schedules were so tight that this was the only Friday available that month when they both had a morning free to talk with me.

We settled down to conduct the joint interview at the dining room table in part of the single room that made up most of the middle floor of Anna and Roger's house. Anna and Roger sat facing each other, while I and my tape recorder were situated at the head of the long table. During the interview, either Anna or Roger generally took the lead in responding to questions I asked. This was spontaneous and something that did not require negotiation. Anna spoke at greatest length in response to my opening question, which was to describe the evolution of their collaborative relationship. Anna spoke more than Roger did about the conflicts in writing style. Anna and Roger were of one voice in describing how they negotiated intellectual differences and how that contributed to the quality of the scholarship each produced. While they were very expansive in some areas, such as in describing their research, they were less expansive about some questions that probably would have required them to conjecture about aspects of their relationship that they had not previously considered.

My first observation about Anna Ranero and Roger Strohm's relationship from watching them together during the joint interview, was of a gentleness toward each other. They both struck me as being quite thoughtful and careful about the words they chose not only in addressing me but also in addressing each other. They allowed each other time to finish their thoughts and rarely interrupted each other.

Anna and Roger's interpretations of events did not differ dramatically. This relatively singular voice is not something I expected to find when I spoke with them together, but I came to discover that it was characteristic of the couples I interviewed who have been engaged in successful, long-term, collaborative relationships with a spouse or partner. I interpret this to be one reflection that their relationship is egalitarian.[1] It is also probably a reflection that they are accustomed to constructing a seamless public voice in their writing. It is in dramatic contrast to both the style of writing and the style of speaking of the couple presented in the next case narrative in this book.

During one part of the joint interview, when we were talking about their working styles and how they differed, Anna made an offhand comment that may offer some insight into why some academic couples make the decision not to have children. Both Anna and Roger had described themselves as getting obsessed or very preoccupied with a project they might be working on. Anna commented that she really could not imagine how academic couples with children managed it. Compared to her own approach to writing, which she characterized as "inefficient," she said that such couples "must not have any wasted movements to be productive as some are." Roger agreed, proposing that couples with children must be better able to work with divided attention and smaller units of time. For Anna and Roger, it appears that their **lifestyle**, the way they organize their home to accommodate their work, as well as their decision not to have children are strongly influenced by their personalities and strong and distinct preferences about how they do their thinking and writing.

Two Different People

I saw a slightly different side of both members of this couple when we relocated after the joint interview to conduct the follow-up session in each of their offices on campus. I met with Anna first. She now holds a full-time position in college-level administration. We met in her roomy, well-appointed office in the administrative suite of a relatively new building near the center of campus.

Perhaps to counter an impression that she felt might have been communicated during the joint interview, Anna spoke of how she and Roger differed. She described herself as being more competitive and more outer-directed, while he is more inner-directed. "Roger plays with ideas for fun," Anna said, "but I do not do it for fun. It is something I am required to do." The comment reminded me once again of how strongly the reward structure of the research university had shaped their lives. This and other comments led me to conclude that her motivation to participate in this particular research project was a sense of professional duty or obligation rather than an agenda for social change or a view of their relationship as being anything out of the ordinary. This was not true of either of the other two cases I have presented in this section of the book.

What I learned from watching Anna in this setting confirmed my impression that she is shifting to a different stage of her career. I concluded that with the exception of the work she might continue with Roger, she has reached a stage where she is much less likely to be deeply engaged with the single line of research she has pursued relentlessly since graduate school. Anna spoke of some ideas she would like to try out about undergraduate advising. She would like to experiment with some more creative forms of writing. She appears weary, and possibly disillusioned, with some aspects of the publish-or-perish game and relieved to have it behind her. Anna clearly aspires to what she labeled as a more balanced life.

My one-on-one meeting with Roger also added some details to my impression of him. We met in his tiny office on campus, which was completely barren of any decoration or personal item. This is where he conducts his office hours and meets with students, but this is clearly not a place where he spends much time. From my conversations with Roger, it is my guess that he will continue much as he has in the past, living a life preoccupied with ideas if not necessarily with publishing. At this point in their relationship, I sense that Anna and Roger will occupy more distinct working spheres than they have in the past. I suspect that whether they will continue with the work they do jointly has more to do with Anna's interests than with Roger's.

Conclusion

Some of the strongest impressions I got from the time I spent with Anna Ranero and Roger Strohm were from the topic one or the other chose to emphasize by speaking at length about it repeatedly and on different occasions. For Roger, it was the reward structure and how he and Anna productively negotiated intellectual differences of opinion. For Anna, it was the battle to be seen as distinct from Roger. She returned to this topic on a number of occasions, speaking of the importance of "maintaining a separate self" and "being on an equal footing." It seemed important to her to underscore their differences. Although she spoke at length about how her area of research and Roger's are different, it is a difference that Roger acknowledged was hardly clear even to colleagues in their department. The number of references Anna made to this topic suggested to me that the extent of the overlap in their areas of research was problematic for her. The issue of having a distinct scholarly identity may have been aggravated for Anna because the nature of her research interests has provided little opportunity to collaborate with people other than Roger. Unlike the other couples I spoke with, neither spoke at any length about **collegial networks** or about collaborating with others.

A number of changes Anna and Roger opted to negotiate about their new faculty appointments point to some of the challenges they must have faced in having faculty appointments in the same department. That they sought positions in different departments when they relocated, that Anna is completely retooling herself to teach in another college, and that she chose to decline voting rights in the psychology department all lead me to suspect there must have been some uncomfortable elements to their original arrangement. It is my suspicion that, if asked, Anna and Roger would admonish a young couple about the drawbacks of having positions in the same academic department.

7

The Second Case: Different Chapters, Same Textbook: Collaboration between Psychologists in the Same Department

My work has been driven by outside pressures: getting tenured, get-ting promoted, and being respected. I think the fact that we are col-laborating together is going to make it much more likely that we will continue to be productive because we have both reached a stage in our own careers where the outside pressures do not matter any more. We have many outside interests that can pull us away from our work. Now it has to be the intrinsic interest and satisfaction in scholarly work that makes it happen. *–Roger Strohm, July 1997*

Now both full professors in different departments at the same research university in the Midwest, Anna Ranero and Roger Strohm are both highly productive scholars by any measure. Within one year of each other in career age, but seven years apart in chronological age, the evolution of their collaborative relationship reflects the impact of pres-sures internal to the couple and the traditional academic **reward** struc-ture to develop autonomous research identities. The case highlights the contribution that some long-term collaborative partnerships can make to sustaining research productivity against competing demands as well as to the production of new knowledge and theoretical perspectives.

The Evolution of Their Personal Relationship
When I met them, Anna Ranero and Roger Strohm had been together as a couple for 26 years. They first met in the late 1960s when Anna was visiting the campus of a research university on the West Coast when she was choosing a doctoral program in psychology. Both admitted during the joint interview that I conducted with them that at the time there was no immediate chemistry between them. Reminding me that this was a time when the style for women her age was long hair and blue jeans,

Anna said that Roger thought she looked like quite the prim school teacher in her skirt and heels. At the time, Anna was a junior high school teacher and an instructor in Introduction to Psychology at a local college.

Both Anna's and Roger's research deals with how people make judgments and decisions. Anna's research focuses on risky choice—how people make judgments and decisions under risk. Roger's specialty is how people make decisions about the meaning of sentences and how they resolve complexities and ambiguities inherent in language. Making a statement that reflects how closely allied their fields are and that would become this chapter's title, Roger said: "We are both cognitive psychologists. Our areas of expertise would be like different chapters in the same textbook."

Making choices for different but equally uninformed reasons that they now chuckle about, Anna and Roger ended up working together in the same methodology-oriented research laboratory in cognitive psychology during their doctoral programs (overlap in **training**). Each worked under the tutelage of the same advisor, whom they described as a mathematical psychologist—that is, someone who uses mathematics to describe systematic structures in human behavior. Known to be a stickler for semantics and the kind of person who required dozens of drafts before being satisfied, their advisor was one whose list of former advisees was longer than the list of advisees who stuck with him. Roger observed in his own wry way: "That kind of training was successful at teaching good writing skills, but it was not the kind of thing that made writing a lot of fun."

When Roger left the laboratory to begin a faculty career in the early 1970s, he and Anna had been dating for more than two years. The job market was very tight (**geographic mobility**). He received two offers, both relatively late in the academic year. His preference was "to enter a faculty position in a good, small place where they did some research but it wasn't the be-all, end-all." Instead, he landed a position at a Big Ten university. It was the kind of competitive department, he said, that brought in four new assistant professors with the expectation of awarding tenure only to one. About the effect of the newfound position on their relationship, Anna said: "It was not clear what was going to happen to our relationship. We had never talked about a future together. I, for one, was terminally tongue-tied about such things. There was no question about one of us giving up on our careers. We were too committed to our work to consider that. The relationship could have gone either way."

Completing her doctorate within the year, Anna entered the same constricted job market, convinced that it was highly unlikely that she and Roger would end up in the same place. She hesitated about submitting her credentials to the same university where Roger was employed, believing it unlikely they would hire another faculty member with such similar training. Two fortuitous things happened, however. First, her curriculum vitae happened to land on the desk of the person who had been the advisor of Anna and Roger's advisor in California. Secondly, the university had developed a proactive policy of hiring minorities even if there was no advertised vacancy. The university was particularly interested in recruiting members of underrepresented groups and guessed, incorrectly, from her name that Anna is Hispanic. Anna said, in an understated way that I grew to realize was characteristic of her, "If it hadn't been essentially an extra position, they wouldn't have looked at me. That was a very good piece of luck."

Anna and Roger chose not to disclose their personal relationship during her campus interview. He said: "It was a deliberate decision on my part. It is not that we lied about it; it is just that we chose to keep quiet about it. The reason I decided that was because the year before, a woman in the department had tried to get her spouse hired and it had complicated things. It seemed to me that it certainly was not going to do any good and it had the potential to do some harm." When Anna received an offer for a tenure-track faculty position in the same department as Roger, she accepted it immediately. They made their personal relationship public after she relocated.

Anna remained at that research university for 16 years; Roger was there for 17 years. Each was tenured and promoted to full professor during that time. She eventually served as department chair. A variety of factors eventually coalesced to pull them away. Anna observed: "One of the things that happens when you are in one place for a long time is salary compression and, in some cases, inversion. There was no way to right that according to the university's way of thinking." As department chair, she recruited new faculty members at salaries that were higher than those of highly productive senior faculty. Similarly, Roger commented that it is hard to be fully appreciated when you have grown up career-wise and gone through the ranks at one place. He said: "It is easy to come to feel inadequately appreciated. Being that long in one place, you begin to wonder if you are in a rut. We had gotten to the point of saying, either we are going to stay here forever or we are going to move now. Finding two tenured positions in a first-rate place is very unlikely."

The turning point in Anna and Roger's decision to relocate to another university came after Anna received a telephone call from a colleague. The colleague asked Anna if he could nominate her for an endowed chair in a college of business at another research university. Going so far as to experiment with it on a trial basis by serving as a visiting professor at another university, Anna had previously weighed the advantages of a faculty position in a business department. Faculty in economics and business do most of the research on decision-making. She accepted the invitation to be nominated, but made it clear from the outset that she would not consider relocating unless something appropriate was available for Roger. Anna commented that she felt she had not been aggressive enough in making this point on other occasions.

Both Anna and Roger were invited to interview on campus at the same time for faculty positions in different departments. No spousal hiring program or policy was in place at the time. They were attracted to the campus because of the sense of community. They said that they were encouraged by the amount of interaction they saw taking place between department heads and the deans of the different colleges during the campus visit. They found this refreshing in comparison to their university, where everyone was "off doing their own thing."

Anna and Roger made it clear that they really had not intended to relocate and that they would not have done so if they had not both received attractive offers. They each negotiated a faculty appointment that crossed departments. He has an appointment in psychology and computer science; she has an appointment in the college of business and a zero-time appointment in psychology. Sensing concern that they might collude to operate as a voting block, as there had been at their previous institution, Anna declined voting rights in the psychology department. A zero-time appointment makes it possible for her to supervise graduate student research.

Their Collaborative Relationship

Anna and Roger did not collaborate as doctoral students. Their first coauthored publication did not appear until after they each had earned tenure. Even though their research areas overlapped from the earliest days of their training, Anna and Roger tried to develop independent research identities. Over time they have coauthored eight out of what Roger estimated to be 40 or 50 journal articles each has published. Neither has written a book nor do they have concrete plans to do so, because it is not a convention in their discipline.

Feedback about manuscripts and about ideas has always been an integral element of their working relationship. They give each other detailed feedback about manuscripts, just as a departmental colleague might. In the early days of their relationship, before they became so familiar with each other's work, however, the feedback was not necessarily technical. Anna said: "I think it is fair to say that for a long time neither of us completely understood what the other person was doing. We read each other's papers much like an informed outsider would. We tried to help each other by giving each other feedback, but it was not and could not be technically oriented."

Roger spoke about the importance of feedback more in terms of the exchange of ideas and about how they "bounced ideas off each other." He said:

> We have always used the other person to bounce our own ideas off. There is no question that Anna has made contributions to me in helping to clarify my thinking in my own area, and I would certainly like to think that I have done the same for her. Even though we were not official collaborators for a variety of reasons, certainly we were having an influence on each other's thinking. In that sense, we were collaborative thinkers even when we were not collaborative writers.

Their research areas are close enough that, as Roger observed, "any idea that either of us has, which we naturally bounce off the other, is likely to provoke not just remote reactions, but ones that are near to the other's interest." For about 15 years, just about all of the time Anna and Roger had at least one writing project that they were working on together. It would be one out of four or five projects each was working on at any given time. Each project took two or three years to complete. What usually happened, Anna said, is that: "An idea for a piece would arise and we would do it and close it off. Then something would arise later, usually on a completely different topic." Anna characterized the times when they wrote together using the following words:

> It is almost like an interdisciplinary effort. Although we are both psychologists, the boundaries within disciplines are sometimes just as strong as those between disciplines. At the points where we collaborated, we each would be able to see suddenly that by thinking about the other area, something became clarified in our own. In these cases, it was a two-way realization. It wasn't just looking to

the other person's area to clear up problems in one's own, but really a coming together of the whole being more than the sum of the parts.

Both Anna and Roger described the excitement of realizing for the first time the ways in which the theoretical aspects of their individual research programs would fit together in a unique, new, joint project. The project would be bolstered by long familiarity (**intellectual intimacy**) with each other's work. Roger commented:

> Each of us has naturally broadened our theoretical approaches to more kinds of things, so probably it was inevitable that sooner or later we would have to face how our different areas fit together. Sooner or later, since we are in the same general domain, we probably always knew that we were not going to be able to erect a rigid wall to separate the two.

Anna said that it has only been in the last three years that they have begun to be "forward-thinking" or "to think in terms of a progression of our joint agenda in the same way that we have always done for our individual programs." Roger agreed with her point during the same conversation, saying: "This is clearly a joint project. It is a fusion of our separate areas." She added, referring implicitly to a highly flexible **division of labor**: "This is something we have chosen to do. The joint part is joint because the best parts of what is new in it come from both of us. That is not something that one person does the technical work and the other one does everything else. Theoretically, it is very much a product of us both."

As a reflection of the theme repeated throughout our conversations, it was apparent that it was particularly important to Anna that they were on "equal footing" in a joint project. Anna commented:

> Taken together, each of us has expertise in relevant areas, but very disparate corners of the areas that are relevant. This really is a case where we are pooling a lot of individual knowledge that I, at least, would not have gotten on my own. At this point, we both know one another's areas well enough that this is a choice that is good for the project and it is good for us individually. This is a place where we are on equal footing. Each of us has something very distinct to contribute.

Recognition

Both Anna and Roger repeatedly made the point that up until very recently, they were very sensitive to the need for **recognition** as independent scholars or, as Anna said, for maintaining "a separate self." Roger described the department where they were both first appointed to a faculty position as a place where the people who did not pick up on the rules of the game quickly did not survive. He said: "There was a high threshold for performance. There were a lot of different things that you thought you had to do right if you were going to have any chance of surviving. You definitely came in with a research program. You pretty much focused on taking advantage of the start that you had made and building on that to establish yourself as a person in that field."

There were a number of reasons why Anna and Roger made the decision not to collaborate together as junior faculty. Anna said: "We were fairly new exemplars of couples who had appointments in the same department. There was a lot of uneasiness there that it would not be possible to distinguish who did what. It was quite a deliberate decision that we did not work together." Roger elaborated this point when he said:

> We did collaborate fairly early on and fairly steadily over the years, but it was always the minority of the work that each of us was doing. The things we did together were only on lines of research that were not directly within either of our individual lines of research. We were concerned not to have anybody be able to characterize one or the other of us as being derivative of the other. The hazards of the department that we were in and in a lot of departments like that is that in any long-term collaborative relationship the question arises about whose work it really is. It is the belief that there is only enough work there for one. It is a concern if you have any single connection that dominates your work, but it is particularly a hazard if you have a long-term collaboration with your advisor. We were sensitive of that from the beginning and knew that we needed to establish beyond a shadow of a doubt that each of us had an independent line of research we were identified with.

According to Roger, who of the two spoke at greater length on this issue, it is absolutely essential in a competitive research environment to become well known for one thing. Their collaborative work did count positively in the evaluation of their credentials but, he said, "It was only really paid attention to because we had already established ourselves as having an identifiable reputation in the field" (**reward**). At another point Roger said: "Somebody who only had, say, a collection of side interests and never had a single thing that they were known for, it wouldn't matter how much they had published and how good they were in each of those things, if they spread themselves that thinly they wouldn't make it."

Referring to the impact of their collaboration on the quality of their work, Anna observed that even though their early collaborations were not in areas that were "near and dear to our individual hearts or major pieces of our individual egos," as separate pieces of work: "they are amongst the best individual pieces of work either of us have done. You might think that would be motivation enough for us to have given up our separate lines of research and just done it collaboratively, but again, there were other political and social factors that entered in that decision."

Negotiating Differences in Collaborative Styles

Despite their shared intellectual heritage, Anna and Roger are not unlike many of the couples I interviewed in their description of having to negotiate differences in **working and writing styles**. After first experimenting to neither's satisfaction with actually trying to craft sentences sitting side by side, they shifted to a writing process where one or the other usually takes the lead in writing a first draft. Then, as Anna worded it, "The other person goes in and digs and tears apart the things that do not work." She said that as tough as it is, each one has to sit down and struggle with the manuscript. When one or the other has more expertise in a section, they will occasionally divide up the initial drafting, but they both prefer the sense of coherence across the manuscript that appears when one person takes responsibility for the writing.

One area of the writing process that has been contentious is how they give each other feedback about ideas and manuscripts. Anna said: "I think that in terms of bad feeling, we have had more bad feelings about learning how to literally get the words onto paper than we have had about the real heart of the work. That just keeps getting better and better." As Anna described it, when they first started reading each other's manuscripts, she tended to be fairly forthright. She jotted her comments and notes all over the paper, expressing her reaction in an uncensored way, almost exactly as she was thinking it. She might write "I hate this" or "This is dreadful" in the margin. Roger, on the other hand, would go through her papers putting a faint mark or a question mark in the margin, leaving it unclear to her exactly what his reaction was. Anna explained: "I come from a family of Brazilians. We argued loudly and often. He came from a family of Norwegians, where a raised eyebrow is a strong statement." Over time they grew to understand the differences in style, so that she can now say she hates it and he is no longer threatened. Roger has learned to be more forthright, but there are still differences in their collaborative styles. Anna said: "The longer we work together, the more sensitive we are about how to critique each other's work and how to suggest that something is going the wrong way."

There are also differences in Anna's and Roger's preferred style for working out a problem that they discussed openly during the joint interview. As you might guess from the way they give each other written feedback, Roger said that he prefers to "go off and think about it for a few days to get a feel for the factors and the whole." Roger likes to work through a problem on his own. Anna also likes to work out a problem on her own, but her preferred style is to talk it through out loud. She said: "Even when we are working on very different projects, I have always used telling someone about it as a way of thinking further about it. Articulating it out loud to another person helps me to think about it." Roger acknowledged that he had to learn that when Anna described a problem she had encountered, she was often really in "talk mode" and was looking for a sounding board rather than answers. Roger said: "That was another thing we had to learn. Sometimes she will start to tell me something and it is clear that she has not really worked it out. I used to think that she wanted me to help her. I realized eventually that she wants to talk to me, but she does not want me to interrupt her." Anna emphatically agreed with this comment, referring, once again, to the importance of independence. She said:

> I do not want him to try and fix it. I am usually not telling him enough of the whole story that he would be in a position to fix it. When we started working on this stuff, I was always afraid that he would fix it and that it was no longer my own thing.

Working Styles

Anna and Roger also differ in their working styles and in the type or *quality of time* they require to write. Anna said that when she is working on a project she can become totally preoccupied with it. She described the way she works in the following words:

> When I am writing a paper, I get obsessed by it. I never know exactly what day I can finally get started. There is sort of a magic moment when I get hooked. Especially on the writing projects, if I

could live in my bathrobe for the next four or five days, I would. I would sleep when I was desperately tired and I would work constantly while all of this stuff wants to come out. It is constantly on my mind. I can never set it aside to rest, or at least back in those days, I could not set it aside to rest for a minute. So, it was a matter of picking and nagging and pushing on ideas that still required time to think through. It drives him crazy because I cannot let it go. I want to talk about it constantly.

Roger admitted that he, too, can obsess on a problem and that it is difficult for him to write when he has only small chunks of time available. His preference is to have a full day but he said he did not have the "days-on-end kind of obsession." Roger said that there are times when he needs to get away from a problem, to give it time to percolate in the back of his mind.

The way that Anna and Roger negotiate these differences in working style is shown in how the *space* is arranged in their home. Reflecting her preference for working in the morning and his preference for working at night, they each have distinctly defined work space on different floors of their three-story house, out of the public view. Roger teaches most of his classes in the late afternoon. His preferred working pattern is to have dinner and relax for a while. He starts working at 9 o'clock at night and may work for four or five hours. His work space is on the ground floor of the house, two floors below the bedroom. The distance provides a sound barrier. Anna, on the other hand, prefers to work early in the morning. Her study is in a room near the bedroom on the third floor. With this arrangement, Roger explained, they both have the isolation and private space needed to do their work. When they are working together, such as in reviewing a jointly authored manuscript, they do it at the dining room table in the joint space that is the middle level of their home.

Negotiating Intellectual Differences

Anna and Roger both spoke of times in their collaborative work together when there was a "gut feeling" that some aspect of their thinking was wrong. They both agreed that over time they had learned to trust that feeling. "If it feels wrong, it probably is wrong," Anna said. Describing situations like this, Anna said:

We work in areas where there are many different ways to approach a question, and sometimes from the very start the terms and the symbols and the concepts that are part of the implicit model are just the wrong batch. Sometimes it is simply necessary to say, "I can see that we can do it this way, but it is losing the sense of what we are really trying to get to." There have been places where sometimes we have tossed out fairly well developed hunks of work because it truly wasn't right. Even if it seemed to be doing a good job on one basis, there wasn't any fidelity to the original sense of how the process is working. Whenever that has happened, we have come out the better for it.

Aspects of their **personal relationship** also contribute to how Anna and Roger have learned to negotiate their intellectual differences over time. Both used the same words to describe those qualities: stubbornness, trust, and respect. Anna referred to stubbornness, for example, when she said: "For me, if it is going to be a really productive, theoretical collaboration, you have to be able to talk and to argue. The other person has to be able to hold their ground when they are right long enough to convince the one that thinks they know everything in this area." Part of what underlies this is respect for the other person's knowledge or expertise. Roger spoke of respect when he said:

In the collaborative projects that we have done that were not within our respective areas, it was very often the case that we would have ideas about how the work should go or what was the solution to the problem we were working on that the other person disagreed with. We think a lot alike, but we do not think exactly alike. There are times when we have said to each other, "I think that you are wrong, but that is your business." That is the sort of respect you have in a successful relationship.

Roger said that although they both had a strong drive to be independent thinkers, they would not want to appear in print as opponents. He described the process of negotiating differences in opinion in the following words:

We are both stubborn enough that neither of us has been willing just to let go in situations like this. I cannot remember if there ever has been a project that we just finally abandoned because we could not resolve it. In fact, usually we do find a way of resolving it, and when we do, we have learned that we are both happier with the resolution than we would have been with our own individualistic approaches. We have the same attitude, for example, in picking furniture. What I think is okay, she might hate. What she thinks is okay, I might hate. But what she loves I am going to love. We just do not settle until both of us are happy. It will make the other person happier too.

Roger said that even though he considers himself really to be a "lone worker and a lone thinker," his collaboration with Anna is not surprising because they have a shared **worldview**. It is "because she and I think an awful lot alike, which, of course, is part of our attraction," he said. At another point in the interview, he said: "Nobody is quite as compatible to my way of thinking and I think that is probably the other way as well. So there is probably more opportunity for speaking with one voice."

When Roger compared collaborating with Anna to collaborating with colleagues, he spoke of the role of the personal relationship and emotional bond in sustaining their commitment to be successful collaborators. Roger said:

> The emotional means that we care more about the collaboration being successful. With another collaborator, if we could not agree, we would probably find a compromise or trade-off rather than insisting on thinking hard enough to find the way to make it mesh. That is part of the reason that I think that the work she and I have done together is among our best work. It would be good if we could manage to make ourselves do that with our more casual collaborators, but it is just too much work.

Over the course of their long personal and working relationship, Anna and Roger negotiated differences in working styles by accommodating the way they gave feedback, arranging the work space at home to fit their different work rhythms, and trusting differences of opinion on substantive issues as a marker that an idea demanded more thought.

Future Directions

Anna's and Roger's working lives have changed since they relocated to another university. Although both acknowledged that in the past there was little division between their **private and public lives**, they see themselves as leading what they labeled "a more balanced life" now. Roger has a number of hobbies. During the tour they provided of their home, he observed with some pride that Anna has acquired a hobby for the first time: flower gardening.

Although neither of them said this outright, they both have reasons why they might abandon the habit of dedicating so much time to scholarly writing. Anna described her approach to writing in the past in ways that did not suggest she found it pleasant. She said it was "not an orderly way to work," "easily disrupted," and so intense that "you put off going into one of those kinds of fits." Anna described the pace of her life as being more sane now, saying:

> I don't want to do a whole lot of research now, given my administrative duties. I don't want to give up teaching. I don't have time to aspire to more than a piece a year or a piece every year and a half. I find that is a wonderful, sane schedule. One of the things that I have grown to dislike about academe is this constant upping of the ante of how many pieces you are supposed to publish in a year—people counting how many lines on a vitae rather than evaluating its contribution. I have found that administrative responsibilities have freed me to do the research that I would have done anyway, but at a pace that is good for me.

Roger also described himself as a person who has always found writing difficult. Roger still finds theoretical writing "engaging," but writing up an experiment has grown to be "trite and routine." It seems likely that the opportunity to write with Anna helped to make the process more enjoyable for him. It is the thinking, more than the writing, that he likes. He said of himself: "I have always enjoyed thinking and talking and working out ideas and, to that extent, writing out notes. I have not really enjoyed the mechanics of writing all that much, at least not enough to make me want to do it as part of my life." In informal comments made more than eight months later, Anna described him as a man who likes to work in the intellectual domain. She said he is someone whose goal always has been to "Get his system of thinking in order."

As the quotation opening the chapter suggests, both Anna and Roger have reached a point in their careers where they no longer feel driven by external demands to publish. Roger noted the influence of both seniority and the institutional culture on their ability to collaborate together when he said: "We are both sufficiently senior now that we do not have to worry much anymore about being identified with the other. Secondly, this university does not seem to care that much anyway."

Anna and Roger have reached a point in their careers when many things are pulling them in directions away from their scholarly writing, while their mutual preoccupation with ideas and the collaborative relationship that they have developed over 20 years are forces that may sustain it. Toward the end of my campus visit, each spoke once again of how they learned to deal with what seemed initially to be contradictory viewpoints, and how it was this process that improved the quality of their work because it compelled them to extend their thinking. Roger made the following comment informally when I visited him in his office on campus:

> In earlier projects, when we found something that seemed contradictory we always found that if we worked hard we could figure it out. Very often the truth lies somewhere in the middle of two extremes. We have grown over time to trust the conviction that if we disagree, we must both be wrong.

Anna said:

> I don't think he is impatient with me anymore. He knows it is very important to me to work it out myself. We do not want to agree on something we do not understand. Each of us has to reach a thorough understanding independently. Early on in our relationship it was difficult to be patient enough to understand each other's viewpoint.

These comments punctuate the point that independent thinking does not have to be sacrificed to maintain a successful collaboration.

8

Don't Ask, Don't Tell:
A Response to the Second Case

PETER MAGOLDA

I remember the day—July 22, 1985—as if it was yesterday. With Marcia, my spouse, driving, I divide my time between absorbing the landscape and mentally preparing for my day-long job interview for the position of Director of Student Services at a southwest Ohio community college. I can see for miles—corn to the left, soybeans to the right, endless farm fields on either side of the two-lane roads. From my perspective, the job is not an ideal fit. From the search committee's perspective, I suspect the same could be said about me. I mentally generate a list of the positive features. First, the job appears challenging especially because it blends academic affairs with student affairs. Second, this college attracts mostly working-class, non-traditional-age students, which would be a refreshing change from the privileged traditional-age students with whom I work. Third, this campus is only 20 minutes from the town where my spouse, who is a faculty member, works and resides. This commute would be better than our current arrangement, which requires us to shuttle between Vermont and Ohio. Most importantly, I would be employed in higher education, something I had taken for granted prior to joining the ranks of couples in academia (**geographic mobility**).

The ribbonlike highway conforms to the gentle, rolling hills that are characteristic of southwest Ohio. The narrow road requires Marcia to decelerate as a bouncing eighteen-wheeler approaches. Brick ranch-style homes with neatly trimmed lawns and manicured flower gardens are sporadically situated between old farm homesteads with unkempt acres of fields separating the residences from the highway. I quickly conclude that Ohio's natural beauty cannot match Vermont's. Still, residing in the same household with my spouse outweighs these aesthetic shortcomings. I hum a melody of a song to mask my nervousness about my pending interview and inevitable relocation to Ohio (with or without a job). The pressure is enormous knowing that failing to secure this job would complicate our lives. Suddenly I realize the appropriateness of the song I am subconsciously humming: 10CC's "The Things We Do for Love." Fortunately, I know Marcia won't ask the name of the tune; I don't tell.

The passing crossroads are decorated with Americana that symbolize the competing values of yesteryear as well as the growth-and-change agenda of the 1980s. A dilapidated roadhouse tavern tattooed with "For Rent" and "Keep Out" signs sits opposite a newly constructed minimart. For the past few weeks I have been sorting out competing values related to work and home: job security versus job satisfaction, long-term versus short-term benefits, and my quality of life versus my spouse's quality of life. Two important and intertwined aspects of my life—my spouse and my job—do not yet fit together. Which values will prevail? Suddenly, words like "growth" and "change," staples in my work and home vocabulary, alarm me.

I mask my disappointment as we near the campus. The four 1960s-ish buildings flanked by asphalt parking lots remind me of a high school. I joke about the ease with which I will locate my host. Marcia forces a chuckle. Since my host will drive me to the airport following my interview, I bid Marcia farewell, exit the car, and stand in the empty parking lot with my garment bag in one hand and my briefcase in the other. The scene reminds me of my youth, when my parents would drop me off at a summer camp that hardly resembled its promotional brochure photographs. Camp usually worked out; I hoped the same would be true in this instance.

Marcia and I usually talk openly about our hopes and fears and encourage and support each other when making important decisions. In this instance, we deviate from this norm. Becoming an academic couple— entangled in the same web of uncertainty—takes getting used to. Marcia refrains from asking questions about my job search in general and this job in particular. Similarly, I refrain from sharing my views with her. My life as part of an academic couple is not yet an open book, even for my spouse. In retrospect, these dynamics were partially due to us knowing each other's thoughts and partially due to us not wanting to verbalize our uneasy inner thoughts about securing dual careers in higher education. Not until months later, after I successfully secure a job, do we abandon our "don't ask, don't tell" policy.

The purpose of this chapter is for me to respond to the Anna Ranero and Roger Strohm case study, which offers a rare glimpse into the long-term relationship of a senior academic couple. My primary task is to assess, on a personal and conceptual level, the evocative power of the narrative and the extent to which it is consistent with or different from my own experiences. In the analysis that follows I utilize one of my areas of expertise—interpreting documents and material culture through an anthropological lens—to enrich understanding of what it is like to be an academic couple working in the same department and to illuminate the issues the members of the couple encounter as they navigate their complex work and home lives.

Following are five vignettes. In the "You Can't Judge a Book by Its Cover" vignette, I discuss the political relationship between academic couples and higher education institutions during job interviews. In the "Textbook Example" vignette, I explore what collaboration by academic couples looks like from the vantage point of the couple and those who evaluate the couple's output. In the "Matching Bookends" vignette, I explore the expectation by colleagues, students, and acquaintances that academic couples simultaneously act in unison and as independent entities. In the "Go by the Book or the Book Will Be Thrown at 'Ya" vignette, I focus on issues that are on the minds of colleagues who work with academic couples, including conspiracy, collusion, and block voting. In the "Balancing the Books" vignette, I explore two conceptualizations of balance: balancing work responsibilities and balancing work and home responsibilities. In the "Closin' the Book" vignette, I discuss the problems and promises that await academic couples in the future.

Smart and Smart (1990) concluded: "all of the [dual-career] couples we spoke with said they talk with one another about their work, ideas, and experiences, often solving work problems together through discussion. They understand each other' s pressures and try to be supportive."[1] This statement typifies Roger and Anna's relationship throughout their academic careers, except for the precouple phase of their relationship. As they describe it, in the early phases of their relationship, neither Roger's nor Anna's lives were an open book to each other. Anna's comment, "I was terminally tongue-tied," suggests that the "don't ask, don't tell" strategy that my partner and I employed in the 1980s was already alive and well in the 1970s. The politics of the job exploration process can lead to a sense of powerlessness that contributes to these noncommunicative phases of an academic couple's relationship.

Austin and Pilat (1990) discuss the stresses (for instance, fear of the unknown, fear of disappointing a partner, and so on) associated with dual careers in academia, and recommend that the couple make this exploratory process a productive challenge rather than a debilitating obstacle.[2] Roger and Anna's first job search more closely resembled what Austin and Pilat refer to as a debilitating obstacle. Their second was closer to what Austin and Pilat refer to as a productive challenge. Examining Roger and Anna's second academic job search, 16 years after their first, sheds some light on the politics of couples' job explorations. In their second search, Anna and Roger knew what they wanted from each other and from potential employers. They were in a better bargaining position. This shift was in part due to the power derived from asking and telling.

You Can't Judge a Book by Its Cover

Midwestern hospitality prevails during my Director of Student Services interview luncheon in 1985. The search committee temporarily suspends the formal interview. Instead, we casually converse about non-work-related topics such as Ohio's humidity and the Cincinnati Reds. The free-flowing humorous exchanges about work and family reveal much about individuals' personal and professional passions. Likewise, the committee is getting to know me as a person, not simply as a candidate.

Following an awkward moment of silence, a senior member of the search committee leans toward me and makes a statement (posed as a question). He asks: "If it wasn't for your wife's job here [in Ohio], would you be applying for this job?" I immediately conclude that this question is of the same magnitude as a Final Jeopardy question. That is, answering this question correctly will determine if I win or lose the job (which I lost). I repress my initial retort that they cannot legally ask me that question, and reply: "That's an interesting question. . . ." I fumble to explain that my desire to relocate in the same geographic region as my spouse influenced my decision to apply for this particular job. Further, I declare that I would never accept a job offer unless I were certain I am qualified and fully committed. I want to establish myself as an individual, not as a "trailing partner." My inquisitor appears unconvinced, as am I. Implicitly, his question challenges my qualifications, integrity, and motivation for applying for the job. This interviewer makes erroneous assumptions about me and my candidacy based on superficial criteria, like trying to judge a book by its cover. This was an important question that I wish he had not asked and I had not answered.

The question, and the overall issue of academic couples, receded between 1985 and 1989 while I worked in administration as Coordinator of Academic Advising and Assistant Dean on the campus where Marcia had a position as faculty member. It receded even further while I was completing my graduate studies (1989 to 1993) at a nearby institution. It returned with full force in 1993 as I pursued a tenure-track position in my spouse's department. At that point, Marcia had been in the department for 10 years and was already a tenured full professor. My interviewers—faculty and graduate students—knew Marcia. Since I had previously taught part-time in the department and had attended numerous departmental socials, the interviewers also had some knowledge about me.

In 1985, my stance pertaining to interview questions about academic couples was "don't ask and don't tell." In 1993, halfway through this faculty interview, I reverse my position. Faculty friends and graduate student acquaintances interview me as if I am a stranger. Although I detest an "old boys' network"–style interview, being treated as an alien is also troubling. I want them to explore the many chapters of my life and not refrain from this exploration because the cover of my book looks familiar to them. I want them to ask about my views of working in the same department with my spouse. I want to tell them my views on how I and my partner are alike and different. Initiating these kinds of conversations is a challenge. The interviewers walk on eggshells until a first-year graduate student inadvertently mentions the M word: Marcia. Over gasps emitted by the woman's peers, I seized the moment to share my views about working side by side with my spouse. At that moment, my "don't ask, don't tell" stance seems antiquated.

The previous analysis section focused on the relationship between partners during the job exploration process. This section explores the relationship between academic couples and higher education institutions during job interviews. I use the Ranero-Strohm case study and my story to explore the theme of "you can't judge a book by its cover" and the recurring theme of "don't ask, don't tell." I examine both themes and cases through a power and politics lens.

In this section I explore one political issue: whether couples should disclose their relationship to an employer. Neither Anna nor Roger acknowledged their personal relationship to Roger's colleagues during Anna's job interview in the mid-1970s. This was a deliberate decision on their part. The history of Roger's department, including the lack of support for an academic-partner candidate the year before, influenced his decision not to tell; he hoped they wouldn't ask. One need only look at my interview luncheon exchange to understand Roger and Anna's rationale for keeping their relationship a secret. This acknowledgment can lead employers to make stereotypical assumptions about issues such as the candidate's motivation and competencies, which may disadvantage the candidate.

Only after Anna accepted a formal job offer for a tenure-track position in Roger's department did they publicly reveal their relationship. One could reasonably conclude that Anna earned the job solely on her own merit—that is, the department evaluated her as an independent and competent scholar. Accepting a job knowing it was based on the review of one's own credentials (not the partner's credentials) satisfies the candidate and partner. Yet this deception could create an atmosphere of distrust between the couple and their colleagues.

The Ranero-Strohm case study and my story reveal how tentatively proponents and opponents act when interacting with academic couples during the hiring process. After accepting my department's offer to join the faculty, I discussed the unusual dynamics of my interview with both students and faculty colleagues. Most confessed that they wanted to solicit my views on being part of an academic couple and offer their own views. Legal and/or ethical uncertainties muted my interviewers' intentions. An interviewer cannot legally inquire about a spouse or partner unless the candidate volunteers information about him or her. As a candidate I, too, was uncomfortable openly discussing my spouse relationship, fearing that interjecting her into the process would jeopardize rather than advance my candidacy.

What is worse—not acknowledging the relationship or acknowledging the relationship and then being required to answer couples-related questions? Each option has advantages and flaws. The latter option is viable only in situations where an institution's espoused and enacted values regarding academic couples are congruent. Smart and Smart (1990) describe examples of couples-friendly programs at two institutions that illustrate this kind of situation. Oregon State University offers a faculty fellowship to the spouse of a new faculty member that he or she can use to do research or seek employment with the aid of the family employment program. Washington State University has a partner-accommodation fund to create new positions for well-qualified spouses or partners.[3]

These kinds of initiatives benefit the institution and couples. For example, the Oregon program might attract a high-caliber couple who individually would not consider applying for the job. Supporting couples during the recruitment and selection processes might also lead to stronger loyalty bonds and a prolonged commitment between the couple and the institution. The Oregon State University and the Washington

State University exemplars go a long way toward leveling the power playing field in the job search process.

Unless such power-leveling programs are in place, only academic couples with strong bargaining power (for instance, both are prolific, independent scholars) can negotiate acceptable deals for themselves. Roger and Anna's most recent job relocation exemplifies this scenario (that is, she would not consider a job without a suitable job for Roger). Higher education must develop policies that encourage both candidates and institutional representatives to abandon their "don't ask, don't tell" posture that reduces the chances that one would judge another's book by a cursory glance at the cover.

A Textbook Example

In 1998, Marcia and I receive an invitation from an editor of a journal to cowrite a review of the Ferber and Loeb (1997) book about academic couples (see Magolda and Baxter Magolda, 1998).[4] The proposal—an academic couple reviewing a book about academic couples—intrigues us. Since this small project will not interfere with our existing writing commitments and will not consume much time, we agree to do it. It is a textbook collaborative opportunity for the both of us—writing about a topic that interests us and overlaps with our areas of interest and expertise **(training and interest)**.

We know from experience that the thought of one of us looking over the other's shoulder while our stream-of-consciousness evaluative comments are typed frightens us. We opt for the divide-and-conquer strategy, one we have successfully employed in the past. We agree to read and review the text independently, then compare reactions. We meet, identify points of agreement, select a focus, and negotiate writing tasks.

We use the subtitle of the Ferbers' book, *Problems and Promises*, to organize our commentary. We extrapolate from our notes a list of issues that fit into this problems-promise framework. I agree to craft a short story that will introduce us as an academic couple and illuminate the issues we intend to raise in the review. Marcia agrees to craft a crisp chapter-by-chapter overview and to synthesize our reactions. After independently completing our writing tasks, we retreat to our separate work spaces to fine-tune each other's drafts. Our feedback to each other is straightforward and unambiguous. It is akin to the type of blunt feedback Anna gave Roger's papers in the early days of their collaborative relationship. Later we connect our independently generated sections and draft an introduction and conclusion. We encounter one sticking point: I want to set the review aside for a few days, then tinker with it one more time before submitting it. Marcia rereads it and deems it ready to go. She prevails and we submit it. The editor accepts it, offering only a few copyediting suggestions. Marcia's instincts are correct in this case, highlighting one of the advantages of our different approaches.

In this section I use the Ranero-Strohm case study and my story to explore what a textbook example of collaboration by academic couples looks like from the vantage point of the couple and those who evaluate the couple's collaborative output (**reward**). The recurring theme of "don't ask, don't tell" is again linked to new issues—this time, collaboration and the culture of individuality in academia.

In my narrative, the book review Marcia and I wrote is "textbook" because it was related to our separate research agendas but was not the centerpiece of either. This was also true in the Ranero-Strohm case study. In that case study, each partner had already established an independent research identity and had met research productivity benchmarks prior to their collaborative ventures. By the time this couple initiated their "textbook" collaboration, they had exceeded their department's reward criteria for productivity (that is, tenure).

The two examples in this section illuminate the traditional reward structures upon which excellence is based in academia, how these unwritten expectations are transmitted to faculty, and how faculty members respond to these demands. These cases also reveal the contradictory values higher education administrators expect faculty to embrace—most notably, collaboration and individuality. Higher education's "rhetoric for success" includes ideals such as collaboration, cooperation, and partnerships. Yet the reward structures value, for example, a single-authored book more than a coauthored book. Higher education remains suspicious of collaborative partnerships, especially if they involve academic couples, even if evaluators can satisfactorily answer the "who did what?" question. The image of independent scholars with a unique and distinct scholarly persona and agenda continues to be the textbook example of the ideal faculty member.

Many of the tensions that academic couples reveal about their experiences in academia (even in those institutions that have couples-friendly policies) can be summed up as a progressive policy (that is, hiring and supporting academic couples) entrapped by a prehistoric accountability system. As these case studies suggest, a textbook collaborative venture necessitates that those in power be explicit about values upon which success will be determined. More importantly, as Roger suggests, those in power need to modify traditional criteria so that collaboration is more highly valued. Anna and Roger's case study reinforces the idea that collaboration and quality are not mutually exclusive concepts.

Matching Bookends

In 1997, I drop off a book to an advisee at her residence. I know her well. As I enter her apartment, I inquire about a photograph of an adorable baby prominently displayed on a credenza. I learn it is her child, who died a few years earlier. My surprise shocks her. She explains that she wrote about her child's death in numerous student development papers required for my spouse's seminar. I am surprised to realize that the student expects that academic couples should operate as two bodies with one mind. This tension—couples acting in unison and independently—is further developed in the short story that follows.

Around that same time, Marcia and I share an office in our home. My new computer forces us to separate our work space. The computer's CD player allows me to listen to music as I (and Marcia) work. This arrangement pleases only me. Marcia's notebook computer makes it possible for us to experiment with a trial separation; she works on our screened-in porch during the spring and summer months. Both of us know this solution is temporary; separate work spaces are inevitable. In the end, Marcia retains property rights to the original study and I move down the hall. I obtain the laser printer in the settlement; she negotiates visitation rights.

Music is not the sole reason for the split. We have a number of other differences (**working style**): I work best early in the morning and late in the evening; Marcia's optimal work time is from mid-morning to mid-evening. Marcia is a more linear thinker and efficient writer; I am more cyclical. I work on multiple tasks at the same time; she favors working on one task at a time. She brackets out distractions (for instance, phone calls); I try, but seldom succeed. In the classroom, Marcia is more formal and tactful; I'm more informal and plainspoken. On the surface, we are more dissimilar than alike. Our colleagues, students, and friends recognize us as distinct individuals (that is, two bodies, two minds, or mismatched bookends), while they simultaneously expect us to be two bodies with one mind—matched bookends.

This section explores an unusual paradox: an expectation by colleagues, students, and acquaintances that academic couples act simultaneously in unison and as discrete entities (**recognition**). Roger and Anna, like many academic couples, view themselves as different chapters from the same textbook. Others accept this image while simultaneously advancing an image of a single chapter in the same textbook. Meeting these contradictory expectations creates unique dilemmas for couples.

Roger and Anna worked hard throughout their careers to untangle this paradox. That is, they tried hard not to be seen as "two peas from the same pod," while acknowledging that in many ways they were from the same pod (for instance, attending the same school and having the same dissertation advisor). Early in their careers they distanced themselves from each other in teaching, research, and administrative domains while proclaiming their ideological similarities and mutual regard for one another—bookends of sorts, sometimes matched, sometimes not. Maintaining a separate (but not too separate) self while staying connected was a conscious and constantly monitored process for Anna and Roger.

Much of the Ranero-Strohm case study description showcased Anna and Roger's balancing act. Their distinct research agendas, their separate work space (offices on separate floors in their home), their different idea of office aesthetics, their preferences for processing information (Roger being more methodical than Anna), their different personality types (Roger being more introspective than Anna), and their preferences for teaching and writing are examples of how they differed from one another. Yet they collaborated on research and used their personality differences to their advantage when writing.

A danger in this contradictory set of expectations is that the couples simplify things by splitting the differences and moving toward the center. That is, they temper their unique qualities both as individuals and as a couple in order to satisfy these external demands that want couples to be all things to all people. This strategy would eliminate desired diversity. Maintaining their differences as individuals enhances their partnership and their contributions to the institution rather than them offering duplicate assets.

Go by the Book or the Book Will Be Thrown at 'Ya

In 1993, Marcia and I begin to work together in the same department and same graduate program (College Student Personnel). As part of our responsibilities, each year we serve on the program's admission committee, which is charged with evaluating applications and interviewing candidates. In 1996, after denying admission to an applicant, the department chair received a letter from an individual who served as one of the applicant's references. The advocate wrote:

It is also a concern of mine that both a husband and wife sit on the review/selection team. I am sure both are honest people. However, having a husband and wife on a review/selection team looks wrong and I believe strongly that one of them should be removed. It is important to remove any doubt about fairness of the process.

Toward the end of the letter, the advocate argued that "a wife would not vote against her husband." Implicit in his letter is the claim that neither my partner nor I are "going by the book" (that is, functioning as two independent and objective evaluators) and a subtle request that those in power throw the book at us. There is also the suggestion that partners will operate as a voting block.

Another totally different example with the same subtext occurred in 1995 when our department interviewed a preeminent African-American scholar for a faculty vacancy. The candidate expressed interest in the position but said that he could consider accepting our offer only if his spouse secured employment in her academic discipline. This is not dissimilar to Anna's response when she was approached for a new position. While department chairs, deans, and search committee members worked hard to extend an offer to the couple, thorny issues such as salary demands and exceptions to departmental procedures (hiring a spouse when there is no faculty line available) resulted in a failed search. Ironically, faculty members in the spouse's potential department accused university administrators of not going by the book because their negotiations conflicted with affirmative action policies. In essence, the faculty threw the book at the administration by denying its proposal.

This analysis focuses on conspiracy, collusion, and block voting, which is an abridged list of murky issues lurking just below the surface of many people's consciousness when they think about academic couples working in the same department. This fear is best summed up by a humanities professor at Johns Hopkins University who noted a frequently thought but seldom spoken axiom: "People who sleep together tend to vote together."[5] Concerns about such issues as operating as a voting block are seldom as overtly presented to couples as they were to my spouse and me in the accusatory letter. Yet academic couples are unlikely to be naive about these issues. Anna, for example, chose to decline voting privileges in the Psychology Department, where she had a joint appointment. She did this in order to counter the perception of voting as a block with Roger.

Ferber and Loeb (1997) note that "colleagues are often apprehensive about partners forming political alliances, particularly when both are members of a small unit."[6] Similarly, Smart and Smart (1990) captured this near-universally accepted belief held by academic couples when they wrote:

> Couples who work in the same department said they often fear that their colleagues will suspect them of voting as a block, of supporting one another regardless of circumstances. Their colleagues will also think they do not keep confidential material scrupulously, but rather give each other inside information.[7]

Even in the rare instance where the issue is verbalized, responding to the perception that couples are a threat to departmental democracy is difficult. For example, my initial reaction to the advocate who accused my spouse and me of wrongdoing was to dismiss his Neanderthal viewpoint. Yet when I carefully considered the author's arguments, I interpreted his letter to reflect that academic couples, acting as one, pose a threat to the integrity of academic decisions. My department chair's well-crafted response (with input from both my partner and me) reminded me how difficult it is to convey persuasively the ways academic couples operate.

Embedded in this issue is a real concern that couples, like other political allies, do not abuse their power or act unethically. Those who think and act as if couples collude and conspire, but never verbalize these concerns, do a disservice to the couple and to the organization. Equally problematic are strategies like the one employed by the student advocate, who found the couple guilty of collusion without ever allowing them to confront their accusers or respond to the charges. This "don't ask, just assume" strategy is problematic. These case studies suggest that all parties need to ask and tell.

Balancing the Books

In recent years our department sponsors a two-day overnight faculty retreat. This ritual is one of many in early August that marks the start of a new academic year. Many of my colleagues bemoan the loss of work time, the time away from family, youth-hostel accommodations, and the overly ambitious and vaguely defined agenda. Postretreat appraisals are guardedly positive. Participants rate the informal time together during meals and the late-evening informal conversations most favorably.

One evening during the retreat, colleagues sitting around a table begin to discuss the upcoming year. As time goes by, the question of balance eventually dominates the conversation (**private and public lives**). Discussants agree that faculty workloads have expanded, faculty members are underappreciated, and faculty members (individually and collectively) need to take action to recapture those balanced lives of yesteryear. A consensus on a definition of balance and acceptable ways to achieve and maintain balance is not forthcoming.

To jump-start the discussion, participants generate a list of the balanced and unbalanced colleagues; Marcia and I make the unbalanced list, as do a handful of other colleagues. The conversation stalls after the group concludes this playful exercise. Fortunately, a sage senior professor interjects that being balanced is not synonymous with being productive. The difficult part, as the group discovers after a 60-minute debate, is defining balance.

I confess that during this discussion, I become suspicious of balance zealots for two reasons. First, it appears that they use balance as an excuse to justify why what they (or someone else) thought they should do did not get done or will not get done. Verbalized, the argument sounds like: "I would like to do this because it is a great idea, but for the sake of balance, I am going to pass." Second, the proposed strategies to achieve balance are too formulaic. That is, balance is portrayed as a metaphorical scale. To achieve balance, you delete this and add that. Unconvinced by these arguments and exemplars, I probe these assumptions, as do others. Sharp disagreements emerge as the discussion unfolds. In the true spirit of academia, after a long debate we agree to disagree. That is, we adopt an impure libertarian stance of "you do your thing and I'll do mine," with the hope that things will balance out.

In this section I explore two conceptualizations of balance that emerged as I studied the Ranero-Strohm case study. The first focuses on how the individual faculty member attempts to balance work responsibilities within the confines of a particular job. The second centers on balancing work and home responsibilities. I use the Ranero-Strohm case study and my short story to examine this question of balance more carefully, with the hope of better understanding what balance looks like for academic couples and whether striving for balance is a good idea.

The issues that Roger and Anna raise as it relates to finding balance within each of their respective jobs seems no different from my own experiences and those of my colleague who sat with me one evening discussing work/home balance. For most college faculty, the most obvious work duties to balance are teaching, research, and service. As Anna and Roger's story suggests, achieving a balance is an idiosyncratic process that is influenced by the individual's interests and expertise and the institution's expectations. Since Roger and Anna originally accepted a position at a Big Ten institution, it was not surprising that their institution placed a high premium on research. For Anna and Roger, this expectation was compatible with their own professional agenda and academic training, which also valued research, particularly early in their careers.

The boundaries between work and home are probably more clearly delineated for faculty members who do not work with their partners. For some academics, differentiating between home and work and calculating work/home ratios are complicated tasks.[8] The Ranero-Strohm case study clarifies this point. For example, since both enjoy writing and spending time together, an activity such as conceptualizing a paper is probably difficult to categorize as a work task or a social event. This delineation is further complicated by their hobbies, which are also home-based (for instance, Anna's gardening). Computing a work/home ratio to assess balance for academic couples is no easy task.

A personal example further illustrates this important point. When my partner and I attend a professional conference, one could easily categorize this task as work. Yet attending conferences with my spouse not only allows me to present my research findings, attend meetings and presentations, and assist students with job placement (that is, work tasks), it allows me to travel, visit with friends, spend time in a hotel with my spouse, dine out each evening, and get away from the daily grind of work (leisure tasks). This conference activity does not fit neatly into either the home or work category. Yet my conference experience is fundamentally different when my partner does not attend. In these instances the conference feels like work. Adjusting the balance is difficult when the variables that need adjusting are ill defined.

Spending insufficient time with significant others (partners, children, and so on) is an activating event that may lead some faculty members to conclude that their work and home life need to be better balanced. For these individuals, work and home lives conflict and seldom overlap. For academic couples like Roger and Anna, their work and home lives frequently overlap and are often in harmony, partly because of the amount of time they spend together. Since their research areas of expertise overlap, each has an in-home consultant, which allows them to become significantly involved in each other's work.

When assessing balance, context matters. An analysis of this case study suggests that there is little benefit in trying to identify who is balanced in higher education and who is not. Nor is it a productive task to try to reach consensus on a grand definition of balance. Anna's and Roger's thoughts about balance suggest that striving for balance is a good thing provided the couple defines balance and has control over the adjustments. There is no algorithm for determining balance in these different domains. It is a personal endeavor; each decision an individual and couple makes has consequences.

Closin' the Book

This case study illuminates at both a personal and institutional level some of the promises and problems that academic couples and higher education institutions must face in the next millennium. The case reveals what universities have to gain and lose in terms of sustaining productivity and knowledge creation by hiring faculty couples who are in the same field.

One of the significant gains is in realizing the potential of collegiality. In an ideal academic community, professional colleagues provide intellectual stimulation for each other, offer constructive and critical feedback, and through their support help sustain motivation for intellectual work. Academic couples like Roger and Anna epitomize this form of collegiality. Their insights into and empathy toward their partners' work provide necessary affirmation and diminish work-home conflicts. Their care for each other extends to extensive investment in their partners' success and satisfaction with their work. This investment heightens productivity and job satisfaction in ways that probably heighten long-term commitment to an institution.

Higher education institutions must revise their perceptions of and their approach to academic couples to realize the potential gains in productivity, job satisfaction, recruitment, and retention. Many of the dilemmas experienced by academic couples and the institutions that hire them stem from the fear of open discussions of how academic couples operate. This "don't ask, don't tell" approach creates problems in recruiting, retention, job satisfaction, and productivity.

Moving to an "ask and tell" approach, or an open dialogue about the phenomena of academic couples, has more promise for the future. Specifically, open dialogue among faculty to explore fears and dilemmas around academic couples would help faculty groups clarify their views prior to interacting with candidates in the selection process. Couples-friendly views expressed during the selection process would heighten the probabil-

ity of honest disclosure on the part of candidate couples. This open dialogue could extend to the issue of academic couples collaborating.

Rethinking criteria for collaboration in general and between academic
couples in particular is necessary to extend the bounds of productivity.
Contemporary value of diversity should be extended to valuing difference
exhibited by academic couples rather than expecting them to be the
same. Supporting our differences might diminish the paranoia surrounding couples colluding. Eliminating some of these dilemmas (for
instance, collusion) could remove barriers to productivity and balance.
This might lead to a textbook example of the good life in academia.

9

Introduction to the Third Case: Experiencing Africa: A Creative Writer and an Anthropologist Collaborate

The third and final case, describing the collaborative relationship between an anthropologist and a fiction writer who coauthored a book together, differs in several ways from the preceding two other case narratives presented in this section of the book. Unlike the majority of the couples participating in this research, the members of this couple, Laura Bauer and Allen Harris, are in two disciplines with entirely different research traditions. They are more than a decade younger than the faculty presented in the previous cases. Laura and Allen also differ from the other examples presented in that they are actively engaged in the parenting of two young children. The fact that they work side by side in a shared study is also not the most common arrangement among partners. It is a metaphor for how their professional and personal lives are comingled.

I collected data for the case narrative from multiple sources over the course of nearly two years. I interviewed Laura and Allen separately by telephone in October 1997 and visited them in their home to conduct a joint interview more than 16 months later. These sessions, all tape-recorded, produced more than 90 pages of transcripts. In addition to the interviews, I read several journal articles that Laura published about their experiences as a couple doing fieldwork in Africa, as well as several short stories and a book that Allen authored. The interview data were supplemented by the observations I accumulated during the evening and day I spent with them, when they generously welcomed me into their lives as scholars and parents. Finally, I had the unusual opportunity to access their viewpoints by reading and re-reading the memoir they coauthored about their experiences doing fieldwork in Africa.

Intellectual Intimacy

Laura and Allen share a deep personal and **intellectual intimacy**. By that I mean that they voiced an unusually detailed familiarity with each other's ideas and work as well as reflexivity about how it is produced. This intimacy is accomplished not only through 25 years of shared life experiences but also by close physical proximity and constant, ongoing interactions about each other's work from the very first days of their relationship. They have worked side by side in shared work space throughout their careers, an arrangement that accommodates the enjoyment they find from reading out loud to each other from what they are working on.

The intellectual intimacy or familiarity Laura and Allen have with each other's work is evident in a number of additional ways. One way it is displayed is in the accuracy with which each can describe the other's viewpoint. On repeated occasions, I would hear her describe how he felt or he describe how she felt using words that were very similar, if not identical, even though uttered in an entirely different setting, sometimes months apart. I also saw it expressed in the detailed knowledge each displays of particular papers or stories the other wrote, sometimes 20 years ago, and what went into crafting or producing them. They can speak for each other without being the other.

While there have been periods when part of their intense interdependence was accompanied by physical isolation, it is clear that both Laura and Allen are social people, deeply committed to their immediate family and engaged in wide **collegial networks**. A facsimile machine and ready access to e-mail and the Internet at home ease the sense of isolation they feel from the writers' community elsewhere. They are an active presence in the academic community, often entertaining and attending events together on campus.

The way that Laura and Allen choose to divide the labor in their household, as well as to collaborate, requires an investment of time that might seem incomprehensible to many people. Their habit of drafting and redrafting what they write is part of this. They calculated, for example, that they wrote between 25 and 30 drafts of every section in their coauthored book. This investment of time is also evident in the amount of time they spend reading and sharing their work with each other. Allen said that he had probably read aloud to Laura every section of just about everything he has written anywhere from two to four times. The time investment is one of the ways that Laura and Allen continually demonstrate their commitment to help each other accomplish their ambitions. As the demands of children and work make their lives increasingly frenzied, this time investment grows more and more difficult.

Voice

One of the aspects of this couple that was most interesting to me is the way that Laura and Allen represent their viewpoints—what I label as "voice." I believe that it is one of the ways that **egalitarianism** is manifested. When I interviewed other couples for this research project together, it was generally the pattern that they alternated speaking and spoke on different topics, using some well-practiced but probably unspoken agreement of which one of them was the expert on a particular topic or which one of them cared the most deeply about it. In all cases, the couples seemed careful to make room for each other to speak.

Laura and Allen used a different approach to representing their mutual story. It was the same approach they used in their jointly authored memoir about their experiences in Africa. Just as they alternated sections in their book that they clearly marked with which one of them was speaking, during the joint interview they sat very close to each other and handed the microphone back and forth. Where one member of the other couples I interviewed took the lead in telling the story of their collaborative relationship without any apparent negotiation, and it was told briefly, Laura and Allen took turns telling the story chronologically, and the story occupied several hours and was expansive in the telling. I think they have practiced the oral tradition of storytelling as one aspect of their appreciation of Third World cultures.

Laura and Allen did not erase differences in viewpoint that emerged as the narrative of their relationship unfolded. They organized their joint narrative chronologically using dates but almost never agreed about a date. As with the strategy they used in their memoir, I interpret this as a way to negotiate differences and reduce conflict. They do not amalgamate or synthesize their voices. They allow each other the time to tell their versions of a story without ironing out the creases, so to speak, between their different versions of the same story. It is this practice of giving each other ample room to speak their version of the story and to leave their version largely unchallenged that I characterize as a representation of egalitarianism because it kept both on equal footing.

Resources and Practices of the University

Financial support from external funding agencies as well as from the university through policies such as awarding research leaves and grants was evident throughout most participants' curriculum vitae but interestingly, was something they rarely made reference to. Although all the participants in the case studies received resources in various forms to support their research and writing, the extent of this kind of support is particularly prominent in this case. Between 1985 and 1998, for example, Laura was able to secure eight semesters of release time from teaching through grants, leaves, fellowships, and/or sabbaticals. She had the help of a research assistant for six years. Allen was also awarded a year's release from teaching to work on their jointly authored book, as well as other grants and appointments as a research fellow. Different sources of funding have provided the opportunity for them to spend most of their summers doing fieldwork and/or working on their research rather than teaching. This evidence of support for both of their respective scholarly agendas is part of what keeps them at a university that is far more rural than where they ever envisioned living out their careers.

For several reasons, I suspect that resources provided by external funding agencies as well as the university seem to be particularly instrumental to Laura's publishing productivity. First is that the nature of her discipline requires travel and intense data collection, recording, and analysis. A second reason is that she is one of those faculty members who writes in long, relatively concentrated units of time, unlike Allen, who rarely walks away from the work of writing or thinking about writing. He regularly devotes eight or nine hours a day, three days a week, to writing. Laura is not on that kind of schedule unless she is on sabbatical or leave.

There are aspects of both Laura's and Allen's teaching assignments that are traditionally both associated and not associated with high levels of publication productivity. Allen largely teaches undergraduate students, something that is not characteristic of prolific writers. Laura works largely with graduate students, something that is more characteristic of prolific writers. However, Allen has been able to organize his teaching schedule so that most of his responsibilities on campus are concentrated during two days of the week. He crams his teaching, committee work, and consulting with students into these days. He grades papers at night. That allows him to concentrate on his writing during the remaining three days of the week.

The Case Response

The response to this case is written by Dr. Stacey Floyd-Thomas, an African-American woman, religious scholar and ethicist, and a self-declared womanist. Floyd-Thomas's comments add the heretofore-absent voice in this text of a minority faculty member and of those who are just embarking on a faculty career. Observing that the sense of isolation that Laura and Allen experienced during their fieldwork in Africa was bracketed both in time and geography, Floyd-Thomas comments that this sense is an ongoing aspect of her daily life with her husband as they adjust to being black with an emancipatory agenda at a predominately white institution. This supports the hypothesis that an academic partner may be particularly instrumental to faculty members who are isolated from like-minded colleagues because of the geographical location of their institution, their race or sexuality, lack of same-sex collaborators, or the nature of the topic or research method(s) utilized.

Floyd-Thomas's comments endorse the argument that a shared **worldview** is a central component of an academic couple's attraction to each other, as well as of the work they share. Floyd-Thomas observes that she and her husband chose academic careers as the best vehicle collectively to accomplish their goal to empower the black communities "from which [they] came."

Floyd-Thomas's response extends the discussion of the impact of an academic partner beyond the realm of research into the realm of teaching. She adds to the mixed views about the compatibility of research and teaching by analyzing how she feels her interactions in the classroom contribute to her teaching. She sees that her very presence as a teacher in the classroom is central to her emancipatory agenda. She contrasts her commitment to teaching to that of Laura and Allen, who organize their lives to maximize their research productivity, taking advantage of opportunities for research leaves and sabbaticals that absent them from the classroom and from mentoring relationships with students.

Conclusion

After Laura, Allen, and I finished our nearly day-long interview, gymnastics, swimming, homework, and an evening of hosting guests remained on their schedule of activities for the rest of their long day. Like their refusal to establish a division of labor to handle household matters, the lack of compartmentalization between their personal lives and work and between the worlds each inhabits is partly how they accomplish the intellectual intimacy that makes them so integral to each other's work. The nature of the work they do allows them to do much of it at home. It seems unlikely that people who require neat compartmentalization between their personal lives and work will be able to achieve the egalitarianism this couple has battled to maintain.

10

The Third Case: Experiencing Africa:
A Creative Writer and an Anthropologist Collaborate

I think that in some ways, every novelist is an anthropologist—a geographer of the imagination. The act of writing fiction is an anthropological act. *–Laura Bauer, February 1999*

Laura Bauer and Allen Harris first met as undergraduate students in 1971 when she was 17 and he was 20 years old. By the time they got together as a couple two years later, their professional identities—she as an anthropologist, he as a writer—were beginning to be etched as central to each of their identities and to their attraction to each other. Their life as a couple and as a family, as well as their work, was very much shaped by the experience they shared of living in a remote village in Africa between 1979 and 1980 while she was doing the fieldwork for her dissertation. Since then they have returned to Africa several times, including once with their young son. Africa is an ongoing lifelong project for them. Ten years after their first visit, they coauthored a prize-winning memoir describing their experiences in Africa. The book is widely read and has drawn both national and international attention.

Neither Laura nor Allen was born with a silver spoon in his or her mouth. Neither came from a family of academics. Of Eastern European immigrant descent, Laura grew up in Queens, New York, in a secular Jewish family. From a Scottish, Catholic background, Allen grew up in a middle-class family in a suburb on Long Island, not far from Laura. Laura supported herself through college and graduate school on scholarships, while Allen found a way to make ends meet through a creative range of unconventional part-time jobs. A comfortable way of life is something that they have come to experience only recently. From the earliest days of their relationship, both Laura and Allen sought a creative model for marriage and family that was different from anything they had experienced themselves as children.

Laura and Allen's resumés show **career symmetry**. Although he had held a similar appointment at another university, they were both hired as assistant professors in different departments at the same university in the Midwest in 1985. They were both awarded tenure in 1991 and promoted to the rank of full professor in 1998. Both have amassed impressive publication records. At the time I interviewed them, he was working on his sixth book of fiction, and she was devoting a year full-time to finishing a fifth and sixth book concurrently.

The Overlap of Their Disciplines

From the first, there was a strong component of intellectual excitement in Laura and Allen's attraction for each other. They are each fascinated with ideas, including each other's. Laura described their initial attraction and the overlap in their **training and interest** in the following words:

> We each had more than a passing interest in each other's career. I had a very serious interest in creative writing when I was younger and at one point fantasized about being a poet, although that was only one of many fantasies I had. Writing was really important to me. When I decided to go into the social sciences, there was a certain regret that I would have to read a lot of bad writing. I get a lot of vicarious pleasure from being married to a writer and getting to cast more than a sidelong glance into the world of good writing through him. Likewise, he had taken a lot of anthropology as an undergraduate and we had actually studied with the same teachers at different periods in college. He was very influenced by anthropology before he got involved with me and found as a writer that it was a really interesting way to look at the world.

Similarly, Allen's attraction to Laura lay in part in her identity as an anthropologist. He described them as "partners in our ambitions." The product of a college education where feminists and high-achieving women surrounded him, he was very clear, according to Laura, that he wanted a wife who was never going to be a housewife. Part of Laura's appeal was her personal qualities, including that she is what he described as a very loving person. But the fact that she is an ambitious person was critical to him as well. Along with his lifelong interest in learning about other cultures, Allen found the thought of a partner who is an anthropologist exciting.

The Contribution to Productivity

Laura and Allen spent three years of their 25-year-long relationship writing their coauthored book. Although this coauthored book is probably what links their names in the minds of their colleagues, it is really only a small element of the many ways they collaborate and the ways that their relationship shapes their writing. During the course of the individual and joint interviews, they described the contribution of emotional support and mutual advocacy, informal feedback, exchanging manuscripts, and serving as a test audience for each other's work.

Emotional Support and Mutual Advocacy

Both Laura and Allen spoke of different ways that their **personal relationship** contributed to their work as writers and scholars. Their time in the field was a very trying one, Allen said. They were often together 24 hours a day. The experience was intense not only because they were in a radically different culture, but because they were in a small, isolated village without running water and 30 miles from the nearest electricity. They went through a lot together and worked very hard, he said, at trying to be helpful to each other.

Both Laura and Allen see their relationship as mutually beneficial. When, at one point in our telephone interview, I observed that it seemed their relationship was mutually supportive both in terms of their domestic and professional lives, Laura replied that she certainly saw them as great mutual supporters who are fan clubs for each other. They do all they can to support each other's careers and career trials, she said.

Informal Feedback about Ideas

Of the two, Allen spoke the most about the importance of the informal **feedback** they provide each other. During the intense intimacy of collecting data in an isolated location and an entirely unfamiliar culture, Allen provided someone for Laura to bounce ideas off. Because he had almost always been present as events unfolded, he could offer his interpretation of what was going on. This experience seems to have created an awareness that one way their disciplines overlap is in the demand for acute observation. Laura referred to this overlap in the quotation that opens the narrative, as well as when she said:

> Anthropologists are in a sense like writers and writers are in a sense like anthropologists. Both groups are observers. We both like to think about people as psychological entities and what makes

them tick. We both like to analyze relationships. That is something one does in the kind of field work that I do.

Exchanging Manuscripts

Another way that Laura and Allen provide feedback to each other is through the exchange of manuscripts. Each is always the other's first reader. They read each other's work constantly. During the first 10 years of their relationship, they read all of each other's drafts. Since they have both become so busy, they still read each other's work but not as intensively or frequently as they used to. Allen described a characteristic exchange these days:

> When Laura gets to a point in an article where she thinks she really needs some input, then she'll show it to me. I'll do the same thing. I'll be working away on a chapter and when I think I've finished or if I want to see if I've finished something, I'll read it to Laura.

Serving as an Audience

A defining characteristic of Laura and Allen's working relationship is that they read their work out loud to each other. A shared study and similar work schedule help to make this possible. Speaking of the time when they wrote their book, Laura said: "We both like to read; we're both kind of hams. He loves to give readings. I like to give talks. We like to read to each other. We often read a scene back and forth that we'd written, or if we had forgotten a detail, we'd ask each other about it."

Like many creative writers, hearing the words on the page read aloud is especially crucial to Allen. He does this not only with Laura but also with other colleagues. Laura said that it was not uncommon to hear Allen on the phone at midnight reading his work to a fellow writer. Allen described the importance of hearing how something he has written sounds:

> Laura is a very good listener. I like to read out loud what I've written. I'll read it off the computer screen when I'm sitting at my desk and she is right behind me at her desk. You can't hide anything when you read it out loud. Any little repetition or awkwardness will come out. I literally have read two, three, or maybe four times every section of my last novel to Laura and every story I've written. She's beginning to hear a lot of different sections of this new novel. She's like an audience for me.

It is important to Allen that his readers are able to apprehend what he has written on first reading. Another way in which Laura serves as an audience for Allen is to test if what he has written will resonate with a reader. Reading his work aloud is a way for him to determine if a scene works. He said:

> In that sense, I have been very much influenced by ethnopoetics and Third World literature. A lot of Third World people do not have a written language. Their literature is oral. Those are very, very complex tales that are told out loud in real time. That's why I read it out loud to Laura. I don't want her to spend 15 minutes reading a paragraph, going over and over things. I want her to hear it in real time. If she gets it and gets engaged in the scene that I'm writing, then I know that I'm on the right track.

When I asked Laura to clarify what Allen meant when he described her as a good listener, she said that what she largely did was to sit, listen, and appreciate. In the early drafts she might have comments or ask for clarification if something seemed confusing. She acknowledged, though, that she might ask him to clarify something that he would refuse to clarify because as a fiction writer, she said, he will sometimes want to keep things more ambiguous, where she would like it to be more precise.

Their Coauthored Book

Laura and Allen plunged headlong into the intense work of writing full-time on their coauthored book in 1991, 10 years after their first visit to Africa and the year they were both being reviewed for tenure. He had just completed his second book, a collection of short stories; she had just completed her second book, a traditional ethnography. Both had already achieved a certain amount of visibility and recognition in their disciplines. After negotiating an advance contract on the book, they each applied for grants from a new unit on campus designed to promote interdisciplinary collaboration. The idea that they were crossing the social sciences and humanities was very appealing to the granting unit. A one-semester sabbatical combined with a one-semester grant freed each of them from teaching for a full year to write the book.

Their coauthored book is a memoir of their experiences as field researchers in Africa. Allen describes the book as being about how fieldwork is far more difficult and challenging than most anthropologists are willing to admit. Laura sees it largely as a way to inform graduate students about the realities of doing fieldwork. In it Laura and Allen openly share their frequent cultural missteps and the ongoing anxiety about completing the project successfully. The book is directed to both academic and popular audiences, which is one of the things that made it difficult to write and created some initial difficulty in finding a publisher.

Collaboration in preparation for writing the book had been going on for years before it was written. Laura and Allen did a lot of thinking and talking about the experience before they could begin to write about it in a serious way. They tested out their stories on friends at cocktail parties and dinners and found that certain ones were proven "crowd pleasers." They started writing the book in 1989 when they prepared the detailed outline. They distributed a sample chapter to about 20 publishers before finding one that would issue a contract they found acceptable.

Allen took the lead in laying out the chronology for the book by combing through the carbon copies he had made of hundreds of letters he had written to friends while in Africa. He made copies of the letters, marking every section that he thought they might be able to use to build the book. That gave him a sense of the unfolding narrative and how to organize it by chapter. In addition to the letters, they used photographs, his date book, and the thousands of pages of Laura's field notes to fill in details of the narrative. This explains how they were able to supply accurate details such as the weather each day and the title of the books he was reading on any given day.

The approach that Laura and Allen chose for the book was a new one for both of them, but in different ways. For Laura, it required learning how to write a narrative, including how to build a scene, a sense of character, ongoing drama, and dialogue. For Allen, it was writing something that was overtly autobiographical and completely without fiction. As a creative writer, he was used to the freedom of the imagination rather than the challenge to recount events exactly as they happened. Each was constantly challenged to revisit the evidence to recall as precisely as they could exactly what happened. When they had the frequent, humbling experience of recollecting an event differently, they would return to the evidence to try to reconstruct exactly what had happened.

After trying a more traditional approach of writing the narrative in the first person plural, Laura and Allen settled on an unusual way to handle their distinct voices: they divided up the story chronologically and told their version of the unfolding story in sections within alternating chapters, making explicit in each section who was speaking. They wanted each of their viewpoints to be distinct and to allow the differences in their interpretations to emerge. They felt that this approach was ethnographically accurate. Allen described the approach they used to writing the narrative this way:

> Laura would go from day one to day five, for example, and I would pick up from day six to day nine or whatever. Because the things we were talking about were continuing stories, you would be reading this continuing story from Laura's perspective and then I would pick up and talk about it from my perspective. We never challenged each other's particular perspective, but we would just say, "okay, now it's Allen's turn to tell the story."

Laura and Allen felt that the approach they chose visibly reflected equal contributions. Each wrote an equal number of sections and almost exactly same number of pages. They chose to list their names as authors alphabetically to reflect that they were equal contributors. There was a great sense of equality in the project.

Both Laura and Allen were aware that there were professional risks in publishing a book in a form that was unconventional in both of their fields. Allen anticipated that creative writers might criticize him for writing a nonfiction book. Laura knew that a personal ethnography was a somewhat unconventional form of scholarship in her field and that collaboration with a fiction writer, coupled with a lack of footnotes and an index, might lead to the charge that the book was not scholarly. Each tried to anticipate the criticism the other might receive. Allen, for example, fought for an index to make the book look more scholarly. Laura argued against the index because she was concerned about how his colleagues in creative writing might view it. In describing his concern for the reception that Laura might get from her colleagues, Allen said:

> I understood that this project was risky for Laura as an anthropologist and that she would be criticized in lots of ways that I would not be. Because of that, I reined myself in probably more than I would normally with that kind of project, because there were certain kinds of eyes, invisible eyes looking over our shoulders. They were really looking over Laura's shoulders, but I was there too. We had to be very scrupulous about the accuracy of the details.

The book Laura and Allen coauthored achieved a certain amount of commercial success. They gained national and international visibility through the numerous readings, book signings, and radio and television talk shows they did to promote the book. The book has been widely reviewed. It was marketed in paperback a year after it first appeared in hardback. Six years after it first appeared in print, the book has taken on a life of its own because of the attention they have received from it. They continue to receive invitations to speak and countless e-mails, many from students enrolled in the over 100 courses that have utilized the book as a textbook.

Collaboration as an Element of a Shared Worldview

The topic of family and small communities is something that both Laura and Allen have given much thought to, both personally and professionally. One way they manage to weave their work and family life together is as a topic they both write about, if in very different ways. The issue of families and relationships among couples weaves in and out of much of Allen's fiction, just as motherhood across cultures appears early in Laura's writing and is the topic of the edited book that is Laura's most recent writing project.

Laura and Allen share a **worldview** that encompasses attitudes about family, collaboration, politics, and philosophical orientation. Laura described their shared worldview this way:

> We have always been very interested in each other's work. Although we appear on the surface to be in totally different disciplines, we see the world the same way. There is very little that we disagree about when we talk about intellectual issues. We're focused in the same direction when it comes to politics. We like to talk about politics. We both care about political issues deeply and see the world the same way. We have the same basic philosophical orientation.

A cornerstone of Laura and Allen's shared worldview is the idea that collaboration on multiple fronts is central to a successful marriage. Describing this viewpoint, Allen said:

> I think that being a couple is the essence of collaboration in every single way. I think that a successful marriage is based on collaboration. Whether it's who cooks one night and who does the dishes or who takes the children to the doctor or any number of possibilities. What you do in bed at night. It's all collaboration. A professional project is an official version of all the kinds of collaboration that go on anyway in a relationship.

While not overlooking the potential for conflict that it can engender, Laura voiced a similar opinion about the contribution of collaboration to a marriage. She said:

It's easy for partners to separate and go in their own ways. Our work is so complex and the demands on our time are so varied and intense that I think it is really valuable if spouses work on just about anything together. When it's something that has an intellectual product that they both care very deeply about, it can really enrich the relationship for a long time.

Laura and Allen's view of the family as a collaborative unit extends to their children. One way that they acted this out occurred during the trip where they returned to Africa with their son, then aged six. At the close of each day, Laura turned on the tape recorder and asked their son about his reactions to events of the day. When they returned, she and Allen were asked to write a paper about taking children into the field. While they were writing the paper, they realized that their son had a voice too. They wrote the paper using excerpts from the tapes, keeping each of their three voices distinct. All three names were listed as authors on the article. They presented the paper at a national anthropological association conference. All three of them took turns at the podium reading their respective parts of the paper.

Egalitarianism and the Division of Labor

A self-described feminist, Laura used the term **egalitarian** to describe her relationship with Allen. When I asked her to clarify the term, she pointed to the fact that they do not have a **division of labor**. In this, she was speaking particularly about how they manage the tasks of maintaining a household. Describing this nontraditional division of labor, Laura said:

We don't really have a division of labor between us. We do everything. We have a very hectic life. We don't have a routine where he always does this and I always do that. We never know who is cooking from day to day; we never know who is going to make the beds. It's just whoever is there first does it. We have a very flexible, spontaneous relationship. We have very few ground rules in terms of who does what.

Allen described their division of labor as flexible. He said that it is not uncommon for him to begin the preparation for a meal and then for Laura to take over when, for example, their daughter asks him to read her a book.

When I observed during our telephone interview that the kind of division of labor they had would suggest people with very similar skills, Allen agreed but put the emphasis on the commitment they had to each other and to their family. It is something that has always characterized their relationship. He said:

> We're very committed to our children. We do things without nego-
> tiating. It's just if one person can't do it, then the other person
> does. We've always had that working relationship in all aspects of
> our lives. It hasn't changed with children. It hasn't changed the
> writing we do.

Space

How Laura and Allen manage a household without a clear division of labor, as well as in a definition of family that includes collaboration, is mirrored in the large, book-lined *space*, central to the free-flowing first floor of their comfortable home, which they share as a study. They each have a desk and a computer only a few feet apart. It is part of the public area of their house. It was one of the reasons that they chose the house. Laura said that they had been commuting for a year when they bought the house and that they missed each other a lot. They knew, she said, that they would be spending a lot of time in the study and they would miss each other if they had separate studies. Similarly, Allen said that even though they now had a home where they might conceivably have private studies, after all those years of working together it just did not seem comfortable not being next to each other when they are working.

The shared study has been central to the way Laura and Allen collaborate, particularly in their habit of reading their work aloud to each other. Over the course of the year they spent writing their coauthored book, they were on very similar schedules, often working side by side for eight hours during the day and then for several more hours after putting their son to bed. They spent the day passing things back and forth, interrupting each other to see how a passage sounded or to clarify a detail about a scene one of them was writing. They would take a break in the middle of the day, often taking long walks around the neighborhood discussing the unfolding book and negotiating how to resolve different issues. Afterwards, they would return to the study to work through the afternoon.

Sources of Conflict

Despite its compatibility with the way they work, Laura and Allen have had to negotiate differences in **working and writing style** that a shared study uncovers. Tidiness is one of the ways Laura and Allen differ. By their assessment, he is the neat one; she is the messy one. Another difference is that Allen describes himself as a restless writer who might write for half an hour and then need to get up to roam around a bit to think through something. She, on the other hand, can sit at a desk for hours working on a single thing. They have negotiated the issue of tidiness through compromise: Allen has become a little messier and Laura has become a little tidier. They manage the interruptions because Laura insists that she is the kind of person who can work just about anywhere. Interruptions, she maintains, rarely bother her, while they do, on occasion, derail Allen.

Like the majority of people who collaborate, differences in writing styles generate conflict between Laura and Allen. Most of the differences stem from the different disciplinary conventions they utilize. The conflict in writing styles was most pronounced during the last month of their joint writing project, when they were intensively revising under the pressure of the publisher's deadline. This was not a comfortable time for either of them. The book was running long, but Laura resisted pressure from Allen to cut a lot of material. She pointed to how their disciplinary conventions came in conflict using these words:

> He wanted me to cut details that he felt were extraneous. If we were trying to build a scene with one point in mind, he would want me to include one example as emblematic, whereas I had 15 examples. My urge as a social scientist was to include a lot of evidence. If not 15 examples, at least four or five. Initially, we had a lot of skirmishes over that.

Although both see themselves as having very high standards about the quality of writing, Allen's thoroughness about editing was an additional source of conflict as their joint writing project was drawing to a close. Both recognized this was an aspect of their collaboration that was uncomfortable for Laura. She acknowledged that Allen had much higher standards for writing than she did. While she might be satisfied with what she had written after 10 drafts, he thought that another 10 drafts were necessary. "As a writer with a capital W, he just has a far deeper love of language than I do, even if I do consider myself a good writer," Laura said.

Despite the equal footing they sought by dividing up the narrative into equal pieces, the experience of writing the book together was one that Laura did not always enjoy because it placed her, at least temporarily, in a subordinate role. While Allen described himself as the junior partner and helpmate when they were in the field, she saw herself as the junior member in learning how to write narrative for the book. The undisputed better writer of the two, for a brief period of time Allen became the senior author who basically had the last word. The conflict in writing styles is something that might work against future collaborative projects they might consider. Nevertheless, since completing the book they have successfully collaborated on writing several papers together, two of which have been published in an anthropological journal.

Issues of Recognition and Reward

Being in two different academic fields offered Laura and Allen an unusual platform from which to collaborate and probably helped them to avoid some of the challenges many faculty couples in the same discipline face over **recognition**. Both were strategic enough to establish distinct scholarly identities before coauthoring together. When I asked Laura if establishing a scholarly identity distinct from Allen had been an important issue for her, she said she had never really thought about it. She went on to say:

> It doesn't strike me as an issue. I mean clearly we have our own distinct identities and in some ways the worlds we inhabit career-wise are quite different. Writers look different from social scientists. They do different things, they have different schedules and different networks. It was never a struggle for me to see myself as distinct from Allen or vice versa.

When I asked Allen the same question in my private conversation with him about whether one was seen as riding on the other's coattails he, too, seemed barely able to grasp the question. He said that if anything, they rode on each other's coattails.

Laura and Allen both agree that although this was not their intention, Laura initially received more recognition and visibility for their coauthored book. For reasons obviously not related to the way it is written, they both agreed that it has done more to advance her career than it has Allen's. This has begun to change somewhat now that literary scholars concerned with issues of narrative are writing about the book. By the same token, the book caused controversy in her department while it was largely ignored in his. According to them, the controversy generated by the book was more about an anthropologist collaborating with a fiction writer than because it was coauthored by a couple. The book's commercial success seemed to reinforce the charge that it was not scholarly, even though it won a major academic award.

Conclusion

After completing their book, both Laura and Allen moved on to other major writing projects. The experience of constructing a book-length narrative proved influential to Allen because it gave him the skills and confidence he needed to tackle writing a novel. He has since published one novel and is currently working on another. The one of the two who has frequently collaborated, Laura is now on leave to complete two books; one she is writing on her own and the other she is editing with a colleague.

Laura and Allen are vague about future plans for collaborative writing projects. Allen imagines returning to Africa when their daughter is older. He sees the potential for a sequel to their popular book. Meanwhile, he too is on sabbatical to complete his sixth book, a novel. They both are grateful that their university is so supportive of faculty who produce books. It is this support, as well as the fact that they hold comparable faculty positions, that keeps them in a relatively rural setting even though they would be more likely to find a larger community of like-minded scholars and writers in an urban setting. Whatever they do, it seems clear that they will continue to be highly productive faculty who manage a lifestyle, as hectic as it is, that somehow manages to interweave both work and family.

11

Seeing and Being Seen: Examining the Inner Visions between Race, Relationality, and Research:
A Response to the Third Case

STACEY FLOYD-THOMAS

We knew intuitively that the only way of reaching our goals was to find collaborators that saw our world, held our convictions, and dreamed the same dreams. We found that in each other—a partner with whom we were able to encode all the symbols of our lives into our work and home.

L ike Laura Bauer and Allen Harris, my husband Juan and I met during the formative years of our professional identities. The setting for the meeting, interestingly enough, was a summer academic program where we lived intimately with several prolific academic couples. At the dawn of both of our graduate careers, having such exposure to couples who were able successfully to integrate their personal, professional, and philosophical selves allowed us to observe, critique, and imagine that such a pairing might be not only possible but also attractive.

Sharing similar visions of black empowerment and communal concerns as a baseline for our relationship, our complementary visions and personalities facilitated and made more realistic the notion of a future together in both the academic and romantic sense. Looking back on it now, the situation seems at once strange and ironic. *Who would have ever thought we would become a working academic couple in our own right?* And yet here we are, an academic couple who has been privileged to see the intimate inner visions and inner workings of several other academic couples at various stages of their own relationships. Only now can I see the seams of how Juan and my lives have become one, so to speak. As our relationship evolved from platonic friends to a married couple, we were exposed to many academic couples (several of whom were black) whose

112

lives we could use as "living laboratories" to experiment and envision how our individual lives and collective relationship could, should, or would be. Every detail, from deciding whether or not to share office space, to deciding to hyphenate both of our names, to how to negotiate a job offer, was informed by our association with other academic couples.

Consequently, I feel very self-conscious in the writing of this chapter. Presently I am not part of a prolific academic couple *per se* nor a long-standing marriage, as are Laura Bauer and Allen Harris or the other cases presented in this book. Juan and I are newlyweds who are just now undergoing the transition from graduate students to assistant professors. However, Juan and I are hoping that serendipity will continue to grace our relationship. Our partnership, I hope, will one day contribute to our productivity and have us seen as senior scholars because we have not only an academic community awaiting the yield from their investment, but a familial and cultural community that demands one.

Collaboration as Self- and Collective Reflexivity

Collaboration among academic couples mandates moments of reflexivity. This is especially evident in the choices facing academic couples and the attitudes demonstrated by their subsequent decisions. The moment of reflexivity could begin as simply as a mutual assessment of how much each partner's discipline may overlap or accentuate the other's, but it does not necessarily stop there. Other reflexive considerations can rest on the particular approach each person takes in doing research or how the couple envisions an equitable division of labor in their professional and/or personal lives. All of these quandaries could culminate in how the couple might desire or despise the notion of working at the same institution (or possibly even the same department) as a credible option for the future together. As I hope to illustrate, collaboration is an intrinsic and ultimately inevitable fact of life for many academic couples. The collaborative work of these couples often begins long before they ever decide to share office space or authors' credits.

Juan and I, like Laura and Allen, share the fortune of being academic couples who work at the same university (in fact, we are in the same college and have campus offices in same building). Whereas Laura, an anthropologist, and Allen, a creative writer, are attracted to each other's work because they both involve "observing cultures," Juan, a historian, and I, an ethicist and religion scholar, are inspired by each other's academic approach in uncovering deeper understandings of how things are as we try to envision how things could be improved. Therefore I would suggest that an initial phase of becoming an academic couple is firmly wedded to a shared **worldview** that moves each person deeply. In this fashion, the issue of intellectual compatibility can often be the tie that binds the relationship as strongly as familial and romantic bonds. As much as each person is a spouse, lover, and helpmate, she or he is also a person with whom the other partner can share views on the world in general and life in particular. From this perspective, academic couples can potentially form relationships that are holistic and reflexive based on how they envision themselves as individuals and as a couple. For instance, rather than being "partners in our ambitions," finding each other's ambitious aspirations in his or her disciplines exciting in how they enrich "lifelong interest in learning about other cultures," like Laura and Allen, Juan and I are partners in our *convictions*. What I mean by this is that we saw the academic profession as a vehicle or a means by which we could collectively empower the black communities from which we came. An academic career was not an end in its own right.

Many of the issues Juan and I have contended with as colleagues, friends, and spouses largely stem from the occasional realization that we are, in fact, operating under somewhat different assumptions based on our own orientations. Whereas we share many core values and beliefs, much of our experience together is greatly informed by those significant differences in our personal backgrounds. I am the youngest of four children and was raised in a predominantly white, middle-class, suburban neighborhood in Texas. My husband was raised as an only child in a black, working-class, urban neighborhood in New Jersey, just minutes away from New York City. He probably has a more similar family background to Laura and Allen than do I. While I was socialized totally within the confines of a stable two-parent household with steady interaction with my extended family, my husband became a "latchkey kid" as a result of his parents' divorce during his preteen years.

Consequently, our orientations and perspectives also affect how we live and collaborate with one another (differences in **working and writing styles**). Juan generally calls me "an organizational and motivational mastermind" not only because I have an obsession with time- and labor-saving devices that will make life run more smoothly but because I also have a way with provoking people to work toward a common goal that will bring ease and efficiency to their lives and struggles. As he says, I "can get to and show other people the way to the bottom line of any situation in a heartbeat." Juan, on the other hand, is a borderline workaholic whose love of long-suffering labor, determination, and focus are to be alternately feared and envied.

With my obsession for efficiency and expediency and his compulsion for arduous reflection, our outlooks are at once divergent and comparable, which results in the constant challenge in our relationship as an academic couple. Yet this paradox has also at times made perfect sense. For instance, while I was in the midst of doing my dissertation, Juan's support and coaxing (as well as his tireless editing suggestions) (**feedback**) made the experience somewhat less than miserable. Meanwhile, Juan tells me how much my analytical suggestions and insights aid in his work because I help him "approach situations in a more efficient and realistic manner" where he would have otherwise spent tireless time and energy running around in proverbial circles. In this way we are complementary in that we mutually complete each other (enhancing each other's strengths) to bring the other to perfection. Note that I say "bring the other to perfection" and not just the other's goal/task, because I think this is often the assumption that others make when it comes to collaboration with a spouse or partner.

Generally speaking, it is often assumed that in a spousal collaboration one is carrying the weight of the other and that therefore the product or outcome of a text, for instance, is largely due to the other. I hardly believe that is the case. Laura and Allen's case attests that under some circumstances, collaborative writing can be much more time-consuming than singularly authored work. Causing someone, as in Juan and my case or Laura and Allen's, to go back and reassess, reedit, or redo something in the other's writing does not suggest that that person is "carrying or doing the work for the other." Rather, it suggests that both are in a state of constant reflexivity about how to become a more "perfect" researcher and scholar. To work collaboratively, therefore, suggests being reflexive and vulnerable enough to allow another to critique and comment on your approach/expertise. And of course being vulnerable and open bespeaks an inclination for the establishment of **intellectual intimacy**, a point that I will now address more fully.

Intimacy and Advocacy

As a result of collaboration, intimacy is a crucial factor for academic couples. As was stated in Laura and Allen's narrative, intellectual intimacy was fortified through shared life experiences and familiarity with each other's work, but most importantly by the physical proximity and constant ongoing interactions as friends, lovers, colleagues, and partners. Issues of shared space, voice, worldview, and labor tend to accentuate the intimacy between the people in academic couples. But it is my observation and contention that support as well as advocacy are the most essential criteria for collaboration with a spouse or partner.

It was made clear in their narrative that the evidence or need for emotional support and mutual advocacy became most critical and visible when Laura and Allen were doing fieldwork in Africa. Allen stated that experiencing Africa "was intense not only because they were in a radically different culture, but also because they were in a small, isolated village." Therefore "they went through a lot together and worked very hard, he said, at trying to be helpful to each other . . . in an isolated location and an unfamiliar culture." I found great irony in that reality, not because I question its validity or seriousness but because the way in which Allen described the setting of their field experience in Africa is very like how Juan and I understand our day-to-day reality within an academic world. Such a reality exemplifies in contradistinction how Juan and I differ from Laura and Allen. What brief phases of discomfort or sequestration did in or for the lives of Laura and Allen in the way of intimacy is incomparable to how Juan and I are forced to face the same levels of reflection and engagement continuously within the academy. In this way, our relationship is not only "mutually beneficial," like Laura and Allen's, but it is vital. As complementary partners in what sometimes seems like an alien setting, daily one of us gives hope, sustenance, and affirmation when the other finds his or her station or perspective tenuous or disconcerting.

This reality is not one that I think only Juan and I hold, but is a shared experience of those black academic couples who have been our models and muses and whose footsteps we follow. Such an experience brings clarity to why, of those African Americans in academia who are married, 40.7 percent of women and 47.7 percent of men are married to another academic in higher education.[1] Whereas it is important to assess how collaboration is associated with prolific scholarly output, it is more vital to understand the basis on which partners feel able to invest as much time and energy into their work as they do. Juan and I are sensitive to the expectations and demands placed upon us as scholars of color, especially in predominantly white academic contexts. Having been conditioned by the joint assumptions that failure is not an option and that everything we do contributes to the common good, Juan and I find the support and advocacy we give one another not only beneficial but actually essential. In this regard it becomes critical for us to broach the subject of race and representation as it pertains to the particularity of being a black academic couple.

Race and Representation

Juan and I, as a black academic couple aspiring to be prolific, are very conscious of the way we understand what we see and the ways in which we are seen. In his description of the black intellectual's warring with a sense of double-consciousness, W. E. B. DuBois, the most prolific black academic in American history, calls the paradox of seeing and being seen a "second sight" that allows one to "see one's self through the eyes of others."[2] However, in recounting his own experience of being apart from his familiar community and striving to create an identity for himself in an academic one, DuBois noted that a sensation of double-consciousness for black people caused a peculiar and pervasive crisis that moved far beyond self-consciousness. This ability not only to see yourself through the eyes of the other but always to see oneself through another's eyes causes the black intellectual to measure her or his "soul by the tape of a world that looks on in amused contempt and pity."[3] Critical theorist Pierre Bourdieu states that this self-deprecating act of reflexivity is a calculated result of the "performative magic" and "symbolic violence" that is inherent within institutions of education. He says:

> "Become what you are": that is the principle behind the performative magic of all acts of institutions . . .[4] [However,] it *signifies* to someone what [one's] identity is, but in a way that both expresses it to [her or] him and imposes it on [her or] him by expressing it in front of everyone . . . and thus informing [that person] in an authoritative manner of what [she or] he is and what [she or] he must be. This is clearly evident in the insult, a kind of curse . . . which attempts to imprison its victim in an accusation which also depicts [one's] destiny.
>
> .The educational system provides a good example of this process: the development of this system involves a certain kind of objectification in which formally defined credentials or qualifications become a mechanism for creating and sustaining inequalities, in such a way that . . . this mechanism provides a practical justification of the established order. . . . It enables those who benefit from the system to convince themselves of their own intrinsic worthiness, while preventing those who benefit least from grasping the basis of their own deprivation.[5]

Such a disposition, DuBois contends, causes the genius and power to effect change of black individuals to become falling stars that die "before the world has rightly gauged their brightness."[6] Reflecting on these, I realize now why DuBois and other prolific black scholars (especially couples) were so important to me. They not only echo the saliency of my understanding the warring ideals of being black and American but they also describe the central conflict of what it means for those of us who enter into the academy. As my muses they seem to be saying: *"Don't let go of your vision and capability in spite of what the mirrors within the academy/America might show you. Do your best to note your strengths and apply them to empower our people. Don't be consumed with others' visions of you. Focus on your own."*

When Juan and I first met, we shared accounts of college and plans for graduate school and spoke of the ongoing and undefeated battle of shunning how we were seen so we could effectively complete our goals. We knew intuitively that the only way of reaching our goals was to find collaborators who saw our world, held our convictions, and dreamed our dreams. We found that in each other—partners with whom we were able to encode all the symbols of our lives into our work and home. That marked our attraction for one another. Whereas our common interest in an academic career enhanced our relationship, it was our worldview of making a difference for black people while not changing our past lifestyles that caused us to choose such a path. Our attraction for each other grew out of our mutual search for a partner who shared a common vision and held a complementary worldview.

What began as two friends sharing jokes and childhood anecdotes became a relationship grounded in the fact that Juan and I understood our world and ourselves in a way that resonated with the other. With that in place, all the other accomplishments of our life together—career, travel, family, and so on—have been much easier to negotiate because we almost instinctively view ourselves as an academic couple that has been extraordinarily fortunate. However, we feel that the first and foremost indicator of our good fortune is being happy and productive partners above all else.

Granted, Juan and I realize that our present as well as future lifestyle affords us opportunities and luxuries that our parents or contemporaries may not have. However, we realize much is at stake. As a religious scholar who was reared in a black Christian household, the biblical verse "To whom much is given, much is required" is paramount in the expectations imposed upon Juan and me as a black academic couple. This is to say that for all of our theoretical and intellectual pursuits there must be a practical end. Where at first this may seem like a lot of mixed blessings and burdens, this actually makes us better scholars and collaborators.

In this sense I think it is evident that, as an academic couple, Juan and I could be more readily defined as complementary rather than **egalitarian**, as Laura and Allen define themselves. As a self-avowed womanist, I shudder at hearing myself say that. One could assume that I am saying that my husband and I do not consider each other to be equals. But according to the definition in the description of Laura and Allen, I must admit that Juan and I (more me than him) rarely, if ever, leave the other's version of the story largely unchallenged as to ensure "equal footing." We are both so consumed with how our lives and work impact those around us that we always want to be responsible and truthful in our actions, especially when doing collaborative work. As a historian and an ethicist whose work revolves around the untold stories and rejected moral agencies of black people, we are obsessed with "getting it right." More than anything else, teaching in all its nuances serves as a constant touchstone for Juan and me as we strive to become more prolific and estimable as an academic couple.

Perspectives on Pedagogy

When asked why we decided to take up an academic profession, Juan felt that it was a logical progression that fortified his natural inclinations and talents (that is, mentoring, tutoring, writing, and studying) while being useful to the task of racial uplift. I think the appetite for an academic career was created for me as a student who was always wishing that someone who looked like me could be teaching the class that I was in. For these reasons I am always astounded when prolific academicians shirk teaching. As I read how Laura secured eight semesters of leave to follow her intellectual pursuits in research, I found it quizzical that such a feat would be desired. As a black professor, I feel that my presence may at times have more of an impact on people in the classroom than outside it. But even more, it is from the classroom that I get my inspiration for research. In the dialogical moments in teaching I can keep the pulse on what inspires, puzzles, or frustrates students.

As interdisciplinary scholars, Juan and I see our pedagogy, research, and service as inextricably bound. Likewise, not only the teaching moment but the university setting is crucial to how we specifically understand our ability to effect change and simultaneously enhance our own lives. This is a major sticking point for Juan and me. As a person who is used to urban, multicultural, and big university settings, Juan thinks he might be better suited at such a place. On the other hand, I am forever lamenting over my personal experience as one of the few black faces in a sea of white, feeling certain that I can best enhance and represent the lives of students in such a context. But in either case, unlike Laura and Allen, we both have an understanding that our physical presence in the classroom, administrative meetings, and student functions is essential to how we envision ourselves as scholars.

Our understanding of prolific scholars was largely shaped by those scholars and academic couples who not only were productive in their research, but whose concomitant stance of academic excellence in teaching and university-building were equally profound. To be prolific, in my opinion, is to be cutting-edge, exemplary in productivity, yielding fruit. For those whose academic reflexivity is engulfed in fighting against the miseducation of a people, we cannot separate theory from praxis, research from teaching. To do so would threaten our ability ever to become prolific. Katie Cannon, prolific religious ethicist womanist scholar, states that this notion of what she calls "emancipatory praxis" is a challenge to systems of domination that calls us as scholars to fight all forms of miseducation (racism, sexism, classism, and so on) "in an effort to create a more just society.[7] This work—[as Cannon] warns—is difficult daily labor . . . unglamorous, incremental, unsentimental, and often invisible. It demands vigilance and courage" not only in our research, but our teaching and outreach as well.[8] Why can't this emancipatory praxis be done via the auspices of research and the publication of several monographs? It is not enough to write the wrongs; we must right them. As Paulo Freire suggests, in order to transform our society, we must adhere to a pedagogy of the oppressed:

> a pedagogy which must be forged *with* not *for* the oppressed (whether individuals or peoples) in the incessant struggle to regain their humanity. This pedagogy makes oppression and its causes objects of reflection by the oppressed, and from that reflection will come their necessary engagement in the struggle for their liberation. And in the struggle this pedagogy will be made and remade.[9]

In her own admission, bell hooks, world-renowned scholar and author of more than 20 books, states that she "never wanted to be a teacher [since she was little all she] wanted to do was write."[10] However, after reading Friere's work and becoming an avowed feminist in graduate school, she realized that writing was not enough. She noted that within the academy there is a "sad reminder of the way teaching is seen as a duller, less valuable aspect of the academic profession." For hooks, Freire, Cannon, and other marginalized yet prolific academics, herein lies the "serious crisis in education." hooks says it well:

> Students often do not want to learn and teachers do not want to teach. More than ever before in the recent history of this nation, educators are compelled to confront the biases that have shaped teaching practices in our society and to create new ways of knowing, different strategies for the sharing of knowledge. We cannot address this crisis if progressive critical thinkers and social critics act as though teaching is not a subject worthy of our regard. The classroom remains the most radical space of possibility in the academy. For years it has been a place where education has been undermined by teachers and students alike who seek to use it as a platform for opportunistic concerns rather than as a place to learn. . . . [We should] celebrate teaching that enables transgressions—a movement against and beyond boundaries. It is that movement which makes education the practice of freedom.[11]

In recognition of education as "the practice of freedom," Juan and I constantly toil with the dilemma of how to invest greater meaning into our teaching. While we all exist in an academic context governed by the "publish-or-perish" paradigm, the pedagogical experience serves as the lifeblood for the research and other commitments that my husband and I take very seriously. The freedom that comes from face-to-face interactions with students is currently more desirable than the need for unlimited sabbaticals and the like. I am not saying that my husband and I do not appreciate an occasional respite from the daily grind that teaching can become, but we have never envisioned how we could be professors without actual students to teach.

On the one hand, this might illustrate some naïveté on our parts that might be dispelled once tenure, children, and other long-range concerns of maturity begin to materialize. On the other hand, this might also illuminate the fact that there seem to be certain things conferred upon and demanded by our white counterparts that Juan and I have been led to believe are inaccessible to us based on the fact that we are *black* academics. The prospect of engaging with students and having them begin the learning experience anew for themselves is a wonderful component of being an academic couple. The teaching moment allows us to heighten each other's enthusiasm and appetite for the class lecture or seminar discussion. Here the world sees the academic couple in its fullest realization, with each partner sustaining and encouraging the other enough to make it possible for him or her to face the unexpected perils and thrills of the teaching moment as it, too, is a collaborative moment.

PART 2

The Social Nature of Faculty Scholarship

12

"Different, but the Same":
Introduction to the Invited Chapters

It is the same thing in writing with a research collaborator. They write one section, you write one section. Or they write a draft and I work it over. It is different, but the same. This is how you do it in this business. –*Woman, Professor, Molecular Biology*

The first part of the book reflected the perspectives of the participants and focused on the social and material aspects of couples' personal relationships and lifestyles on publishing productivity. The second part of the book consists of three chapters that set the findings within the broader context of relevant research literature. Written by academics who have demonstrated an expertise on the topic, the chapters in this part of the book explore elements of the institutional setting, particularly the academic reward system, and the even wider social setting of collegial recognition and networks associated with publishing productivity. The chapters provide some background that is necessary to understand fully the implications of the comments and observations made by participants presented in the case narratives. They place the motivations and behaviors of individual faculty in a wider context. They underscore that faculty research and productivity are a social process.[1]

The chapters in Part 2 expand on what I have referred to previously as the subtext of some of the comments made by members of academic couples. They explore some of the more contentious issues raised by academics who collaborate extensively with a colleague who is also an intimate spouse or partner. These are topics raised by participants but most often discussed in a somewhat understated or oblique way, and where participants, who were generally very thoughtful in their replies, were especially cautious and circumscribed in their choice of words. This is one of the signals that alerted me to the sensitivity of some of these issues.

Summary of the Invited Chapters

The chapter about scholarly collaboration by Ann Austin cogently makes the point that collaboration among academics who are life partners shares many qualities with other collegial configurations. Included in the qualities that it shares is the process used to produce coauthored work and its contribution to innovation and knowledge production. On the other hand, the advantage afforded by ongoing proximity and ease of access to informal feedback about ideas is one instrumental way that these relationships differ from other collegial configurations.[2] Collaboration among life partners also differs from other collegial partnerships that do not include an intimate intellectual and personal bond, in that an unusual longevity that rarely characterizes other types of collaborative pairings may provide the opportunity for theory-building.

Collegial networks provide an important avenue for visibility and recognition for faculty. The chapter by Jeff Milem, Joe Sherlin, and Laura Irwin makes the point that it is a mistake to think of members of the couples presented in this text as removed from colleagues or to assume that the relationship is so inner-directed that it functions to isolate them from like-minded colleagues. The chapter considers several aspects of collegial networks that have not been approached before in the literature. One is that the function and composition of collegial networks vary for faculty by career stage. The second innovative perspective about collegial networks introduced by the chapter authors is to distinguish between campus-based networks and extracampus networks.

Milem and associates argue that these different networks, one rooted in colleagues on campus and one in colleagues off campus, serve very different functions for faculty. Networks with colleagues on campus primarily serve personal needs for affiliation, especially for marginalized groups such as gay and lesbian faculty. They are an indispensable source of community and information about policies and practices on campus, such as those about tenure and promotion. Colleagues off campus are more likely than colleagues on campus to be from the same disciplinary background. They offer access to collaborators, information about publication and grant opportunities, and both recognition and visibility by such practices as citing colleagues. This chapter underscores the point that successful academics, including those with a partner in the same profession, are engaged simultaneously in multiple personal and professional relationships.

In her chapter about academic reward and recognition structures, Jane Loeb confronts some of the more unpleasant accusations faced by academic couples who collaborate. One of these is the charge of collusion. Loeb reviews practices in a variety of disciplines for acknowledging contribution of coauthors. She notes that the ambiguity about judging individual contribution to coauthored work can be exacerbated by the "Matthew effect," where a disproportionate credit accrues to the most visible or the most senior author. She suggests that the Matthew effect may be an impediment for both members of a couple receiving comparable recognition for collaboratively produced work. She cautions young couples who are inclined to collaborate that the scenario most fraught with difficulty is when the members of the couple are in the same field, there is an overlap in their areas of research, and one is either significantly younger than the other or in a position with less status or prestige. Issues of recognition, especially for achieving the distinct scholarly identity required for tenure at most research universities, are less pronounced for members of academic couples who work at different institutions or whose fields of study employ completely different research methods or conceptual approaches.

The invited chapters incorporate references to the case narratives that appear in Part 1, but they are written in such a way that they can be understood without a thorough reading of the cases. This accomplishes the goal of something that has not been done before—that is, incorporating recognition of academic couples as a collaborative unit in the existing research in three areas: collaboration, reward and recognition, and collegial networks.

My editing of the invited chapters was primarily to reduce redundancy between the invited chapters and between them and the case narratives. It was also to point to connections that might weave together the different parts of the book.

Multiple Viewpoints about the Impact on Productivity

The authors of the invited chapters present several viewpoints about some issues central to collaboration. For example, there is a difference of opinion about whether scholarly collaboration enhances either the quality or the quantity of faculty publishing. Jane Loeb, the author of the chapter about reward and recognition, is more confident about the link between collaboration and quality than is Ann Austin, the author of the chapter on collaboration.

Participants in the research project, particularly those who worked with a spouse or partner on only a project or two, also offered different opinions about the impact of collaboration on the quality of scholarship.

A small number of participants confessed to a tendency to compromise or to settle on a consensus view in order to protect the personal relationship. These were the participants least likely to see the connection between collaboration and quality. A male sociologist in the larger interview sample who had written several journal articles with his spouse in the early years of their relationship is an example of this. He said:

> A marriage just involves a whole lot of things. To add that dimension to it just doesn't work well for many people. Not that my wife and I fought a lot over these articles, but I know there just were times when I felt I was going along just to avoid conflict in the marriage. We don't fight a lot anyway, but this was adding a dimension which invited disagreement and I just wanted to avoid that. There are certain things in a marriage that you know upsets the other person, so you don't talk about those things.

Other participants who had coauthored with a life partner saw handling intellectual differences of opinion differently and consequently are more positive about the association between collaboration and quality. The expression that the "whole is better than the sum of the parts" is one that came up often among these participants. It was not uncommon for participants to describe differences in writing style and disciplinary background as an advantage because they require being more attentive to analyzing the nuances and meanings of words and concepts.

Socialization as well as training in the scientific method provides scientists with the tools to resist reaching both premature conclusions and premature consensus for the sake of avoiding conflict. A member of one of the couples (both geologists) in the interview sample for example, pointed to her training in the scientific method and traditions in their academic discipline as a safeguard to prevent reaching an intellectual compromise for the sake of the relationship. A senior faculty member at a research university in the Midwest, she observed that people in her discipline are trained to juggle multiple working hypotheses and to offer alternative explanations for everything. She used these words to describe the process:

> When we go out in the field, people will generally take the opposite view. . . . They see how inventive they can be in coming up with another hypothesis that explains the observation. . . . In our discipline, it is good science to be as argumentative as possible without

bringing personality into it. If you have five geologists on a field trip, by the end of the trip you will have at least 10 hypotheses to explain something that you have observed.

This argument is reflected in the case narratives of academics who have collaborated in producing scholarly research with a spouse or partner—that is, that deeply ingrained disciplinary training and a genuine commitment to the personal relationship propels them to negotiate differences in both opinion and working and writing styles. Part of what is modeled by the couples presented in this book who have succeeded at the process of collaboration is how to disagree productively if not necessarily always amiably.

Impact of Collaboration on Quantity

A similar difference of opinion about the impact of scholarly collaboration on quantity of publications exists among some of the chapter authors. Yvonna Lincoln, describing a traditional division of labor that is similar to the one presented in the introductory quotation that introduces this chapter, argues that coauthoring enhances output because of the time saved by an efficient division of labor. Ann Austin points out in her chapter, however, that time-saving and efficiency are not accurate descriptors of the outcomes of all types of collaborative arrangements.

Whether collaboration saves time and thus enhances quantity depends to some extent on the approach taken to allocate authority for the text. Most of the participants who had collaborated with a partner for 10 or more years described utilizing more than one approach to joint projects they undertook.[3] Participants described other situations where they shared authority for all parts of the text rather than dividing up responsibility for different sections of an article or chapters in a book. In such cases, they sometimes described discussing the subtle nuances of individual words and the wording used in every sentence. This is clearly evident in the third case narrative presented in Part 1. Time devoted to talking through intellectual differences, while it may produce a better product, is not an approach selected for reasons of speed or efficiency. As is amply illustrated by both the first and last case narratives, the time members of these couples invest to negotiate differences reflects a mutual commitment to quality of the product, to the personal relationship, and to each other's success as scholars.

13

Reviewing the Literature on Scholarly Collaboration: How We Can Understand Collaboration among Academic Couples

ANN E. AUSTIN

> Both of us are driven by ideas. Both of us are very content, and have been all of our lives, with the excitement of the life of the mind. It makes us very companionable because it is something that we can really understand about each other. He is as likely to be standing in the shower and me standing outside the shower door talking to him about some idea as we are to be doing that in some sort of proper circumstance where we are sitting down writing. The fact is, that can go on anywhere, anytime, day or night. That is the thing that makes it so much fun. *–Martha Hanson, one of a pair of geographers*

In recent years, interest in collaboration has been increasing both among academics choosing to use this form of work and among researchers studying how scholars go about their work. Information is somewhat dated, but collaborative research appears to have been on the increase over the past half-century.[1] In terms of research about collaboration, a small but steady stream of work has taken up the project of examining how collaboration occurs, by whom, under what circumstances, with what challenges, and with what results.[2] A particularly interesting kind of collaboration is that which occurs between academic couples— those who share a personal relationship and a household as well as intellectual work. As a context for examining the work and lives of academic couples who collaborate, this chapter highlights the literature on collaboration more broadly. The chapter addresses several related questions: How does the literature on collaboration inform study of academic couples who collaborate? Conversely, how do cases and literature on academic couples expand understanding of collaboration more broadly? In

130

the context of the literature on collaboration, what further questions for research does exploration of the lives and work of academic couples who collaborate suggest?

The chapter is organized around themes in the literature. The first section provides an overview of how collaborative work has been conceptualized and categorized within the literature. Then I discuss findings concerning the relationships between fields of study and extent and kind of collaborative scholarship. The third section examines what has been discovered about the outcomes of collaborative work. Does it enhance productivity and, if so, under what circumstances? The fourth section deals with the process of doing collaborative work and explores contributions from the literature concerning how collaborators approach their work and the specific challenges and issues they often encounter. In each of these sections, I synthesize findings and themes in the literature on research collaboration and then offer some thoughts concerning how the literature relates to couples who collaborate or how cases about such couples may offer additional insights into the nature of scholarly work and how it is produced in collaborative situations. The final section of the chapter highlights themes that have emerged throughout the chapter concerning couples who collaborate, and offers questions for further research that would add in important ways to the existing literature base.

Forms of Research Collaboration

Various authors have suggested ways in which to categorize the different forms that collaborative work can take. Smart and Bayer (1986)[3] identified three kinds of collaboration: complementary, supplementary, and master-apprentice collaboration. In their categorization, complementary collaboration defines relationships in which the researchers choose not to divide the project into pieces, each taken up by one of the collaborators, but rather to work together on the project at the same time. Much communication characterizes this kind of work, as the collaborators share ideas and stimulate each other's thinking in order to move to new insights. Responsibility is shared, and the process is very participatory for each collaborator. In contrast, in supplementary collaboration, tasks are divided among the partners, often based on each person's specific expertise. The master-apprentice model is most commonly found in collaborations between a professor and graduate students, where hierarchy is apparent because one partner has more expertise than the other(s).

Brady (1988) identified two kinds of collaborative writing: "partial collaboration" and "full collaboration."[4] Like Smart and Bayer's supplementary collaborators, Brady's partial collaborators divide writing responsibilities, with each writing those sections for which he or she has primary authority. Full collaborators, on the other hand, parallel Smart and Bayer's complementary collaborators; that is, full collaborators do not clearly divide the labor but work closely, seeking consensus and engaging in considerable discussion and negotiation. Requiring a great deal of time, this kind of collaboration is less frequent. While academic collaboration usually brings to mind jointly authored products, there is also "subauthorship collaboration," in which assistance is provided in the form of data gathering and analysis, editing, and sharing of research equipment or facilities, though coauthorship is not necessarily the result.[5]

As an alternative to categorizations as a way to conceptualize forms of collaboration, Baldwin and Austin (1995) examined the metaphors that collaborators in the field of higher education use to describe their relationships. Marriage and family metaphors (including "sisterhood," "like close cousins") were used by some of the collaborators to suggest very close relationships with high levels of sharing and personal connection; some using this metaphor commented that while they do not always agree with their partners, they have the ability to help each other keep perspective.[6] "Good friendship" that included "ongoing conversation" was a similar metaphor articulated by others in the study, who commented on the dynamic interactions that characterized their relationships. Another participant metaphorically spoke of collaboration as a "symbiotic organism where all partners depend on and benefit from each other." This kind of relationship is "not a zero sum game"; partners are not bargaining for position or advantage but are seeking ways to work that benefit each partner.[7] Other participants in the study used work-related metaphors—construction, weaving, and partnership. For example, referring to collaboration as being like construction work, one said: "One person lays the foundation, the second puts up the walls, and the first person finishes the woodwork." Like a "partnership," to use another participant's words, each collaborator maintains his or her own separate identity.[8]

How does collaboration among academic couples relate to these categorizations and descriptions? The categories of complementary and supplementary collaboration, full and partial collaboration, and subauthorship can probably be used to understand the possibilities for collaborative relationships among couples as appropriately as these categories are used to explain the kind of work relationships between other academics. In the case studies offered in this book, some couples are completely full or complementary collaborators, and others use complementary and supplementary collaboration depending on the project. Additionally, all described ways in which they engage in subauthorship collaboration on projects in which one partner is the author alone, such as through daily assistance in reading drafts and offering feedback.

The metaphors offered by collaborators who are not personally linked are interesting in the ways in which they use personal relationships—marriage, family, friendship—as ways to explain the dynamics of collaboration. Perhaps what we learn from considering these categorizations and metaphors is that collaboration among academic couples shares much in terms of form with other kinds of collaborations—that is, it can be complementary, supplementary, or involve subauthorship. However, collaboration among academic couples literally involves the marriage/family/close personal relationship that is used only metaphorically to describe collaborations among noncouple collaborators. The nature of the close personal relationship (the unique aspect of the collaborative relationship of academic couples) and how it affects the collaboration and its outcomes are a theme throughout the chapter.

Collaboration in Various Fields

Research on collaboration has shown that it occurs in some fields more than in others. The "hard sciences" such as chemistry and physics tend to have more collaborative work than the "soft sciences" such as political science and sociology. Collaboration is fairly unusual in the humanities.[9] Collaborative work is most common in mature fields where strong paradigms are in place, such as the sciences.[10]

Disciplines with more developed paradigms, such as the "hard sciences" of physics and chemistry, are characterized by some degree of consensus about theory, methodology, and appropriate training. Members of such disciplines feel a sense of shared purpose, knowing what research questions need to be pursued and how to pursue them.[11] In fields with high paradigm development, theoretical structures are in place and the steps to follow in doing research are widely understood and somewhat routine. Therefore the tasks can be identified, divided and delegated, and organized around time lines.[12] Given their strong paradigms and clear theories, work in mature fields can focus more on theory-testing than on theory-building. Thus collaborative teams have a base of knowledge and skills from which to explore, revise, and confirm or disconfirm the field's dominant theories.[13] Collaboration is also more common in fields where sophisticated instruments and facilities are needed and where research is financially well supported. These characteristics also are most often found in disciplines with high paradigm development.[14]

In fields with less consensus around theory, methodology, and training, such as sociology, political science, or to an even greater extent, English and history, researchers have less theoretical reason to approach and organize tasks in particular ways, and thus division of labor is more difficult to accomplish.[15] In the humanities, for example, scholars often work independently in libraries and archives where, as individuals, each researcher interacts subjectively with the material; in a field that depends on the experience and interpretation brought by individual scholars, delegation of tasks among more than one researcher is difficult.[16] Collaboration also tends to be less frequent in new or less mature fields or in new subfields in established areas. In such fields, scholarly work more typically involves single-authored theoretical work that defines boundaries and proposes conceptual frameworks.[17] Collaboration is less frequent for purposes of defining fields as compared to testing theoretical propositions already articulated.

Since individual disciplines include work on a variety of topics, not surprisingly the extent of collaboration varies across subfields. In new areas where sophisticated instruments are used, much collaboration is occurring.[18] Within the field of anthropology, collaboration is more frequent in the subfields of biophysical anthropology and archaeological anthropology than in sociocultural and linguistic areas.[19] Data-oriented journals in psychology publish more multiauthored papers than those journals emphasizing conceptual analysis, literature reviews, and professional activities.[20] These examples suggest that patterns of collaboration are likely to change as fields change and move from theory-development to theory-testing and, in some fields, to use of sophisticated equipment.

In addition to collaboration within fields, collaboration occurs across fields. Luttaca's (1996) dissertation work on interdisciplinarity involved a sample of individuals from the sciences, social sciences, and humanities who had collaborated with colleagues from other disciplines.[21] She found that most of her respondents worked with only one or two colleagues, rather than with large teams. Such collaborative relationships came about through serendipity or because a colleague sought to work with someone with a different perspective or needed specific technical knowledge from another field. Typically, researchers' own disciplinary assumptions and preferred methods led to challenges in the interdisciplinary work. Lattuca concluded that researchers who were trying to create conceptual interdisciplinary products often explicitly critiqued disciplinary positions and offered philosophical reasons for doing interdisciplinary work. Trying to create more synthetic rather than conceptual work, these researchers perceived different disciplinary perspectives as pragmatic concerns that could be negotiated.

Overall, the research on patterns of collaboration indicates that collaborative work is chosen more often for theory-development than for theory-testing.[22] The explanation for this pattern is that in developed fields with established and well-recognized theories, researchers know what questions are most important, they share consensus on the theoretical propositions that need to be tested, confirmed, or disconfirmed, and they are in agreement about what methods are most appropriate for exploring those questions. With common understanding on such key issues, division of labor and collaboration among two or more researchers can be managed reasonably well. In fields where a strong paradigm is not in place to identify boundaries, define concepts and questions, and guide methodological choices, consensus around what questions to ask, how to divide tasks, and what methods are most useful is more elusive; thus collaboration among one or more colleagues is much more difficult.

The cases presented in this volume of academic couples who collaborate, as well as other research reporting on larger numbers of academic couples,[23] offer interesting examples of collaboration in some of the fields where this kind of joint work is less frequent. For example, Laura, an anthropologist, and Allen, a fiction writer, function as a highly collaborative couple in all aspects of managing their family and professional lives and have coauthored a memoir of their fieldwork experience in Africa that has received wide attention. While some collaboration may be found in anthropology, it is certainly very infrequent among fiction writers in the field of English. Though this case may be somewhat unusual, it certainly suggests that Laura and Allen's close personal relationship is a central motivating force not only in their choice to collaborate but also in the success of that collaboration.

Outcomes of Collaboration

Those interested in collaboration or engaged in it may wonder about whether particular advantages accrue to those who choose to work with scholarly partners. Put directly, what are the results of collaborative work? Some research suggests that collaboration leads to higher rates of publishing.[24] Nevertheless, while researchers have taken up this question of the relationship between collaboration and publication productivity, much remains unclear. In their review of research on collaboration, Austin and Baldwin (1991) reported that while some research links collaboration with scholarly productivity, it is unclear whether collaboration actually leads to increased productivity or, conversely, whether collaborative people choose more frequently than their counterparts to engage in collaborative work.

In terms of collaboration and the quality of research, the relationship is also hard to sort out.[25] Some analysts have suggested that rather than leading directly to better quality, collaboration may help scholars avoid mistakes or realize when projects need further work.[26] In this way, the contribution of the collaborative process may be primarily in the area of quality control. Examining the question of the impact of collaborative research publications, Smart and Bayer (1986) concluded that "sparse and insignificant evidence" supports the assertion that coauthored publications have greater impact on their fields. Overall, collaboration has little impact on "aggregate quality, regardless of field, as measured by citation indices."[27]

Most relevant to the focus of this volume is the research concerning academic couples and that on academic couples as collaborators. While only a relatively few studies have focused on academic couples, those that have offer interesting insights. In recent work, Astin and Milem (1997) found that the effect on productivity of having an academic partner/spouse is positive for women but negative for men: "Women with academic spouses/partners tend to be more productive than do women with nonacademic spouses/partners. However, the direction of the effect is the opposite for men."[28] The reason, they hypothesize, is that married or partnered academic women gain access to information, support, and networks through their spouse/partner that assist their careers and work.

Moving her focus of analysis beyond academic couples in general to a more specific focus on highly productive academics who have coauthored with a spouse or partner, Creamer (1999) examined patterns of coauthorship among these individuals and the relationship of these patterns to scholarly productivity. She identified and labeled three patterns of coauthorship: short-term, intermittent, and long-term. Short-term coauthorship relationships involved broad onetime intersections of interests between the members of a couple. Participants characterized the coauthorship as not unlike other collaborative relationships they had experienced, and they reported that it did not affect their productivity in significant ways. Those who were intermittent coauthors collaborated on more than one project, but with gaps of more than five years between projects. Those studied who fit in this category cited the importance of establishing their independent identities as a reason for the intermittent nature of their coauthorship activity with the partner. Those involved in long-term coauthorship relationships had been consistently publishing with the partner or spouse for more than 10 years. Typically having had similar disciplinary training, they reported that they often worked "on a topic at the interstices of their closely allied but distinct research areas"[29] and that they were able to pursue theory-building. Creamer reported that these scholars spoke of the importance of "mutual trust" and "emotional commitment" in contributing to the duration of the collaboration, as well as the importance of frequent and immediate feedback that came through many conversations occurring over time.[30]

Creamer concluded that short-term and intermittent partnerships with spouses and partners were similar to collaborative relationships with other colleagues and had little effect on the overall career productivity of the scholars. In contrast, long-term coauthorship relationships were more likely to affect the quality and quantity of the scholarship produced. Offering an explanation of why long-term collaboration between academic spouses/partners affects scholarly productivity, Creamer favored the hypothesis that the key factor is the availability of ongoing feedback about ideas. Through this feedback, scholars receive the reinforcement that is an important ingredient in productivity.[31] Furthermore, Creamer explained, among the couples she studied, sharing household responsibilities did not seem an especially important issue, but the efficiency of interchangeable work-related roles was significant. Creamer concluded:

> The most significant role in scholarly productivity of such collaborations may not, as has been supposed, be the indirect contribution of an egalitarian division of labor in the home. Instead, it may be the direct contribution to productivity through access to the many types of highly specialized, intellectual, emotional, and physical labor required to produce scholarship made possible by a partner with overlapping skills and interests.[32]

Although the literature on the results of collaboration still has many unanswered questions, the research pertaining specifically to academic couples suggests that the dynamics of close, ongoing interaction over long periods of time may be a critical factor in enhancing productivity.

Though much research indicates that collaboration is more likely to be used for theory-testing than for theory-building, some collaborating couples, particularly those engaged in very long-term collaborative work, apparently find that their joint work leads to theory conceptualization.[33] In sum, the ways in which academic couples, such as those described in the cases in this book, go about *doing* their work together may be the most important aspect of studying collaboration among intimate partners. Their work habits may offer insights useful to understanding how productive collaborative work can be accomplished.

The Process of Working Together

The process of doing collaborative work involves various issues and dynamics, and specific collaborative relationships are likely to vary in how these dynamics play out. Furthermore, while collaboration can result in significant outcomes, it also can lead to challenges and costs for participants. In this section, I summarize highlights from the literature concerning possible costs and controversial issues that can arise in collaboration, and summarize research that has explored some of the dynamics on which collaborative relationships may vary.

Potential collaborators should be aware of three likely costs: time, financial factors, and socioemotional aspects.[34] Working with someone else requires discussion and often negotiation, and thus may require more time than when a researcher works alone. Sharing tasks, however, may reduce the overall time required for a project. The time needed is greater with collaborators who are more diverse.[35] Colleagues from different fields often find they must take time to learn about the language, research perspectives, or methods used in a different field.

Financial costs accrue in collaborative relationships when partners must travel for meetings or when they employ the telephone, duplicating services, or postal service for exchange of materials. Collaboration can involve socioemotional costs if the participants find they have different goals, priorities, or standards. Differences of opinion around the research may lead to stress or worry.

The process of collaboration requires the researchers involved to grapple with various issues along the way. "Negotiated order theory" has been used to explain the processes through which agencies and organizations interact and work together.[36] It is also helpful in framing the issues that research collaborators must address. Gray (1989) explained: "Negotiated order refers to a social context in which relationships are negotiated and renegotiated. The social order is shaped through the self-conscious interactions of participants."[37] As "negotiated orders," collaborative relationships evolve over time, changing forms as the participants shift roles and their goals and agreements change. Baldwin and Austin's work (1995) pointed to six dynamics around which collaborators negotiate and define their relationships and work processes. One dynamic around which collaborative relationships may vary is the "degree of jointness" in the relationship. The continuum for this dynamic ranges from collaborators assuming very distinctive, separate roles, on the one hand, to partners who engage in seamless, interactive roles. Those on one extreme will divide the work, with one partner collecting data and the other writing, for example. In contrast, in collaborations with high "jointness," collaborators are likely to work without clearly defined roles and to engage in much discussion together about all aspects of the work, exchanging ideas and drafts regularly. One of the collaborators studied by Baldwin and Austin explained such seamless collaboration, which may remind readers of the cases of academic couples described in this volume, in this way: "We have daily communication and say, 'Have you thought of such and such, and read this?'"[38]

A second dynamic on which collaborative relationships may vary is the extent to which the collaborators are explicit in defining roles and responsibilities. Division of labor is always an important issue in collaboration, and choices among partners are likely to relate to each person's interests, abilities, and time, as well as the kinds of tasks that are required on a particular project.[39] While some research collaborators engage in systematic, open, and explicit discussion of who has what responsibilities on a project, other pairs give no explicit attention to these matters. One collaborator in a long-term partnership explained: "We maybe talk about various components: 'You take that piece, I'll take this piece.' But beyond that basic rudimentary understanding, it's basically evolutionary as we go along. . . . Division of work just happens. It's based on trust."[40] Like this longtime collaborator, academic couples described in the cases in this volume—couples who have worked together over an extended period of time—are quite likely to have collaborations where roles and responsibilities are not explicitly verbalized, partly because they are so familiar with each other that it is no longer necessary.

Collaborative relationships may also vary on the degree of flexibility in roles. In some collaborations, partners keep the same roles over time; in others, the roles may vary depending on each person's time availability or level of interest in a particular project or set of tasks. This is the situation among the couples presented in the cases. Among the long-term collaborators studied by Baldwin and Austin (1995), patterns on either end of this flexibility continuum were observed. In the cases of academic couples who collaborate, choices must also be made about whether roles will remain constant or vary.

A fourth dynamic involved in negotiating the order between collaborators concerns similarity of standards and expectations. Collaborators may have divergent or very similar perspectives on such issues as how polished drafts should be before they are submitted, what deadlines are reasonable or appropriate, what standards of quality should guide the work, and how much time should be allocated to different aspects of a project.[41] Academic couples are no different from other collaborators in their need to come to grips with these issues. However, as with other long-term collaborators, longevity of collaboration may diminish the need to speak explicitly about these issues over time.

Related to the issue of negotiating standards is the challenge of establishing authorship order among collaborators.[42] Conventions vary across fields for decisions about who should be recognized as authors and in what order. Decisions may be based on seniority of collaborators, extent and quality of contribution, alphabetical order, or purpose of the publication.[43] Though conversations about authorship may seem awkward, collaborators are generally advised to negotiate at the start of a working relationship about expectations and authorship guidelines for the project. Since all academics face pressures to publish and be recognized for their scholarly contributions, this is an issue that academic couples face as well.

Baldwin and Austin (1995) identified proximity of partners as a fifth dynamic on which collaborative relationships may vary. On one side of this continuum are relationships in which collaborators are located in close physical proximity. On the other side are those in which participants are geographically far apart. As one collaborator studied by Baldwin and Austin pointed out, research partners who are located together "can read each other's faces" and observe moods and reactions, which somewhat diminishes the need for explicit conversations. Through ongoing, constant exchange, ideas can be shared in more informal, spontaneous fashion than among those collaborators who are geographically separated. While academic couples who collaborate could be geographically separated, those whose cases are offered in this book are living in the same households. The cases suggest that they indeed experience the kind of informal, spontaneous interactions described at the high end of this proximity continuum.

The last dynamic that Baldwin and Austin (1995) indicated may vary in collaborations as negotiated orders is the depth of such relationships. The continuum on this dynamic is characterized on one end by relationships that combine personal and professional connections; colleagues who are friends as well as working partners provide examples of these kinds of collaborations. On the other end of the continuum are collaborations organized solely around the work relationship. Those academic couples who engage in joint research and writing, with their lives highly intertwined at both the personal and professional levels, illustrate how scholarly work can occur at one far end of this continuum.

Institutional characteristics affect the nature of collaborations. The extent to which an institutional culture accepts and supports collaborative work, and the policies that relate to collaboration, especially policies pertaining to evaluation and reward processes, will influence choices made by individual researchers about engaging in collaborative work. Certainly this book's cases illustrate how individual preferences affect how collaborations develop and thrive. Also, the couples in the cases are influenced in some ways by institutional dynamics in their choices about their collaborative work. Most notably, all of the collaborating couples chose to wait until after they had each achieved individual recognition before publishing together. Such decisions relate to the power of institutional cultural values that privilege scholars who develop distinct individual identities and contributions, especially in the pretenure periods, as well as institutional reward structures typically organized around assumptions about scholarly work as an individual activity.

Learning from the Cases of Couples Who Collaborate

In reviewing the literature about research collaboration, I have noted ways in which the collaborations of academic couples may, on the one hand, illustrate particular findings in the research literature on collaboration, or on the other hand, raise questions about or expand the issues pertaining to collaboration. What emerges as most interesting about academic couples who collaborate is *how* they do the work and how their work processes influence their thinking and products.

The dynamics of collaboration discussed in the previous section are as important for couples who collaborate to consider as for noncouple collaborators. For example, couples who collaborate must negotiate the explicitness of their roles, the degree to which their roles are flexible, the extent to which their standards of quality are similar, and their individual work habits, just as other collaborators must. Academic couples, like all collaborators, are engaged in "negotiated orders," where many details of jointness, flexibility, and work styles and preferences must be handled. Personal closeness does not preclude these issues as part of the collaboration. All in all, comparing the cases of academic couples with the literature on research collaboration, we learn that the dynamics and issues that affect or relate to the collaboration of academic couples seem to be similar in many ways to those at work for other collaborators.

What can we learn, however, from the cases presented in the book about differences in the experiences of academic couples who collaborate? Are there aspects of their collaborations that are particularly interesting or distinctive? Collaborators often mention that they choose to collaborate because they can produce together something that is better or different from what they can create alone. The academic couples presented in this text also discuss their collaborative work in this way. In discussing his collaboration with Martha to probe a complex problem that crosses disciplines, Greg, the geographer in the first case, noted: "the sum is greater than the parts." Anna, one of the pair of cognitive psychologists presented in the second case, said: "It wasn't just looking to the other person's area to clear up problems in one's own, but really a coming together of the whole being more than the sum of the parts." Like other collaborators, these couples choose to work together because they believe they each bring something that, when combined with what the partner brings, will produce something better than either could do alone.

What is distinctive about these couples, however, is that they create daily lives that are closely intertwined with the collaborative work. Their lives and lifestyles support the collaboration; the collaborative work influences how they organize their lives. The intertwining of the personal professional aspects of their lives appears to contribute to collaborative work in at least three ways: (a) through easy and informal information sharing, (b) through the creation of a shared knowledge base, and (c) through the respect and support that accrues over long periods of collaborative work and life together. I discuss each of these ingredients in the lives of couples who collaborate, arguing that these ingredients contribute to productive scholarly work and to the uniqueness of collaboration among couples.

A key advantage for couples who collaborate is the opportunity they have for informal, ongoing sharing of information and exchange of feedback. The ongoing, informal, spontaneous conversations reported by all of the couples presented in this text facilitate their work individually and jointly. They involve floating ideas, asking for and receiving immediate feedback, and providing what Greg calls "corrective jogs" to improve problems in an idea or piece of writing. While the literature indicates that other collaborators, especially those who are in close proximity, appreciate the feedback each can give the other, one unique aspect of the collaborative process for academic couples seems to be that such conversation and feedback can occur at any time. These conversations are spontaneous, informal, constant, and woven throughout all aspects of the couples' lives rather than relegated to specific work time, as would be more likely for collaborators not sharing an intimate relationship and a shared living space.

A second ingredient in the lives and work of academic couples that does not appear in the literature about other collaborators is the importance of a shared knowledge base, which is often interdisciplinary. Over time, academic couples come to understand each others' fields or subspecialties, and they come to share certain knowledge and perspectives together, especially as they work on a shared project. Noncouple collaborators who work together over long periods are also likely to develop a shared knowledge base that facilitates the speed and ease of their work. However, the closely intertwined lives of academic couples, where conversations occur over long periods and interspersed through other aspects of professional and personal activities, are likely to enhance the *depth* of the shared knowledge base.

The third ingredient in the experience of couples who collaborate over time that does not appear in the literature about other collaborators concerns the benefits of time spent together, including both on a daily basis and over the long term. As discussed, collaborating couples face the same issues to negotiate as other research collaborators—division of labor, writing style, preferred approaches to the work. However, when couples collaborate for a long time—and share a connected personal life—the negotiations appear to be much easier than for collaborators who lack long and close personal connections. For example, when asked how they have managed differences in work style and perspective on various scholarly issues, Martha and Greg, from the first case narrative presented, indicated that time together has helped them to understand each other's areas of expertise and to develop a shared worldview so that they are now in a better position to be useful to each other. Time not only enables collaborators to negotiate differences in ways that make their future work easier but also creates emotional bonds that sustain collaborative work, even if it is difficult.

In contrast to what the literature explains about research collaborators generally, the sustained, personal relationships that academic couples share may be the critical ingredient that enables them to ask hard questions and take up complicated scholarly issues. While research on collaboration suggests that theory-testing rather than theory-development is more typical work for collaborators,[44] some of the academic couples discussed here have taken up theory-development. The support and trust provided by a successful, long-term, personal relationship, the ongoing feedback and conversation, and the shared knowledge base may be the particular factors that lead some academic couples to move into theory-generation. Continuing research on academic couples may show that these relationships have the possibility of being especially productive due to the factors of engaged, spontaneous conversation, shared knowledge bases, and long-term interaction in an environment where personal commitment to the work and the relationship can be counted on.

Continuing Questions

The literature on collaboration is fairly new and still includes many unanswered questions. Knowledge about academic couples is only a small part of this research so the explorations in this volume are useful for expanding understanding of this form of work among academics. This chapter has focused on highlighting key aspects of what is known about research collaboration and showing how this literature provides a framework for understanding collaboration among academic couples. I have indicated that academic couples are likely to be similar in many ways and in many of the issues they face, to their colleagues who collaborate but do not have such long-term personal connections. However, the cases of couples who collaborate also suggest new insights into how scholarly partnerships can work, suggesting that collaborators with close and long-term personal commitments and physical proximity may have unique factors characterizing their lives and work that affect their scholarship in productive, creative ways.

As research continues to focus on academic couples, I suggest some further questions whose answers would add to understanding of scholarly collaboration: How do academic couples who work together over decades sustain their sense of creativity? Is it important for couples who collaborate to continue to work with other colleagues (as have the couples discussed in this book) in order to bring fresh perspectives into their work? How does the collaboration of couples compare with the collaborative relationships of colleagues who share deep, personal friendships but do not have the advantage of ongoing, close, physical proximity? What happens to collaborative work if a couple's personal relationship deteriorates?

The work on academic couples who collaborate also raises an interesting question or challenge for universities and colleges. If collaboration between academic couples can lead to highly innovative work and to theory-development, perhaps institutions of higher education should be purposefully seeking to employ collaborating couples. Additionally, if further research suggests that long-term collaborations among personal friends also has benefits for creativity and quality of work produced, universities and colleges might consider encouraging long-term partnerships overall. Since institutional reward structures often undermine or discourage collaborative work, institutional leaders may want to reconsider the benefits of long-term collaboration and adjust policies to support this kind of work in more positive ways.

14

The Importance of Collegial Networks
to College and University Faculty

JEFFREY F. MILEM, JOE SHERLIN, AND LAURA IRWIN

Most of our close friends are people who write and publish. We have a life surrounded by people who are writers. When we meet people, we ask: "What are you working on?" What we mean is what piece of scholarly or creative work are you doing? –Woman, Professor, Higher Education

Based on the findings of some studies that examine the relationship between marital status and productivity for women academics, some authors suggest that single women are at a greater relative disadvantage regarding measures of faculty career success (tenure, rank, salary, publication productivity) than are women who are married.[1] In explaining these findings, the authors suggest that at least part of the differences in productivity can be explained by the tendency for women academics to marry other academics. Specifically, the authors suggest that having an academic spouse or partner conveys certain advantages to women faculty that are not available to women who do not have a spouse or partner who is an academic. The authors argue that one reason academic women with a male academic partner have an advantage over women without a male academic partner is because their partner is able to facilitate access to other colleagues and/or collegial networks to which they might not otherwise have access. In turn, access to collegial networks facilitates greater career advancement for these women. Astin and Davis (1985b) presented this argument when they said:

> women without a male partner may be more likely to be excluded from the "boys" network, important connections and critical information. Academic women who are married have fewer obstacles to

the social networking and collegiality that plays such an important role in facilitating productivity in academe. (99)

This line of thinking argues that social support networks and specifically colleagues and collegial networks play a critical role in facilitating career success in the academy. While many scholars who study the field of higher education have identified the significance of collegiality as a facilitator of career success,[2] there remains much that we can learn regarding the "hows" and "whys" of this process. It is important to note that, with a few notable exceptions, the majority of studies portray male-female partner relationships as the norm, and largely ignore the diversity of partner relationships within academe. The lack of attention given to gay and lesbian academic partnerships and their relationship to collegiality and collegial networks represents a significant gap in the literature.

This chapter reviews and synthesizes literature that addresses sources of collegial support for faculty in higher education. Moreover, the chapter discusses differences in opportunities for networking that occur for men and women faculty in higher education. This chapter begins with a discussion of literature and research on collegial networks from the larger organizational perspective and then shifts to an analysis of the role of collegial networks in facilitating faculty career success.

Dimensions of Collegial Networks

Our analysis of the literature on collegial networks, particularly in considering differences in the experiences of men and women in these networks, suggests that there are three important dimensions that require discussion and attention. First, it is important to discuss the types of individual *outcomes* that may result from participation in these networks. These outcomes may be either personal or job-related in their nature. Second, collegial networks differ by *type* and, based upon these differences in type, can serve a number of functions. Collegial networks of faculty can be locally based or national in scope, and they are likely to vary in their emphasis on career or interpersonal issues. Third, in order to realize the beneficial outcomes of collegial networks, individuals must have *access* to these networks.

Developing and maintaining collegial networks can result in a host of beneficial personal and career-related *outcomes* in organizational and educational settings. Studies indicate that individuals who are connected to collegial networks enjoy job-related benefits such as greater productivity, higher salaries, and increased opportunities for promotion. Networks also provide important personal benefits such as increased levels of satisfaction, comfort, and support within the work environment. Although involvement in collegial networks can result in a number of beneficial outcomes, the specific type of outcome and the degree to which the outcome is realized can be affected greatly by gender. Although women frequently gain personal support and comfort as a result of their participation in collegial networks, males are more likely to realize specific job-related benefits through their involvement in collegial relationships.

Collegial networks also differ significantly by *type*, as faculty members may simultaneously participate in collegial networks within the department, institution, and discipline or field of study. Local, departmental, and institutional networks generally provide information related to career advancement or institutional politics, while national and international networks within an academic discipline often provide critical entrées into a larger community of scholarly research. Collegial networks may be primarily social, focusing on building and maintaining supportive relationships, or they may be primarily job-related, focusing on collaborative work, information sharing, and career advancement. While women often seek to participate in job-related networks, their collegial relationships are frequently focused on providing personal support. In contrast, men are likely to view the function of their collegial networks as informal or social; however, these relationships actually provide specific job-related benefits.

Access to collegial networks is a third significant theme that is evident in the literature. While men tend to gain access to mentors and networks more easily than women do, collegial relationships tend to be more important to the career advancement of women because women are frequently excluded from key decision-making and informational processes. Women may utilize personal support networks as a means of coping with the larger environment; however, these support networks are frequently comprised of individuals who are not in positions of influence or power within the organization or institution. As a result, many women do not gain *access* to the *types* of networks that allow them to realize job-related *outcomes* within the work environment.

Collegial Support Networks in Organizations

The benefits of collegial networks are well documented in organizational settings. Peer relationships can provide both valuable job-related information and critical personal support in work environments.[3] This occurs through increased access to information and to ideas, contact with key organizational decision-makers and leaders, and knowledge about and access to different routes that facilitate career advancement and success.

Kram and Isabella (1985) suggest that peer relationships offer both developmental and psychosocial benefits to members of the organization.[4] Developmentally, peer relationships render career support by sharing organizational knowledge and perspectives that are important to the growth and development of the individual(s) who receive them. Supportive peers offer potential strategies for addressing problems and possibilities within an organization. They also provide a source of feedback that allows employees to check their perceptions and "evaluate their own experiences" within the organization (117). Psychosocially, peer relationships support employees' sense of "confidence" and "competence" within an organization. They also function as a type of "organizational mirror" for the individual by reflecting back important information about the impact that the individual is having in the organization.

Kram and Isabella (1985) examined the effects of peer relationships among male and female employees in a manufacturing company and determined that a continuum of support functions existed in the relationships that employees had with their peers. Through the use of grounded theory, the authors identified three categories of peer relationships: informational, collegial, and special. At the lower end of the support continuum, *informational* peers share news and information in the organization but offer little in terms of personal or emotional support. Informational peer relationships require less energy to maintain and are likely to be quite common in the organization. In contrast, *collegial* peer relationships offer a wider range of career and personal supports. Collegial peers provide their colleagues with career advice and problem-solving strategies within the organization. They also offer friendship and support that are important to the organizational success of employees. Because collegial relationships require more personal time, energy, and effort to maintain than informational relationships require, they are fewer in number than informational peer relationships. Finally, *special* peers offer the most intimate sources of support because they provide career and personal connections that are not formally bound by organizational roles. The relationship among academic partners described in the first part of this book seem to fit in this category. While they are likely to yield the most meaningful benefits to those who are involved, special peers are the least common within organizational networks because of the significant amount of time and energy that are required to maintain them.

Kram and Isabella (1985) argued that the types of support that peer relationships offer differ based upon career life stage (early, middle, and late) of the individual. As employees work to establish themselves in the early phases of their career, peers provide information that enhances their effectiveness by helping employees understand specific work-related tasks and how they fit within the organization. As individuals move through the "establishment stage" and into the "advancement stage" of their career, peers can help "increase visibility" and "identify realistic advancement options" for employees (126). In the middle career stages, peers help individuals maintain networks and address leadership and supervisory issues that aid in increasing their effectiveness in the organization. Finally, in the latter career stages, peers help employees make successful transitions out of the organization.

Differences in the Nature of Collegial Networks
for Men and Women in Organizations

The literature clearly indicates that the nature of collegial support networks differs in important ways for men and women in organizations. These differences pertain to the opportunities that men and women have to *access* these sources of support. Differences also emerge between men and women regarding the *types* of personal support networks that are available to them. Finally, there are also differences between men and women regarding the *outcomes* of personal support networks in organizations.

In a study that highlighted the disparate outcomes of collegial networks among men and women, Kirchmeyer (1998) assessed the effects of a variety of interpersonal, family status, individual, and human capital variables on career success for a sample of 292 mid-level managers.[5] The managers worked in a variety of fields, including banking, health care, manufacturing, and professional services. Career success was defined by both "objective" (income/hierarchical job level) and "subjective" (perceived success) measures, as well as by a category of outcomes that assessed work experience, job tenure, interruptions in career, and professional degree.

As we might expect, gender differences were apparent among variables that predicted career success. Although supportive relationships similarly affected men's and women's perceptions of career success, women were less likely to realize the objective measures of organizational success, such as increased income and/or career advancement. Women who invested time and effort in what were viewed as "traditional" pathways to success (gaining increased job experience and tenure with the company) gained fewer economic benefits for their efforts. The author argued that the work-related efforts of men and women yielded "different career returns" within organizations. The findings of the study indicate that relational supports for women lead to a more comfortable and affirming work environment but that these relationships have less influence on traditional measures of success in the organization than they do for men.

Focusing on different types of collegial networks among men and women, Fritz (1997) used the informational, collegial, and special peer model of Kram and Isabella (1985) to examine the same-sex peer relationships of 666 male and female employees in 20 organizations in one metropolitan area.[6] The findings (39) indicate that men and women experienced similar numbers of peer relationships within each category. However, men perceived higher levels of mutual dependence and honesty with their informational peers. They were also more likely to be involved in activities outside the work context. When compared to women, men seemed to have stronger and more developed "relational strength," as defined by higher levels of mutual dependency and honesty, in relationships that emphasized information exchange and low degrees of disclosure. In contrast, the collegial relationships of women were more likely to be emotionally supportive and less likely to be constricted by organizational roles. Among "special" peers, women exhibited higher levels of "self-disclosure, irreplaceability, and mutual dependence" (40). As women's relationships with their peers increased in levels of disclosure and intimacy, they gained in relational strength. The authors argue that women may experience a different "relationship trajectory" from that which men experience. Specifically, women are likely to focus less time and energy on informational and casual relationships by concentrating on peer relationships that offer higher levels of support and intimacy. This finding may help explain why women are especially drawn to working relationships with a spouse or partner.

Schor (1997) examined the nature of career-building relationships in organizations and found significant differences in the degree of access to collegial networks among 10 male and 10 female high-level executives in large corporate insurance companies in the Northeast.[7] The subjects in the study had advanced beyond the early career stages that were focused on "establishment" and "advancement" in the work setting (Kram and Isabella, 1985). Hence Schor's study offered insights into the career development of a population that had achieved a high degree of job success. Schor's interviews focused on the "career journeys" of participants and explored relationships that had an impact on their career advancement. Although the types of relationships named by male and female executives in the study were similar (mentors, informal colleague networks, and spouses), the nature of the impact of these relationships differed significantly for men and women.

Both men and women executives believed informal networks were important factors in career advancement, but women reported more difficulty "building and maintaining" these networks. Men felt "automatically" and "unconsciously" integrated into informal networks, while women reported that they experienced more "work" than "net"(54). Women expended significant energy to build networks within the context of work, while male executives were more likely to spend time developing networks in social activities that took place largely outside work. Women reported that they used their networks to gain information about the organization and job advancement strategies. In contrast, men often reported that members of their networks sought them out concerning opportunities for job advancement. Some men in the study reported that network members had made active efforts to facilitate their career advancement; however, no women in the study indicated that they had received any unsolicited career assistance.

Successful female executives were more likely than successful male executives to build "richer, broader relationships around work issues" (p.56). While women invested significant energy attempting to develop job-related networks in order to enhance their careers, men tended to gain these career benefits almost casually and often through informal or social networks. Male executives did not contribute significantly to relationship-building. Within this study, men were able to achieve career success without intentionally working to develop collegial networks. However, women did not have the privilege of choosing not to develop these networks, because collegiality was essential to the success of women. The findings suggest that collegial networks are more important for the career success of populations of women. We suggest that this is also true for other populations that are frequently marginalized in working environments, such as people of color and/or gay and lesbian workers.

In a study that addressed access to organizational networks in a publishing company, Brass (1985) discovered the existence of two separate gender networks.[8] In these networks, women were not a primary focus in male interaction networks, nor were men a central focus in female interaction networks. In the publishing company, supervisors and non-supervisors perceived men to have greater influence. Moreover, men had greater access to the "dominant coalition" within the organization, described as "those individuals who typically occupy the highest levels and who have the most influence and decision-making authority" (329). Finally, women who were able to access the integrated gender networks in the company were rated more highly on organizational influence, had access to the dominant coalition, and were more central to the organization than women in all-female interaction networks. Brass's study suggests that gender relationship networks may be both "separate and unequal" in terms of their organizational structures and benefits. The benefits of access to cross-gender networks appear to be particularly significant for women who want to achieve career success in organizations.

Collegial Networks among College and University Faculty

The existence of collegial networks among faculty was probably first identified by Price's (1963) study of academics, in which these networks of scientists were described as the "invisible college."[9] The study identified the existence of a network or an "in-group" that existed in each of the specialties of science. The faculty who comprised these "in-groups" reported that they were in touch with nearly everyone who made significant contributions to their field. Price's analysis of the impact of these groups suggested that these people were very powerful and were able to determine who received recognition and prestige in their fields. Collaborations grew as scholars found that they could accomplish more in research teams than they could as individuals. As these collegial networks grew in size and stature, faculty sought ways to meet and work with their colleagues across the country and around the world. Over time, faculty allegiance was directed more to the group than it was to the institution. Price and Beaver (1966) extended this line of research by suggesting that collegial networks in an academic field or discipline are actually comprised of sets of subgroups of scientists who collaborate together.[10]

Crane (1969, 1972) reported the findings of a study of the collegial networks of groups of sociologists.[11] Crane's findings suggested that collegial networks are circles of researchers who are tied to certain "high producers" in the field. One of the primary factors that facilitates new membership in these circles comes from student-teacher relationships. Mentors sponsor and support their protégés by providing them access to the collegial networks to which the mentors belong.

Support networks for college and university faculty are most frequently discussed as coming from two primary sources. The first source of support that has been identified relates to mentoring that young and emerging faculty receive from more experienced faculty in their field or at their institution. Another source of personal and professional support that faculty receive is derived from colleagues and collegial networks. Bode (1999) suggests that mentoring and collegiality provide the means by which faculty are socialized into their institutions.[12] However, the literature suggests that these processes also provide a means by which faculty are socialized into their discipline and/or academic specialty areas.

The review of the literature on the professional networks of faculty by Hitchcock, Bland, Hekelman, and Blumenthal (1995) led them to make seven assertions about collegial relationships.[13] These assertions are that:

1. Successful faculty (indicated by promotion and tenure and high research productivity) frequently utilize collegial relationships.
2. Mentor relationships can be especially important to junior faculty when they first enter the academy, while peer relationships tend to be longer lasting and provide reciprocal advantages.
3. An investigation of dyadic relationships does not fully capture the range of beneficial collegial relationships; instead, these networks must be viewed as being national and international in nature.
4. Professional associations are important to the creation and maintenance of collegial networks, but these networks must also be maintained through other avenues such as project work, campus visits, and communications through the electronic media.
5. The beneficial effects of relationships with colleagues are most evident in research improvements, and other career advancements (that is, promotion and tenure) are "secondary gains" that are linked to research productivity (1114).
6. Research may be the initial focus of colleague relationships, but other personal and career effects generally result from these relationships.
7. Collegial relationships change and evolve as one progresses through his or her academic career, as collegial networks build, and one moves "from protégé to peer to mentor" (1114).

Mentors and Collegial Networks

Clearly, mentors can serve as an important source of personal and professional support for younger faculty members. An entire chapter could be devoted to this topic alone. Because this chapter focuses on collegial networks, it is not our intent to engage in a comprehensive discussion of mentors and mentoring. Rather, our discussion of mentors will occur within the context of the role that mentors have in facilitating the access of their protégés to networks of their colleagues.

A mentor is a person (almost always a senior colleague) who takes a special interest in facilitating the professional development of an emerging colleague. Mentors generally provide advice, support, nurturing, and opportunities for involvement in larger networks of faculty within an academic discipline or field of study and/or institution of higher education that serve to promote the career of their protégé.[14] Williams and Blackburn (1988, cited in Bode, 1999) identify four functions that mentors provide. These include role-specific modeling or teaching, "encouraging the dream," organizational socialization, and advocating.[15] Sands, Parson, and Duane (1991, cited in Bode, 1999) describe four factors that are apparent in the ideal mentoring relationship. These include friendship (as a source of socioemotional support), career guidance (encouraging professional development), information source (facilitating the socialization of the new faculty member), and intellectual guidance (providing opportunities for scholarly collaboration). Mentoring has also been described as existing on a continuum (Shapiro, Haseltine, and Rowe, 1978, cited in Bode, 1999) that extends from peer pal to guide to sponsor to patron to mentor. The place that an individual assumes on this continuum is defined by the extent of their involvement and by the potential impact that the individual can have on a new faculty member's career.

Defining Collegiality

In a systematic review of literature on collegial relationships, Hitchcock, Bland, Hekelman, and Blumenthal (1995), asserted that over 30 years of research revealed that "successful faculty in higher education—those who get promoted and tenured, who get recognized for contributions, who produce more and significant research—consult frequently with colleagues" (1108). Collegial relationships describe "relatively stable informal relationships" that are reciprocally beneficial and often cross a variety of organizational and geographic borders (1109). Hitchcock and associates identify two primary themes derived from their review of the literature on colleague relationships. One theme focuses on dyadic relationships and the other focuses on collegial networks. Among dyadic relationships, the development of mentor-protégé relationships has drawn the greatest focus in the literature, with peer relationships comprising the other major category. The review of literature on professional networks conducted by Hitchcock and associates revealed that "[t]here is clear and substantial evidence that faculty who communicate more with colleagues produce more and better research" (1112).

Collegiality differs from mentoring in a few important ways. Mentoring usually involves a one-to-one relationship, while collegiality defines a relationship that a faculty member has with many others.[16] While mentoring relationships generally end after a period of time, collegial relationships continue throughout the career of faculty members. Finally, Reohr (1981, cited in Bode, 1999) argues that status differences delineate mentors from colleagues. Collegial relationships are based upon equal status relationships, while mentors generally enjoy more status than their protégés. Research that focuses on collegial relationships within particular institutions is somewhat sparse, while research on the impact of collegial relationships within a broader discipline or academic field is more abundant.

In considering the collegial networks of faculty, it is important to distinguish between two distinct types of collegial networks. The first type of collegial network is found within a given college or university. These institutional collegial networks have as their primary focus assisting new faculty members in their socialization to a particular institution.[17] The second type of collegial network connects faculty members to other members of their discipline or academic field who share with the faculty member a set of common interests, usually centered on research. Networks of this type tend to be national and/or international in scope and are comprised of a number of different people.

Institutional Networks

In a study using data from the New Faculty Project (see Menges, 1999[18]), Trautvetter (1999) identified four examples in which collegiality operated for faculty at the institutional level.[19] These include: (a) teaching-related assistance; (b) support with research-related activities (discussing ideas for projects, providing feedback on manuscripts, offering to collaborate on work, giving advice on grant writing); (c) social support (lunch, potlucks, receptions, junior faculty support groups); and (d) support with "housekeeping" items (help in finding a place to live, acclimating new faculty to the campus and local area, help with computers, assistance in understanding the campus bureaucracy).

Finkelstein's (1982) study of the types of needs filled by relationships with colleagues gives additional information regarding the assistance that institutional colleagues can offer to faculty members.[20] Specifically,

Finkelstein identified a category of functions that he described as institutional linkages. Examples of ways in which colleagues assist faculty in this area include nominating a colleague for a significant campus, college, or departmental committee assignment, "troubleshooting" on behalf of a colleague with administrators or other faculty members, and providing information on departmental or campus policies and procedures or regarding campus politics. Similar to Trautvetter's findings described above, Finkelstein also recognized the important role that institutional colleagues can play in providing help with teaching and research and as a source of general social and personal support. Finkelstein argues that collegial networks can be invaluable in helping faculty to become accepted and valued at their institution.

In an analysis of data from the New Faculty Project,[21] Bode (1999) reported that most faculty who described the support that they received from colleagues reported that it took the form of social support that generally occurred through informal activities. Only faculty employed at institutions with high levels of collegiality were likely to report that they received any intellectual support from their institutional colleagues. Intellectual support came most frequently from collegial networks that were situated in a faculty member's discipline or academic field.

National Networks

While institutional networks serve a number of valuable functions, a study of highly productive higher education scholars (Hunter and Kuh, 1985) indicates that research productivity may be more closely linked with connections to national collegial networks.[22] The authors asked participants to describe the ways in which they found colleagues for professional collaborations. The three major sources of collegial research collaboration identified by this group of higher education scholars were membership and participation in professional associations, collaboration with former graduate students, and collaboration with institutional colleagues. Hunter and Kuh reported that the final category was much less likely to be identified than the first two were. National networks of scholars were much more important sources of support for the research of these faculty members. Less than 4 percent of the scholars in this sample indicated that they had collaborated with peers at their own institution.

Other research provides information about the ways in which faculty sustain their extrainstitutional networks once they have been formed. Perhaps most important to this process is the chance that faculty have to meet their colleagues at professional meetings and conferences.[23] In addition, faculty communicate with their colleagues on a frequent basis through the use of telephones, fax machines, and electronic mail. Network members often visit their colleagues at other institutions.

Costs and Benefits for Faculty Participating in Collegial Networks

The opportunity for collaboration that occurs in collegial networks presents advantages and disadvantages to faculty who are involved. Fox and Faver (1984) interviewed 20 social scientists in order to assess the strengths and weaknesses of collaboration.[24] Among the reasons faculty offered regarding their decision to pursue collaborative work, the complexity of the task or project was often cited, particularly when the research topic lent itself to division of labor. Faculty also indicated that collaboration reduced the "academic isolation" that those who were engaged in a great deal of individualized research reported that they felt. Finding effective ways to alleviate isolation can be especially beneficial to faculty who are marginalized within particular academic communities (that is, women, faculty of color, gay and lesbian faculty). Faculty reported that collaboration frequently enhanced their motivation because of the responsibility and commitment that faculty members felt they had to the colleagues with whom they were collaborating. It is likely that this is a particularly strong factor for faculty who collaborate with a close colleague or domestic partner.

Fox and Faver (1984) noted that faculty members cited a number of "process costs" that resulted from their collaborations. As mentioned by a number of authors in this text, collaboration requires more time for discussion, negotiation, and adaptation because of the need to incorporate different ideas and perspectives. The expense of maintaining a collaborative network was mentioned, as travel and communication costs for lengthy projects could be high. Maintaining relationships over time and negotiating disagreements could also require significant time and energy on the part of the collaborators. At times, collaborations could produce certain "outcome costs" for faculty members. Slow or inefficient partners and team members reduced productivity and could cause the project to be extended or delayed indefinitely. Moreover, determining the order in which authors' names should appear presented problems to some faculty when it came time to decide what the relative contributions of the participants had been to the study.

The review of literature by Hitchcock and associates (1995) revealed additional advantages and disadvantages of networking with colleagues. Advantages of collaboration facilitated by collegial networks included the ability to take on larger research projects, the addition of scholarly skills and expertise provided by other team members, enhanced creativity, increased understanding of literature related to a particular topic, access to the most recent work in an area of study, and opportunities to gain recognition for and feedback about one's work. In addition to the disadvantages identified by Fox and Faver (1984), the review of literature by Hitchcock and associates suggested that collaborative work could inhibit individual creativity.

Changes in the Roles of Networks over the Faculty Career

Like some of the findings of studies of collegial networks in other professional domains, the data from higher education suggest that faculty networks and the roles that faculty assume within them are influenced by the career stage of the individual faculty member. Starting in graduate school and continuing throughout the early years of a faculty member's career, the individual is most likely to be a protégé in a mentor-protégé relationship. It is through the mentor that young academics may receive their initial entrée to the larger collegial networks that exist within a profession. As young academics' careers advance and their work and expertise become known to other academics and to other members of the professional network, their status and role undergo a transition. These faculty move from the role of protégé to that of peer. The power and status differentials evident in the mentor-protégé relationship are transformed so that over time the faculty member is viewed by other members of the network as an equal. As the academic moves on in his or her career, a third type of role is assumed in the professional network. The faculty member remains as a peer in the larger network, but she or he also assumes the role of mentor for her or his graduate students and/or for younger members of the profession. It is in this role that faculty members have the opportunity to draw their protégés into the network of colleagues of which the mentors are now senior members.

Differences in the Nature of Collegial Support among Male and Female Faculty

The contexts in which collegial networks develop differently between men and women are highly significant. Individuals may gain entry into a larger collegial network through self-initiative or through the initiative of network members. While women may be more likely actively to seek out personally supportive collegial networks, job-related collegial networks may be more likely actively to seek out men. The type of network to which a faculty member has access affects the outcomes that are realized, and all of these conditions are likely to be affected by gender status. Trautvetter (1999, 82) observed:

> Many female faculty reported little contact with their graduate school mentor, had no mentor on campus, and were generally not collaborating on research with anyone on campus. They also gave low ratings for collegiality in research and social activities. At the same time, many female new hires expressed a strong desire for mentoring and more collegiality.

Hill, Bahnuik, and Dobos (1989) studied mentoring relationships and collegial support networks and their bearing on communication patterns and academic success among male and female faculty members at two Midwestern universities.[25] The study identified three major types of collegial relationships among faculty: mentor-protégé, collegial social, and collegial task. The mentor-protégé relationship focused on traditional mentoring behaviors, such as providing professional advice or taking an interest in another's career. The collegial social relationship focused on mutual friendly relationships among faculty, while the collegial task relationships focused on reciprocal working relationships. All three types of relationships contributed to effective communication among faculty, with mentor-protégé relationships having the most significant impact.

The majority of faculty members in the study by Hill and associates (1989) indicated they had been involved in a mentoring relationship (81 percent) with the large majority of mentors being male for both male (96 percent) and female (70 percent) faculty. However, irrespective of mentor status, male faculty members reported higher levels of academic success, an outcome assessed by faculty perceptions of their success and job satisfaction, and quantitative indicators of faculty job performance (that is, salary, publications, rank, and number of authored books). Male faculty members with mentors indicated the highest degree of academic success, followed by male faculty without mentors and female faculty with mentors. Male and female faculty in mentoring relationships indicated that they had experienced higher levels of communication support and information adequacy than faculty without mentors did. The findings of this study suggest that mentoring relationships improve the flow of information and the degree to which both male and female faculty members feel connected to and knowledgeable within their work settings. However, gender status affected the outcome of academic success more significantly than mentoring relationships did in this study.

Despite the documented benefits of collegial faculty networks at the departmental, institutional, and national levels, significant differences exist among collegial networks for male and female faculty. Rose (1985) discovered gender differences in the outcomes realized through the functioning of professional networks among a random sample of male (n=43) and female (n=47) assistant professors in psychology across 60 universities.[26] The study focused on the composition of network types within "national, departmental, and institutional" settings. The study hypothesized that gender differences would be evident in network composition, with women academics maintaining more female colleagues and fewer colleagues of higher status. In addition, the study predicted that females would rate their networks as less effective on a variety of career and personal dimensions.

As predicted, the study conducted by Rose (1985) revealed that men had fewer women colleagues within both university and national networks. While male junior faculty maintained more "extrainstitutional" relationships with contacts from former institutions, female junior faculty classified a higher proportion of colleagues as close friends and were more likely to have collegial relationships with women in "high-status" positions. However, when examining network outcomes, women were less likely to see their national networks as effective in enhancing their "visibility" as a strategy for building professional reputation (Rose, 1985, 541). In addition, female faculty indicated that their colleagues were "significantly less likely to have recommended their work to other colleagues" (Rose, 1985, p. 541).

Although female faculty indicated an equal number of colleagues in national collegial networks, the author stated that a majority of the female junior faculty in the study had a "small same-sex support network, including a role model, as part of their system of collegial ties" (Rose, 1985, 544). In addition, the results indicated that when "visibility" was fostered by women's colleagues, it was more likely to result in service-related opportunities, such as committee involvement or public speaking. Among female junior faculty, the visibility received from collegial relationships could potentially result in time-consuming involvement that was ultimately detrimental to research. Within this study, the outcomes that resulted from participation in collegial networks among female faculty could have had a negative effect on career success.

In a study of faculty job satisfaction among a group of 70 male and 76 female tenure-track faculty, Olsen, Maple, and Stage (1995) argued that existing literature portrays women and minority faculty as less productive in research, maintaining a greater emphasis on teaching, and displaying significant commitments to service within the institution.[27] However, contrary to previous findings, women faculty in the sample did not exhibit stronger orientations toward teaching or service. Although women appeared to be as focused on research activities as their male colleagues and engaged in similar levels of participation in grant and article reviews, they were more likely to feel disconnected from informal networks. As the authors stated, "frequently female faculty were not invited to go out to lunch or drinks after work, or included in other important venues for informal communication." Due to a lack of *access* to informal networks, women experienced more difficulty "acquiring information about the department and informing the department about their own activities, research in particular" (286).

Trautvetter (1999) found that men and women faculty utilized their campus colleagues to serve different needs. Men were more likely to use their campus colleagues as a job-related network, focused on clarifying tenure procedures and departmental expectations. However, women faculty members were more likely to utilize their collegial networks with other women as a personal support network, to create child-care cooperatives, and to explore women's career issues. In the data from the New Faculty Project, Trautvetter (1999) also found that women faculty were likely to report that they did not realize beneficial *outcomes* from contact with mentors or collegial networks. They reported that they had little contact with their mentors from graduate school and had not found a mentor on their new campus. Women were also not likely to report that they were collaborating on research with anyone on their campus. While women in the New Faculty Project reported that they were not connected to a mentor nor were they connected to collegial networks on their campus, they expressed a strong desire for both (Trautvetter, 1999). Reskin (1978) suggests that women are at a disadvantage in forming collegial relationships because of their unequal status in society and in the academy.[28]

Kaufman (1978) focused on the degree to which collegial differences existed between male (n=32) and female (n=46) faculty in a human ecology department in a Northeastern university.[29] Although both male and female faculty members indicated that their collegial relationships existed in predominantly same-sex networks, unmarried women had a lower number of men in their collegial networks than either married women or unmarried men. The researchers asserted that "cross-sex relationships among colleague friends seem more permissible for women who carry the protective status of marriage" (16). When compared to married women, unmarried women had fewer male contacts in collegial networks at every faculty rank. However, among married female faculty, by the time the rank of full professor was reached, their networks exhibited "almost as high a proportion of men in their networks as full male professors" (17). Finally, the results indicated that men were much more likely to have collegial relationships with persons of higher faculty rank, while female faculty members were more likely to believe that their colleagues were "professionally unimportant." The authors stated:

> Furthermore, as the data indicated, if women tend more than men to associate with those of similar or lower rank, and with those whose research interests are different to very different from their own, they are quite likely to further diminish their chances for occupational ascent. (19)

The findings suggest that gaining access to integrated networks may be particularly critical for female faculty as a means to promote career advancement. However, it is not clear whether the integrated networks achieved by senior female faculty resulted from their full professor status or whether female faculty who developed these integrated networks were indeed more likely to achieve full professor status. While we suspect that both explanations may be at work simultaneously, the literature strongly indicates that participation in collegial networks facilitates increased job success.

Examining sources of career support among tenure-track faculty at a Midwestern research university, Parson, Sands, and Duane (1992) found that both male (n=300) and female (n=257) faculty members at all three faculty ranks listed spouses or significant others as their greatest source of support.[30] When asked to rank their top 10 sources of career support, the study indicated that male and female faculty members differed in three important areas. Women cited external friends, parents, and other women in their academic unit as sources of support, while men cited men in their academic unit, graduate school friends, and research relationships with colleagues on campus.

Parson, Sands, and Duane (1992) used factor analysis to identify four major sources of career support for faculty members. These included: (a) off-campus personal supports, (b) support from colleagues in the academic unit, (c) professional supports outside the unit, and (d) the existence of a minority network. When examining the relationships among the factors and selected variables, several significant findings resulted. The findings indicated that married faculty, faculty with children at home who were under 18, and younger faculty were more likely to have off-campus personal supports. When support came from colleagues within the academic unit, full professor status and younger age were significantly predictive variables. For professional support outside the unit, full professor status and being a woman were significantly predictive of this factor. The authors noted that underrepresented women in an academic unit might be more likely to seek support from professionals external to the unit. The findings also showed that male faculty named relationships connected with their professional roles as sources of support almost exclusively, while female faculty were more likely to name personal relationships as sources of career support.

Sources of support differentiated among faculty ranks, as assistant professors were more likely to cite on-campus relationships as strong career supports. In contrast, full professors were more likely to cite off-campus relationships as strong sources of support. The findings suggest that assistant professors in early career stages rely more heavily on institutional networks for career support, while full professors rely on an external network of collegial relationships based on research interests and collaborative professional opportunities for support.

Collegial Support and Faculty of Color

The information on collegial support networks for faculty of color is not nearly as extensive as that found regarding differences in these networks for men and women. However, there is an emerging body of research that gives us some clues about the extent to which these networks exist for faculty of color in higher education.

In one study of faculty of color in higher education, Blackwell (1988) found that only about one in eight African-American faculty reported that they had a mentor.[31] A more recent study of faculty of color in higher education reports a similar finding. Using information gathered from faculty of color in the New Faculty Project, Alexander-Snow and Johnson (1999) found that most faculty of color expressed a strong desire for mentoring at their new institution.[32] However, many of these faculty members were frustrated by the lack of opportunities that they had for mentoring at their current institution. Moreover, they indicated they were also disturbed by the fact that their departments were not committed to providing mentoring opportunities to them.

Many faculty of color experience "severe marginalization" in higher education. This is particularly problematic when we consider the important role that mentoring and collegiality have as the primary means for socializing new faculty to their institution.[33] When faculty of color are marginalized, they have a very difficult time learning the political and informal organizational norms that are important to their success at their institution. If faculty are not able to acquire this information in a timely and efficient manner, they are not likely to be promoted or granted tenure.[34]

Access to institutional collegial networks can help new faculty of color to navigate the demands placed upon them that often result from what Tierney and Bensimon (1996) have described as a process of "cultural taxation" that occurs for many faculty of color.[35] This "taxation" results from the expectations that are placed on faculty of color to provide service to the university and to students because of their racial/ethnic background. Given that faculty of color are underrepresented at most institutions of higher education, they face great pressure from administrators and other faculty members to serve on committees or to be involved with racial/ethnic groups that are important to the success of the institution. Because of the diversity in perspectives and experiences that faculty of color bring to the institution, students frequently seek them out for support and assistance in their own work. Regrettably, involvement in any of these activities does not usually serve the faculty member when it comes time for promotion or tenure at their institution (Tierney and Bensimon, 1996). In fact, junior faculty of color are most frequently penalized by their involvement in these activities.

Alexander-Snow and Johnson (1999) report that faculty of color frequently report pressure from their white colleagues to do research that they find "acceptable." Moreover, because some faculty of color may engage in research that is outside the mainstream of the research that is done in a particular discipline or academic field, they may find it difficult to get this research published in the most prestigious journals in that field. As a result, the work of these faculty of color is criticized because it does not appear in the "right" journals. This adds to the reasons why establishing connections to networks of scholars in the discipline or academic field is of critical importance to faculty of color. These networks can help faculty of color to increase their visibility in the profession and establish the importance of their work in their discipline or field of study.

Summary of Findings about Collegial Networks of Faculty

Our synthesis of the literature indicates that personal support networks and specifically collegial networks provide important sources of support that facilitate the career success of faculty in colleges and universities. Domestic partners in the same profession, particularly when they are in the same or closely allied academic fields, are often part of these networks. These outcomes of collegial networks are well documented in the research literature. However, significant and powerful differences in the outcomes of these networks, in the types of collegial networks, and in access to these networks are evident for men and women faculty. Our analysis suggests that important differences in personal support networks are also apparent for faculty of color in colleges and universities. Specifically, the literature indicates that women and faculty of color are at a significant disadvantage in forming collegial relationships because of their unequal status in society and in the academy. A spouse or partner in the same profession may offset some of these disadvantages.

There are two primary types of collegial networks that are important to the success of faculty in higher education. Institutional networks serve the primary function of helping to socialize new faculty to their institutions. It is through these networks that faculty receive important information about the norms and expectations of their departments and their colleges or universities. These networks can be particularly important in helping faculty understand what institutions value and what they do not value when faculty members are evaluated in tenure and promotion processes. Networks in disciplines or fields of study are more national and/or international in their focus. These intellectual networks bring faculty members in contact with others who share their research and teaching interests and provide faculty with opportunities to collaborate with other colleagues in their academic work. These networks serve as an important source of intellectual support for faculty members.

Finally, the research on faculty collegial networks indicates that faculty assume different roles in collegial networks that are determined by the career stage of the faculty member. Faculty begin as protégés in mentor-protégé relationships. It is through their mentors that most faculty are first introduced to networks in their discipline or field of study. Over time, they assume the role of peer in the collegial networks to which they affiliate. As they progress further in their careers and begin to train their own graduate students, faculty increasingly serve the role of mentor in mentor-protégé relationships. It is at this point that the process comes full circle. As mentors, senior faculty provide their protégés with access to other colleagues as their mentor had done for them when they were first beginning their careers.

15

The Role of Recognition and Reward in Research Productivity: Implications for Partner Collaboration

JANE W. LOEB

I went up for promotion and tenure before she did and when I was preparing my papers, the department head said, "Now when you put your papers together, I want you to code all the things you wrote with your wife, whether you were the primary author, who came up with the original idea, who did the data collection, you know, all this stuff." And I said, "Excuse me, do people do that when they collaborate with other people?" He said, "No, but the university has this opinion that when you publish with your spouse that typically only one of you is doing the writing and then adding on the other person." I said, "Well, number one, unless you are requiring everyone who collaborates with someone to do this, then I am refusing to do it." He said "okay" and nothing came of it. We both got promoted and tenured and nothing was ever said about it. *−Male, Professor, Education*

The vignette quoted above exemplifies the centrality of an academic's individual scholarly identity to institutional reward, colleague recognition, and the evaluation of his or her research productivity. In addition, it portrays the special problems colleagues feel in evaluating an individual's contributions to collaborative work, especially research undertaken with a spouse or intimate partner. This chapter provides a review of the literature on institutional rewards and collegial recognition and their role in motivating productivity, and explores the special place of collaborative work, including that produced by intimate partners. Gender differences are also explored, since they can affect the consequences of collaboration and certainly might do so when heterosexual couples collaborate.

By rewards I mean benefits institutions provide in compensation for past success and productivity. These include initial hiring, promotion and tenure, and salary increases, which have received considerable attention in the literature, as well as internal research grants, favorable decisions about teaching loads, and access to graduate students, which have received less attention. By recognition I mean benefits provided by colleagues both within and outside the institution and by external agencies. These benefits range from simple feedback on one's work, to external grants, citations to publications, honors and prizes, appointments to editorial boards, positions as officer or committee chair in national disciplinary associations, and appointments to major government positions or committees, such as National Science Foundation service. Research productivity primarily refers to refereed articles, book chapters, and books, but also includes reviews and other publications.

The relationships among the three concepts are both overlapping and reciprocal. The reward of promotion also signals colleagues' recognition of one's achievements. External grants and citations are forms of recognition as well as measures of productivity. Rewards and recognition are responses to prior productivity, but also may enhance further productivity.

Institutional Rewards

Once hired, the primary institutional rewards are promotion and tenure, and salary increments. Both are heavily based on publications,[1] although external grants are also usually rewarded[2] and will probably become even more important as underfunded institutions increasingly emphasize revenue enhancement. Further, this is true not just at research universities but also at other universities and four-year colleges. For example, Fairweather (1993) found that at all five types of institutions he studied— research, doctoral, and comprehensive universities, and liberal arts and other four-year colleges—the number of career publications was a positive predictor of 1987 to 1988 salary of full-time faculty members.

The evidence suggests that quantity of publications alone, without regard to their quality, is a strong predictor of salary and rank. Citations of publications and the prestige of the journals in which they appear are generally taken as indications of the quality of publications.[3] However, Long, Allison, and McGinnis (1993) found that among biochemists who earned their doctorates between 1956 and 1967, the number of articles published was more strongly associated with promotion in rank than was the number of citations.[4] Similarly, weighting publications by an index of the prestige of the journal in which they appeared did not improve prediction of promotion. Using a national sample of educational researchers in the late 1960s, Persell (1983) found that both income and rank were positively related to article count but not to total citations or to the quality of a sample of their articles rated by a panel of experts.[5]

Further, it seems clear that the importance of quantity of publications as a primary basis for both salary and promotion has increased since the 1960s.[6] As early as 1965, publications were described as increasingly important.[7] Analyzing four national faculty surveys from 1969 to 1988, Bentley and Blackburn (1990) concluded that the emphasis on research had generally increased at research, doctoral, and comprehensive universities. More faculty held a doctorate and expressed that primary interest in research, and research output as measured by grants and publications, increased. Institutional studies have also shown a changing reward structure. For example, Loeb, Ferber, and Lowry (1978) found that rank of full-time faculty at the University of Illinois at Urbana-Champaign (UIUC) was better predicted by books, articles, and reviews in 1974 to 1975 than it had been in 1969 to 1970.

Institutional reward structures have been shown to differ somewhat for faculty in different disciplines. For example, Biglan (1973a and b) classified disciplines on three dimensions: (A) hard-soft, ranging from the sciences, through the social sciences, to the humanities; (B) pure-applied; and (C) life-nonlife.[8] He found that faculty in the "hard" sciences produced more articles and fewer monographs than those in the "softer" disciplines, but they also had collaborated on research more frequently, which confounds the comparison of article counts. Faculty in "applied" fields published more technical reports than did the "pure" fields. Ferber, Loeb, and Lowry (1979) compared reward structures for four fields (sciences, humanities, social sciences, and professions), finding that 1974 to 1975 UIUC salaries were positively predicted by articles in all four areas, by books in the humanities and social sciences, by reviews for humanists, and by "other publications" for scientists.[9] These differences in the reward structure within institutions undoubtedly reflect differences in the norms of the disciplines themselves and therefore shed light as well on disciplinary differences in the bases for recognition.

Rewards also tend to vary by sex. Studies of conditions in the late 1960s and early 1970s indicated that women tended to be concentrated at less prestigious institutions, hold lower ranks, and be paid less than men. When individual qualifications such as highest degree, years of experience, and numbers of publications were taken into account, these differences were typically reduced but not eliminated. Faculty surveys for 1969 and 1975 revealed a different distribution of men and women by institution type, with women tending to be employed at less prestigious institutions, but there was no significant difference in the distributions of men and women by type of institution in 1988.[10] Apparently substantial progress has been made by Research I universities in hiring women in the last several decades.

In his early evaluation of the equity of academic recognition and rewards accorded to men and women, Jonathan Cole (1979) found little evidence of disparity after he had accounted for differences in individual qualifications.[11] However, he did find that female faculty in biology, chemistry, psychology, and sociology held significantly lower academic rank than did males, after publications and citations had been accounted for. Further, discrepancies in rank tend to be worse in more prestigious departments.[12] Comparing the rank distributions of men and women over time, Bentley and Blackburn (1992) found no evidence of improvement, concluding: "the revolving door is still spinning."[13] However, in a sample of scientists containing some with more recent Ph.D.s than Cole's group, Sonnert and Holton (1995) found very similar ranks for similarly qualified men and women in biology, suggesting progress in that discipline.

Early studies showed salary differences between male and female faculty members even after rank, discipline, institution type, and productivity of publications had been accounted for. For example, a national study of 1968 to 1969 salaries by Astin and Bayer (1973)[14] and an institutional study by Loeb and Ferber (1971)[15] of 1969 to 1970 salaries found very similar disparities, at approximately $1,000 and $850. More recent data suggest the gap narrowed during the 1970s but has remained static since then.[16]

If publications are the primary evidence of productivity on which institutional rewards are based, how are collaboratively authored works evaluated in the process? It can be argued that a single paper makes a discrete contribution that is not dependent on the number of authors, so the credit should be adjusted based on the number of authors.[17] Actual practices are unclear[18] and probably differ by field and institution, although there are suggestions that single-authored papers are preferred[19] and that the first-listed author is often credited with seniority regardless of the authors' intent.[20] Anderson (1996) found disciplinary differences in student and faculty perceptions of the department's preference for individual over joint research, with the perceived preference for individual work inversely related to the frequency of collaboration in the field.[21] Similarly, it is primarily in the fields where collaboration is not the norm where it is said to receive relatively modest credit.[22]

Most fields have guidelines concerning assignment of authorship and the position of an individual in the author list, but fields differ in their conventions, and the results are often ambiguous. For example, in psychology order reflects relative contributions, while in the biological sciences the first author is usually the one who did the empirical work and the primary intellectual force is listed last, and in mathematics order is usually alphabetical regardless of the relative contributions.[23] Given the ambiguity involved in deducing how much credit is due to whom, it would not be surprising if status differences were relied on to apportion credit for joint works. A well-known hypothesis, named the Matthew effect by R. K. Merton,[24] posits that well-known scholars tend to receive more credit than they deserve for work done with others and sometimes even for work for which they were not responsible at all. This is one reason that junior faculty members are encouraged to establish an independent identity before collaborating[25] and that young faculty are especially urged not to continue to collaborate with their dissertation advisors while preparing for promotion to tenure.

It has also been suggested that men tend to receive disproportionate credit when they collaborate with women.[26] An individual's research program and its expected long-term contributions are usually a primary basis for tenure, so an independent identity is crucial. This need for an independent identity compounds the risk of the Matthew effect in early collaboration, especially with the advisor. Women start with lower status than men, on the average, and this lower status presumably adds to such problems for women. These factors would in turn complicate the evaluation of work produced by intimate couples.

Recognition

Like institutional rewards, recognition by one's colleagues in the broader scholarly community is largely based on publications, differs by discipline in the relative importance assigned to different kinds of publications (for instance, books, articles, or reviews), may well vary for men and women even when other relevant factors are held constant, and also varies for those located in more or less prestigious institutions. Davis and Astin's (1987) study of factors associated with the reputations enjoyed by highly productive social scientists used seven measures of reputation, including self-reported visibility, total honors and awards, listing in *American Men and Women of Science*, and four measures of citations of their works.[27] Chapters published more consistently and more strongly predicted these various measures of reputation than did articles or books published. As the authors point out, chapters are usually invited or are reprints of earlier work of value, and in either case they indicate a degree of visibility or recognition. In addition, however, they found that the number of citations received by an individual's publications is related to the quality of the institution at which the faculty member is employed.

Similarly, Crane (1965) found that highly productive scientists at major universities were more likely to have won recognition than were highly productive faculty at lesser schools, while Bentley and Blackburn (1992) have pointed out that nearly all faculty in key positions with national disciplinary associations work at Research I institutions.[28] Thus recognition may more easily accrue to those who are well placed in the higher education system than to those who are not, as Merton (1968) suggests in his hypothesis of "cumulative advantage."

Cole (1979) and Davis and Astin (1987) studied sex differences in recognition. Cole had experts rate the visibility and the perceived quality of the work of scientists in his sample. He found that men were rated higher than women on both indices of recognition, although neither sex difference remained significant after controlling for citations and publications. There was, however, an unexplained difference in visibility and perceived quality favoring men among the most highly productive and highly cited scholars. The more recent Davis and Astin (1987) study of highly productive social scientists found no evidence of gender differences in recognition. They interpret the discrepancy in the findings as a cohort difference, due at least in part to new opportunities for research on women that have increased women's chances for recognition and for building networks. Women's greater presence in academia, especially at prestigious institutions, may also have made women's work harder to overlook.

These two studies highlight the often overlapping nature of indices of recognition, reward, and productivity. Cole used citations as a measure of quality, which is a component of productivity or contribution to knowledge. Davis and Astin used citations as the basis for four of their indices of recognition. While both approaches are appropriate, Cole's use of citations as a control measure would reduce any evidence of gender bias in recognition if there were such bias in the citation process. Ferber (1986, 1988) found that authors are significantly more likely to cite publications by writers of their own sex than are those of the opposite sex.[29] Further, comparing these differences in developmental psychology, labor economics, sociology, and mathematics, Ferber (1988) found differences were greater the lower the ratio of women to men in the field. This would work against women in the fields where they remain a small minority.

More recently, Ward, Gast, and Grant (1992) found that articles in one sociology journal were cited more by women if they had a female author and if they were about gender, while the number of citations by men was unrelated to either of these variables.[30] Since the gender affinity applied only to women, it would not disadvantage them. Among biochemists, Long (1992) found that women's papers averaged more citations each than did men's,[31] while Cole and Zuckerman (1984) found no difference in the average citations per paper for physical scientists and mathematicians.[32] On balance, then, citations do not seem to be accorded to men and women in significantly different numbers. Of course, if women's articles are of higher average quality than men's, merely equal citations would be biased in favor of men, but Cole's finding that quality ratings did not differ for men and women after citations were controlled for argues against this possibility.

Wenneras and Wold (1997) found disturbing evidence of differences in the evaluation of men's and women's work, however.[33] Studying the "scientific competence" rating of male and female fellowship applicants to the Swedish Medical Research Council, they developed separate equations predicting these ratings from six different productivity measures derived from number of publications, number of first-authored publications, and citations of these published works, and from other possibly relevant factors such as nationality, field, and university affiliation. Models using the number of citations to first-authored work, and the sum of the impact factors (average citations per paper in a year) of the journals in which all and, alternatively, first-authored papers were published were statistically significant. In all three cases, both being male and having an affiliation with a member of the review committee were significant positive predictors of competence rating, holding the citation index constant. Affiliations were personal ties to a reviewer sufficient to disqualify the reviewer from evaluating the individual, so other reviewers' knowledge of the affiliation would presumably have been at work.

The authors point out that the United Nations recently designated Sweden as the world's leader in equal opportunity for women, so there is no reason offhand to expect these results to be peculiar to Sweden. The effects were large enough that a female without an affiliation would have been essentially wiped out of the competition. These results suggest not only gender bias in the evaluation of scientific work, but also that considerable advantage can be attained through working with other members of the scholarly community. A well-connected, multiply affiliated individual, including one with an academic partner, would have a better chance of being affiliated with members of review committees than would a person who usually works alone and was otherwise not strongly connected. Collaboration, then, could affect the individual's recognition and access to resources that are important to further productivity.

Concerning the effect of collaboration on recognition, Lindsey (1982) points out that multiple-authored papers generate more recognition, although presumably not more knowledge, than single-authored papers of comparable quality, and Beaver and Rosen (1978) find collaboration to be "a mechanism for gaining and sustaining access to recognition in the professional community."[34] They suggest that when evaluating joint work, the tendency is to give credit to all authors but to withhold any blame because of the difficulty in establishing where responsibility lies. However, as already discussed, first-listed authors receive a good deal of credit, and they certainly do in terms of citations. Until the advent of online, searchable databases, regardless of the number of authors only the first author was cited in the *Science Citation Index* and the *Social Science Citation Index*.

The evidence suggests that paper for paper, women receive as many citations as do men, but there are nonetheless numerous suggestions that when men and women work together, the woman receives less recognition. Based on a historical review of recognition received by members of mixed-sex teams, Rossiter (1993) suggests that women working with men tend to be given less credit and that this is even more common in the case of married couples who collaborate.[35] Pycior (1993), who studied Marie Curie's rise to fame, concluded that success for a married woman collaborating with her spouse is assisted by very careful documentation in published work of credit for individual as well as joint accomplishments.[36] The Matthew effect may be particularly strong when heterosexual intimate couples collaborate.

If the Wenneras and Wold (1997) findings are generally applicable, collaboration with a graduate school or postdoctoral mentor could establish collegial ties that would be beneficial to further recognition. Little[37] or no difference[38] has been found between the proportion of men and women who coauthor with their graduate mentor, but a variety of data suggests that these relationships are more likely to be more problematic for women than for men. There are reports of paternalistic relationships in which female students were channeled toward jobs at teaching or women's colleges,[39] the advisor was ignorant of her research field,[40] she was ignored,[41] or she was cast in a subservient role.[42] All of these situations are consistent with Reskin's (1978) hypothesis that women's lower status can block the usually egalitarian relationship among colleagues, and that cross-sex collegial roles tend to be patterned after familiar sex roles, for instance, father-daughter, romantic relationships, or scientist-assistant, all relationships in which the male is assumed to dominate.[43] These patterns differ markedly from the egalitarian relationships presented in the case narratives, but several studies provide additional support for Reskin's view. Long (1990) found that being married increased the odds of a female collaborating with her graduate mentor, and hypothesized that the student's marriage makes it easier for the collaboration to develop by providing male advisors the feeling of some defense against misinterpretation of the relationship as romantic. In addition, more females than males published all of their predoctoral articles with their mentor, suggesting a tendency for women to get stuck in their mentor collaborations or at least not to establish independence from them.

Studying scientists, engineers, and social scientists, Sonnert and Holton (1995) found that a small gap between men and women in degree of collaborativeness favored women in graduate school but favored men thereafter. He suggested that this is consistent with Reskin's view that some men may have an easier time relating to women in a subordinate role than to those in an equal position. These findings could help explain the tendency for women to receive less credit than men for joint work. It seems reasonable to expect that faculty who tend to collaborate with women in subordinate roles would also interpret other mixed-gender collaborations as structured in the same way.

In addition, young children have different effects on men's and women's access to high-status mentors and to collaboration with them. Long (1990) found that having children under six was a negative predictor of collaboration with a mentor for women but not for men. Also for women but not men, interruption between the bachelor's degree and the doctorate was a negative predictor of the number of articles the mentor had recently published. Sonnert and Holton (1995) found that having children during graduate school increased interruptions for both men and women, though less so for more recent Ph.D.s among women and more so for more recent Ph.D.s among men, suggesting some movement over time toward more equal sharing of parental responsibilities. Together these findings suggest that for women, having children during graduate school may negatively affect access to high-status mentors and collaboration with them, thereby tending to reduce further recognition.

Productivity

The number of publications by faculty members has increased over time, and this has occurred at all types of institutions.[44] Sex differences in publication rates and in collaboration have also been studied. Women are generally found to publish less than men.[45] The gap was often found to widen over the course of the career.[46] A more recent study by Long (1992), however, found a small decrease in the gap beginning about 10 years after the degree for biochemists. The gender publication gap seems to be narrowing for more recent cohorts.[47] Furthermore, in several studies the difference became nonsignificant once rank, institutional prestige, and discipline were accounted for.[48] As described earlier, the quality of men's and women's publications is at least equal, if assessed by number of citations.

Women's role in the family has been looked to as a possible source of women's lower productivity. A number of studies indicate, however, that marriage has no such effect.[49] In fact, the opposite may be true.[50] On the other hand, in studies in which young children appeared to have an effect, it has been negative.[51]

Cole and Singer (1991) suggested a "theory of limited differences" as a mechanism through which cumulative advantage may produce significant gender differences in scholarly productivity from small, often nonsignificant, differences between opportunities, resources, and achievements of men and women academics and their reactions to these circumstances.[52] They posit that long-term productivity results from a series of events, or "kicks," which are positive, neutral, or negative and to which the individual reacts positively, neutrally, or negatively. In the short run, the influence of these "kick-reaction" pairs on productivity is small, but it accumulates. Thus small gender differences in both experiences and in reactions to them are translated into significant productivity differences. While few women will experience and react negatively to any one negative "kick," such as inability to work with a particular professor in graduate school because he won't take on female advisees, the event and a dampening reaction to it may affect the individual's later productivity and perhaps her reactions to subsequent "kicks" as well. In addition, gender differences in the positive or negative effects of particular events could add to cumulative differences in productivity.

Effects of Reward and Recognition on Productivity

While based on productivity, both recognition and reward are also believed to reinforce past productivity and provide the impetus for future work. Both can also help the scholar secure resources such as grants, to assist in scholarship. Evidence of this reciprocal relationship between recognition and reward, on the one hand, and productivity, on the other, is found in an increased rate of publication noted at all types of institutions, even as the reward structure has become more heavily demanding of this form of productivity.[53] Apparently, the institutional reward structure shapes faculty behavior. Further evidence is found in data showing that both employment at a top university and holding higher rank are associated with larger numbers of publications compared to faculty employed at less prestigious institutions or lower rank.[54] Faculty in these favored categories are expected to be more productive, but they also often have access to more resources in the form of more time for research due to lower teaching loads and more internal and external grant support. Not surprisingly, grant dollars are also positively associated with publication productivity.[55]

Long and McGinnis (1981) studied biochemists who stayed with a single employer for at least nine years, and found that after controlling for predoctoral publications and citations, subsequent publications were lower for those employed by a teaching institution or an industrial employer not encouraging publications than for faculty in research universities.[56] These results suggest that the organizational context in which one works helps to shape productivity. Thus the early reward of being offered a job with a research university sets the stage for further productivity. Higher expectations for productivity at research institutions are undoubtedly a motivating factor yet are unlikely to be solely responsible. Crane (1965) found that the university's reward structure was mentioned as a motivator by faculty at several minor universities but not by faculty at a major university.

Research and publication are probably motivated by recognition in addition to institutional rewards, especially at top institutions where greater recognition by colleagues tends to accrue (Crane, 1965). Indeed, Lawrence and Blackburn (1985) studied a sample of full professors at a research university and ascertained that output of publications did not decrease after attainment of the highest rank.[57] Thus motivation beyond promotion in rank is clearly involved. Highly productive senior faculty in the field of higher education interviewed by Creamer and McGuire (1998)[58] indicated that institutional rewards may have been important to their initial motivation to publish, but their scholarship had been reinforced and sustained by feedback from colleagues and by the norms of their discipline, or, in short, by recognition.

To the extent that institutional affiliation is an important determinant of productivity, the factors leading to selection of new faculty by prestigious institutions will also have an impact on later productivity. Long and McGinnis (1985) found that papers published and citations did not significantly predict the prestige of the first academic job for male biochemists who earned their doctorates in the late 1950s and early 1960s.[59] Rather, the prestige of the Ph.D. and the postdoctoral departments and the mentor's performance in terms of recent citations (for those who collaborated with their doctoral mentors) all had positive effects on prestige of the individual's first job placement. So the visibility that accrues from collaborating with a mentor who is well recognized would be expected to increase later productivity by affecting the quality of the employing institution.

Early publications did not have much impact on the quality of the first job, but they are strongly related to later productivity, and publishing while in graduate school is, of course, correlated with collaboration with the mentor.[60] Collaboration with a mentor who is actively publishing at the time can have a big influence on predoctoral productivity, on job placement, and presumably, through both of these, on later productivity, although there is apparently no direct effect of collaboration with the mentor on publications counted later on.[61] The importance of sponsorship in general is underscored by Hunter and Kuh's (1987) report that about half of their sample of prolific authors in the field of higher education volunteered that sponsorship was critical to developing both their skills and their interest in research.[62] The early-career recognition involved in sponsorship, therefore, is probably an important factor, albeit indirect, in later productivity.

If productivity is partly the result of rewards and recognition, then any tendency for men to receive greater recognition or rewards than women do could be a factor in the productivity gap. The fact that women tend to be paid less than equally qualified men and to be promoted more slowly would presumably tend to depress their productivity. Similarly, if men receive more credit than do women for joint work, this could have the same effect. In the past, women were infrequently hired at top institutions, which would depress their productivity both directly and also indirectly through a tendency to receive less recognition than if they had been better situated. While equal numbers of men and women have been found to collaborate with their graduate mentors, the tendency to have problems in these relationships, cited earlier, could also depress productivity.

Sonnert and Holton's (1995) study of men and women who had held prestigious postdoctoral fellowships, thereby starting out at the top of their cohorts, suggests that problems some women experience in their collaboration with graduate and postdoctoral advisors may have negative consequences for later reward, recognition, and productivity. For example, having a more collaborative research style during graduate school was a negative factor in predicting women's but not men's later academic rank. In fact, close collaboration with their advisor in graduate school was a negative predictor of women's career publications, but not of men's. Sonnert and Holton suggest that these women students may have been assigned subordinate, subservient tasks, or others may simply have perceived the collaborative work that way. In either case, it appears that women's subsequent rewards and productivity may have been depressed by collaboration with a senior scholar.

Similar results were found for collaboration with the postdoctoral advisor. Women who collaborated a lot during their postdocs but only with their advisors held lower rank, on the average, than those who either collaborated less or who collaborated heavily but with other collaborators as well. For men, no such relationship exists. Also, having a senior advisor enhances men's productivity in terms of career publications but inhibits women's. Again, perhaps women are not given useful work by eminent advisors, or perhaps the high-status advisor is especially likely to profit from the Matthew effect when the student is female, while she receives little recognition for her work.

Sonnert and Holton (1995) describe these findings as a "collaboration trap" for women, and suggest that men might have an easier transition than women from the junior-partner status typical of students to the more egalitarian collaborative relationship of the postdoctoral fellowship years and beyond.[63] This is consistent with Reskin's (1978) hypothesis concerning the patterning of cross-sex collegial relationships after familiar sex roles, in which men traditionally play the dominant role. These patterned roles in cross-sex relationships may be one reason that collaboration has been problematic for women. It is almost as though collaboration with an advisor is a form of recognition for men—which tends to bring with it further recognition, resources, reward, and productivity, but not for women. For the woman it may be more important to work with multiple collaborators, in part because the individual relationships are less likely to be positive, and also because she needs to work alone or with others to overcome the assumption of having been the junior colleague. Indeed, some of the women Sonnert and Holton (1995) interviewed volunteered that they hesitated to collaborate because of fear their work would be appropriated by collaborators or that they would be perceived by others to be a junior partner.

Collaboration among Partners

So far, we have seen that publications are central to rewards, recognition, and productivity and that women tend to have fewer publications but even lower levels of rewards than their publications would suggest. We have also seen that collaboration can build affiliations with other scholars, which can be a positive factor in the evaluation of one's work, yet lower-status members of teams may receive less than their deserved credit. Women in particular tend to experience difficulties in collaboration with colleagues, especially senior ones. What do the findings suggest about the pros and cons of collaboration between intimate partners?

The advantages and disadvantages of collaboration with a partner are in most ways similar but in some ways different from those of collaboration with other colleagues. One difference is that for both partners, the advantages of informal feedback, bouncing of ideas, reading of drafts, and so on can be considerably heightened by the easy communication arising from both a close relationship and also shared living space. All three case studies of partners' collaborations presented in the first part of this volume exemplify these advantages. Another difference is that for the woman, the fears of being used by a collaborator described by some of Sonnert and Holton's respondents would be alleviated by collaboration with a trusted partner. At the same time, when a male coauthor is given too much credit by others for his contributions to the work, it might be easier for the woman to help him understand the importance of making her contributions clear if he is an intimate partner than if he is a colleague with whom the personal relationship is relatively distant. So on balance, she may expect to receive a more equitable share of the credit both because her partner will not knowingly take advantage of her and because he may be more able to see the need to correct undue assignments of credit to himself.

Working with a partner is also different from most other collaborations between colleagues who are not close personally, in the degree and importance of the risk to the personal relationship. Negotiation of differences is a necessary task in collaborations, as noted earlier, and differences arising over authorship rights or order and concerning the credit accorded the authors are matters to which most academics react with strong feeling. Compared to a partner, it is fairly easy to walk away from a colleague with whom the collaboration is no longer satisfying, although even here bitterness often results from the breakup of a collaborative relationship. It seems that for the sake of the personal relationship, partners need to pay scrupulous attention to establishing a clear agreement on the terms of the collaboration. The case of the cognitive psychologists reported in first part of the volume illustrates the extra need to care for the other person as well as oneself when the collaboration is between partners. This couple reported that when they have an intellectual disagreement, they continue to work at it until they are both happy with the result, rather than compromising as they might do with another colleague.

In many other respects, however, the advantages and disadvantages of collaboration with a partner parallel those of working with other colleagues. Young faculty need to establish an independent identity as scholars. Individuals, not research teams, are evaluated for tenure, and young scholars are expected to develop their own programs to demonstrate their capability for independent research. The difficulty is greater the closer the specialty areas of the collaborators, because individual contributions are less apparent to evaluators. Thus, for example, the early collaborations of the cognitive psychologists described in the case study were carefully limited to projects outside their individual lines of research. In addition, due to the Matthew effect, collaboration with an individual who is more senior or who by virtue of sex, race, or other extraneous but status-related characteristic is assumed to be the senior participant, can arbitrarily reduce the credit that accrues to the junior or otherwise lower-status individual. When partners collaborate, this poses special hazards for the junior partner, if there is a chronological or academic age difference, and for the female. The "worst-case scenario" for developing one's own professional identity may be that of the younger or female partner in a couple in the same discipline whose scholarship is also shared, thus making it difficult to evaluate each individual's contribution and likely that disproportionate credit will be awarded to the higher-status member of the team.

Once an independent record of scholarship is established, collaboration with an academic partner is generally less problematic, as all three examples presented in the case studies make clear. Single- and first-authored papers are generally less important in institutional rewards once colleagues understand the individual's own research contributions. Hence an established scholar has considerable freedom for riskier ventures, including interdisciplinary work as well as collaboration with a spouse or partner. Interdisciplinary work is generally not understood well in either discipline and thus is hard to evaluate. Credit for such work is probably generally skewed toward the author whose discipline appears to dominate. For example, in the case of the fiction writer and the anthropologist, the female anthropologist apparently received disproportionate credit for the equally shared production of the book chronicling their fieldwork.

Multiple collaborations can be helpful in establishing a range of affiliations, and they can also serve to keep a collaboration "young." Wells and Pelz (1966) found that the perceptions of industrial and governmental group members of each other's scientific contributions and usefulness to the group peaked after four or five years of working together, then declined.[64] These findings suggest that a single long-term collaboration might get stale rather quickly. The style of collaboration adopted by two of the couples in the cases presented, of having one project in common while also collaborating with others, serves to reinforce their separate scholarly identities and to establish other affiliations while also keeping the spousal collaboration vital.

Special caution is needed in the case of collaboration of partners, for although many of the issues surrounding the evaluation of collaborative scholarship are similar in kind regardless of the type of personal relationship that exists among collaborators, this type of collaboration does seem to evoke an extra level of distrust. This is illustrated in the vignette that opens this chapter, in the statement that "the university has this opinion that when you publish with your spouse that typically only one of you is doing the writing and then adding on the other person." This view appears to rest on a belief that intimate partners are more likely than others to make a gift of authorship to each other, although the literature suggests such gifts from eminent senior scholars to their protégés are not unheard of. In fact, if a couple are about the same "academic age," neither one can afford such a gesture. Nor can their relationship afford the strain of later regret or dissension over credit for the work. Therefore, it is much more likely that such couples would be scrupulous about giving and taking precisely what credit is due. Each needs to develop an independent identity, and the marriage needs to be free of future disputes or hard feelings about authorship, order, or credit. Indeed, Creamer (1998b) found that most of the collaborative academic couples she interviewed had carefully negotiated systems for allocating credit for their joint work.[65] This sort of care is illustrated by the practices of the creative writer and the anthropologist described in one of the cases. In their chronicle of their fieldwork, they individually wrote alternating sections in their own voices, making each one's contributions absolutely clear.

There are probably instances of improper authorship assignment between partners. Certainly it was relatively common in earlier days for the wife to participate in the husband's work but to receive no credit. (It is interesting that these earlier "gifts" were somehow acceptable to many people, but it is not acceptable when the partner thought to be the weaker academic, often the wife, might be receiving too much credit. Neither should, of course, be acceptable, but it is odd that what was sauce for the gander is apparently not sauce for the goose.) In any case, authorship assignment abuses are probably rare if both parties are relatively junior, and are probably most likely to occur when one has significantly more to gain from it in terms of rewards than the other.[66] Because extensive collaboration with a senior scholar poses clear hazards to the junior scholar, and especially to a woman, it is unlikely that many academic couples would undertake such a risk. Thus abuses of this sort seem unlikely to be widespread.

Future Prospects

Both collaboration and the presence of women and couples on higher education faculties are increasing. It should follow that spousal collaborations are becoming more common as well, and as the visible participation of both men and women in egalitarian professional collaborations with spouses increases, this may well provide a new model for cross-sex collegial roles. To the extent that new arrangements reduce the tendency hypothesized by Reskin (1978) to view professional relationships in terms of traditional, male-dominant sex roles, professional women should begin to find it easier to establish collegial relationships with men and to profit from more favorable evaluations of their contributions to joint work.

Another factor that may help to reduce the tendency to place women in lower status roles and give them less credit than their work deserves is a tendency toward more egalitarian marriages, at least among academic couples. This pattern is evident among the cases presented in the first part of this volume. Astin and Milem (1997) found evidence that academic partners have more egalitarian household arrangements than do couples in which only one is a faculty member. Ferber and Hoffman (1997) found evidence suggesting that egalitarian arrangements were more common among younger than older academics. If academic couples indeed tend to have more egalitarian marriages than others, and if younger academics are in any case likely to have more egalitarian house-hold arrangements than do older ones, more and more male faculty should be participating in marital relationships that can provide a model that is more conductive to establishing collegial professional relation-ships with women than was the older male-dominant marital model. In the future, then, even without actively collaborating professionally with their wives, men involved in more egalitarian marriages may contribute to a climate in which it is easier to establish cross-sex collegial relation-ships and in which women's scholarship is more equitably evaluated. Just the presence of more women in a field should also help. The trends, then, suggest a more positive atmosphere for women and couples in academe in the future.

There are several implications for institutions of increased collabora-tive work and increased partner collaboration. In chapter 13 of this vol-ume, Ann Austin points to the need for higher education institutions to develop policies on the evaluation and reward of collaborative work. In addition, to the extent collaborative work is often interdisciplinary, insti-tutions might assist with the review of such scholarship by, for example, making departmental evaluations of the relative importance of their dis-cipline's journals easily available to other departments.

Wenneras and Wold's (1997) study underscores the difficulty of objec-tively evaluating merit when people who are affiliated in some way make the judgments. It is probable that people tend to elevate somewhat their evaluation of an individual who has a relationship with some other col-leagues who will be privy to the evaluation. Marriage is not categorically different but is an even closer relationship than the common friendships and academic alliances that regularly occur and somewhat confuse evalu-ation of colleagues' work. All of these relationships involve some degree of conflict of interest, yet conflict-of-interest policies in higher education are often rather narrow in scope and typically protect against conflicts between reporting authority and family relationship. These policies might well be reviewed to consider how various forms and degrees of per-sonal relationships might best be dealt with. Where clear-cut and strong affiliations exist, such as marriage or academic "parentage," major evalu-ations such as those for promotion and tenure should probably be more carefully reviewed at higher levels more distant from the relationship.

Future Research

Both the current status and changes over time in collaborative work in general and spousal collaboration in particular deserve study. It would be helpful to know, for example, what institutional policies and procedures are currently in effect for the evaluation of collaborative work. Do practices differ by discipline, for partners compared to others collaborating, or for male compared to female coauthors?

It would be useful to study the ascription of credit for joint work in order to determine whether and to what extent there is a tendency to award more credit to senior and to male coauthors. In addition, does such a tendency vary by discipline, sex of the evaluator, or perhaps cohort (Ph.D. year) of the evaluator? Creamer (1999) pointed out the need to look at the experience of partners by cohort,[67] and work reviewed here suggests that changing marital roles and increased spousal collaboration may reduce the tendency to ascribe the junior role to women in collaborative work. It would be interesting to see if the greater presence of women in a field predicts a lesser tendency to evaluate women's contributions as secondary. It would also be useful to study problems in mentorship experienced by women. Are mentorship problems and the tendency to undervalue women's contributions to joint work less likely where the mentor or evaluator has an academic spouse or has female coauthors, especially female coauthors listed first? Does participation in an egalitarian marriage predict more collegial treatment of women by mentors, coauthors, or evaluators?

Concerning collaboration with a spouse, it would be useful to find out whether it affects salary and rank differently from collaboration with other individuals of the same or opposite sex, and to see whether the effects are the same for men and women. Disciplinary differences in the effects of spousal collaboration also deserve study. As the incidence of women and spouses on the faculty and also collaboration itself continue to increase, these questions merit our attention.

PART 3

Implications for Couples and the Academic Workplace

16

Egalitarianism, Institutional Policies, and Productivity

Maybe the world is changing, but in my generation, the assumption was immediately whatever you had done is not your own writing; somebody else did it, like your husband, and you just got credit for it. I hope it is no longer that way in terms of people's perception about who has done the work. *—Woman, Professor, Higher Education*

While women of color have always worked outside the home, feminist writers and theoreticians have been disappointed in the failure of advances for women in the workplace to translate to the expected changes in the family. Legal victories in the courts, the movement of a large number of (white) women into full-time employment, and growing acceptance for careers for women did not translate to the expected gains in women's status. Working women continue to carry the load for about two-thirds of routine jobs in the home.[1] Working women typically generate additional effort to meet both work and household demands, while most men reduce their work effort to compensate for the hours spent on household tasks.[2] This may explain the finding reported in some of the research literature that a highly educated, comparably employed wife reduces faculty men's productivity while it increases women's publication output.[3]

Egalitarian family forms not organized by a traditional division of labor are one explanation for why having a comparably trained and positioned partner may be mutually beneficial to the productivity of members of academic couples. This final chapter acknowledges commonly cited definitions of egalitarianism. It also proposes an alternative definition that focuses on comparable value awarded to both members' career success as a more likely explanation for the relationship between faculty productivity and egalitarianism. The sources in the literature for many of the arguments presented in this chapter were first formulated in a chap-

189

ter I wrote and published elsewhere.[4] The unusual extent of career symmetry I found among the couples in my study and their interchangeability in terms of roles are part of the cohort differences that make it likely that they are a group of faculty whose lives are far less shaped by the demands of family than were preceding generations. The quote that opens the chapters reflects the view that there are significant differences by cohort among the experiences of women faculty.

Egalitarianism as a Family Form

Several authors have recently published books exploring the topic of egalitarianism as a family form.[5] Rosanna Hertz (1986) called the movement toward egalitarianism as a family form, albeit among a small but growing percentage of couples—an example of social change that is occurring on the behavioral level before it is happening on the attitudinal level.[6] Like Arlie Hochschild's (1997) description of the fierce "time bind" faced by middle-class dual-career couples,[7] Hertz argues that the move toward a more equitable division of labor in the home is driven by the structural demands of the workplace rather than ideology. She comments, rather acerbically, from her study of men's and women's roles in dual-career families:

> This study demonstrates that these lifestyle 'pioneers' did nothing of the sort; they reconstructed new family forms not because they desired to blaze new social trails but because the constraints of work and the value placed on success altered the practice of their daily lives. (197)

Even as these family members' work roles press them toward a less-than-traditional sex-based division of labor, what is left intact as the fundamental ideology is the man as the primary breadwinner and women's responsibility for the home. This is the case even when women's and men's salaries are comparable as well as in cases where the wife's salary exceeds that of her husband.[8] In most situations, women retain the primary responsibility for managing household chores even when the family has the resources to outsource many of these responsibilities to paid help supplied by others. Because of their dependency on the labor of others, Pepper Schwartz labeled these "peer marriages" as a "contingent phenomena."[9] In general, she argues, the combined salaries of most couples do not allow the luxury for one member to stay out of the labor force but is sufficient to provide the resources to employ others to do routine chores, such as lawn mowing and housecleaning.

Traditional Definitions of Egalitarianism

Perhaps reflecting the intransigence of the traditional sex roles and in an effort to measure behavior rather than attitudes, many of the most widely read books about egalitarianism as a family form assess it primarily by the division of labor and decision-making authority in the household. An approximately 60–40 split in domestic responsibilities and child care is considered egalitarian. This has been found to be most characteristic of couples where both members place higher priority on family and their personal relationship than on career success.[10] The depth and value of the personal bond, sometimes to the exclusion of most others, is a central characteristic of these relationships, as is the integration in each other's lives.[11]

A Definition of Egalitarianism that Emphasizes Career Goals

The academic couples I studied share a number of qualities with the heterosexual couples present in the literature on egalitarianism but also differ from them in noteworthy ways. Age and career symmetry, a family life that conforms to the demands of work, a personal relationship characterized by mutuality and mutual regard, and a relatively non-sex-based division of labor in the work they accomplish collaboratively are some of the qualities they share with couples presented in the contemporary literature about egalitarianism. That they have some flexibility over their daily schedules and are among the group of faculty who spend a significant amount of time at home on work-related tasks contributes to the fact that they spend a lot of time together and operate in overlapping private and public spheres.

They differ from most of the couples presented in the literature in that both members award high priority to work and that this was a powerful force in shaping their personal relationship from its inception. They also differ in an ideological commitment to egalitarianism. These are dual-career couples where both members are comparably committed to careers. Their situation is quite different from couples who, for lack of interest, training, and/or opportunity, are not employed in positions where there is any reasonable expectation for personal and financial mobility.

As early as the 1970s, definitions of egalitarianism appeared in the literature that did not reinforce the stereotypical association of women with the home, reproduction, and the private sphere and that challenged a sex-based division of labor as source of subordination. Feelings of mutual respect, commitment, and reciprocity may have more to do with how members of a couple see their relationship than simplistic measures of how they handle decisions or how many hours they spend on household labor.[12] For a variety of reasons, including resources, many contemporary dual-career couples are likely to find domestic roles to be less defining of their relationship than career issues.

In 1976, Letha Scanzoni and John Scanzoni used the expression "equal partner marriage" to describe a kind of egalitarian relationship based on an orientation to careers that challenges the ideology of the man as the chief breadwinner and head of household.[13] Their definition has several components: (a) both members are equally committed to careers and both occupations are considered equally important; (b) the partners have equal power in decision-making; and (c) there is complete interchangeability among the partners in both domestic chores and occupational roles. Marriage is not considered automatically to require parenthood.

Carolyn G. Heilbrun, an academic, prolific writer, and feminist who has also written about how she has managed a life devoted to work within a long-term committed partnership with her husband and life partner,[14] places a comparable weight on the centrality of work in her definition of revolutionary marriage. She defines a revolutionary marriage as: "one in which both partners have work at the center of their lives and must find a delicate balance that can support both together and each individually."[15] According to Heilbrun, equality and "the equality of the man's and woman's quests" characterize these marriages.[16]

Such a definition of egalitarianism that applies to couples who share a comparable vocational commitment may underlie Helen S. Astin's and Jeffrey Milem's (1997) proposition that egalitarian arrangements in the home may explain the positive effect of an academic partner on faculty women's productivity.[17] They argue that dual-career academics are likely to have more egalitarian arrangements in the home than couples whose spouse or partner is in another occupation. In such cases, Astin and Milem conclude, at a minimum, men's occupational attainment is not achieved through the sacrifice of a spouse.

Other findings that high achievers are often matched with a high-achieving spouse[18] suggest a closely allied argument to that presented by Astin and Milem. That is to point to a definition of egalitarianism based on a family form that is organized around comparable investment in both careers and an interchangeability in roles assumed rather than the division of labor in domestic affairs. In this situation, a partner in the same profession can be reciprocally beneficial to *both* members, if not necessarily in identical ways. This is what Peter Magolda suggests in his reply to the second case narrative presented in Part 1 of this book. He maintains that the personal relationship extends to an extensive mutual investment in their partners' success and satisfaction with their work. The same premise underlies Xie and Shauman's (1998) conclusion that *both* women and men faculty "benefit from the human capital of their spouses who tend to be highly educated professionals."[19] In this context, I interpret human capital to mean the advantages afforded by access to the labor of a highly trained individual with shared interests.

The definition of egalitarianism I advocate refers to life partners, heterosexual or same-sex, who are comparably invested in each other's work and vocational success. Both are presumed to share the role of breadwinner. This ideology was demonstrated in numerous ways by some of the academic couples who participated in my research project. The choice by the woman to keep her birth name at marriage could be interpreted as an indication of both the importance of her occupational identity as well as egalitarianism in the relationship.[20] It was also manifested in the refusal to relocate unless it was mutually beneficial; familiarity if not intimacy with each other's work; analogous allocation of family resources to both careers, including to dedicated work space in the household; a non-sex-based division of labor in collaborative work; and respect for each other's time.

Shared Worldview

The egalitarianism demonstrated by some of the highly educated academic couples in my research project was driven by the demands of dual careers, by the value of the personal relationship, and, in many cases, by a shared worldview. The worldview is another way they differ from many other examples presented in the literature about egalitarianism, where ideology was less likely to be central. The geographers presented in the first case narrative, for example, speak of the role of a shared worldview about interdependence in shaping a relationship and a lifestyle. It was not uncommon to find participants who shared an agenda for social change, even if surprisingly few labeled it as feminist when they described it. Modeling a nontraditional family form was often part of this agenda. An agenda for social change may not necessarily have been incorporated in their writing but it was generally viewed as a positive aspect in their relationship.

This worldview and the commitment to equity in the relationship may be one explanation for why this group of academic couples who collaborated together seemed to be even less likely to have children than faculty in general, who are already marked by relatively low marriage and birth rates when compared to the population as a whole. The threat that children are perceived to have to an egalitarian relationship may be one explanation for why so few have children.[21] Another likely explanation is that limiting the number of children is one way to enhance career commitment and reduce family obligations, as is single parenting.[22] This was the situation, for example, in the cognitive psychologists presented in the second case, who said they literally could not imagine dividing their attention between their research and children.

It is possible that the non-sex-based division of labor utilized by these comparably trained academics in their collaborative scholarly projects extends to domestic tasks, including child care. This is the situation for the couple with two children presented in the third case narrative. They described their division of labor as fluid, varying by task, and something that after time was negotiated with little effort. There seemed to be considerable vigilance demonstrated by both partners to reject stereotypical roles and to keep the division of labor balanced. Despite such examples, however, I am reluctant to declare that an egalitarian ideology extends unilaterally to domestic as well as work roles. My hesitancy is due largely to the fact that I made a conscious decision to deviate from traditional research on couples by not focusing exclusively on domestic roles.

My observation of contemporary academic couples leads me to question, however, the assumption that division of labor in the home and the division of labor in work-related projects necessarily mirror each other. As domestic roles are probably even more deeply encoded than are work roles with long-standing rituals organized by sex, I suspect that it is premature to say that egalitarian couples escape all manifestations of stereotypical sex-appropriate roles. If for nothing but convenience, efficiency, and to ease social situations, I imagine that many couples fall back on traditional sex-based roles for some domestic tasks, such as the emotional labor of maintaining connections with distant relatives or caring for elderly parents.

Internally Defined Status

It is certainly possible, if not likely, that while members of couples may identify themselves as egalitarian and believe that their contribution to coauthored work is, indeed, of comparable intellectual worth, colleagues do not perceive it that way. That people utilize different criteria to judge egalitarianism in their own and other's relationships is one explanation for this. They are more likely to judge other's relationships by behavior and to judge their own by attitudes.[23] The protracted battle with colleagues that many of the women in the study, including the woman psychologist in the second case, recounted about being perceived as scholars in their own right reminds us that it is not always easy to get others to see you in the way you see yourself.

The roles assumed by members of a collaborative pair, whether it be among an intimate pair or among colleagues, are shaped in some cases by differences in status, such as in career age or seniority. These status differences are generally associated with a clear hierarchy of authority in the roles assumed,[24] but this is not always the case. For example, the value of the member of a research team's expertise and the extent that he or she has a monopoly on that expertise can alter his or her externally defined status on a research team. While most research teams are hierarchical, with authority held by the principal investigator, intellectual authority and status are more likely to be shared when the members of the team hold highly differentiated skills.[25] This same process may operate for pairs of collaborators, including couples, when both provide skills that are critical to a project. This might be the situation, for example, when one or both members is isolated from colleagues who might otherwise supply a highly specialized skill. It also might occur when a joint project is such a creative amalgamation of combined skills that no one else could possibly step forward to provide it. In such situations, differences in externally defined status such as those that might exist among a career-asymmetrical couple are likely to be redefined internally among collaborators.

Shared Personal and Professional Domains

It is relatively easy to visualize the (white) world enacted in 1950s sitcoms, where women and children occupy one world and men, arriving home late in the evening after an exhausting day of work and a long commute to the suburbs, essentially spend most of their time as if they inhabit two entirely discrete worlds. Even in the literature about egalitarianism that defines it in terms of domestic roles, peer or egalitarian couples are portrayed as occupying overlapping personal and professional spheres. Most couples with peer marriages share some purpose, interest, or activity that serves to knit their lives together.[26] These are people who spend a lot of time together and who live overlapping rather than parallel lives.[27]

Ongoing physical proximity, the commingling of spheres, and the constant exchange of information that is implicit within it are essential conditions of shared authority among couples. Physical isolation is one way a dominant group differentiates a subordinate group and devalues its labor.[28] It is also a strategy that restricts a subordinate group's access to instrumental information, expertise, and work skills. "Almost all of the research on couples who have separate spheres of influence find these partners do not have equal power," Pepper Schwartz observed in her 1994 book, *Love between Equals: How Peer Marriages Really Work.*

One of the ways couples who operate in such close proximity create equality in their relationship is by establishing distinct areas of accomplishment or expertise while also sharing areas of interest.[29] This was the case with virtually all of the senior academics I spoke with, who were often very precise about delineating differences in their own and their partner's primary areas of inquiry. Their joint writing projects were most often at the point where their areas of interest intersected but were not a main line of inquiry.[30] Having distinctly established domains of authority, as well as the strength of the personal relationship and the commitment to each other's welfare, are probably strategies that deflect the jealousy that one might expect among members of couples whose careers are relatively symmetrical.

Early Career Identity

Although about 10 percent of the interview participants who had coauthored with a spouse earned doctorates before this time, a sizable percentage of the participants (62 percent) belong to the generation of faculty who completed their doctorates between 1966 and 1976 (see Appendix C, Table C.1). The lower percentage of respondents who had coauthored with a spouse or partner in the more recent doctoral cohorts is probably a reflection of career age and the opportunity to collaborate. Faculty who completed doctorates in the late 1960s and 1970s entered faculty positions during a time of relative prosperity in higher education. They are probably one of the first generations of faculty couples to have the opportunity for a significant amount of career symmetry where the members hold comparable positions and are relatively equivalent in terms of career age and stage.

Like the samples in other recent publications about egalitarianism as a family form, the majority of participants in this recent project were members of the baby boom generation. Even though the participants may not have been conscious of it, the ideology of the women's movement and the growing legitimacy for careers for women probably influenced their commitment to egalitarianism.[31] With later marriage, higher divorce rates, and smaller family sizes, this is a group of women whose adult lives are far less shaped by the demands of children and family and far more shaped by employment than preceeding generations.[32]

This historical context, I believe, is part of what explains an important aspect of the agency displayed by many of the faculty women who participated in my research project. A professional identity and the expectation of having a meaningful scientific career are evident very early in the experiences of many of the women I interviewed from the relatively recent doctoral cohorts. In this way, the women's careers might be said to resemble closely the careers of typical high-achieving male scientists. This was the situation, for example, of the geographer presented in the first case narrative. Her early sense of vocation is evident in her adolescent reveries of having work-related conversations with a spouse over the breakfast table. There was no question for the woman cognitive psychologist presented in the second case narrative that finding an appropriate position when she first began her faculty career took precedent over her personal relationship. Similarly, that each was developing a clear sense of vocation was a very important element of the development of the relationship of the couple presented in the final case narrative. A well-defined sense of occupational identity and a clear commitment to a scientific career at a relatively young age are characteristics that cannot be underestimated in the professional success of the women presented.

The Role of Men in These Relationships

Without in any way downplaying the agency clearly demonstrated by the women, it is also important to acknowledge the unconventional role the men in these relationships played. Both members of the partnership had to be quite deliberate about their decision to discard traditional sex roles. By doing this, the men relinquished some of the privileges society generally awards heterosexuals, particularly heterosexual white men.[33] Pnina Abir-Am and Dorinda Outram (1987) reach much the same conclusion from their study of historical couples in the sciences between 1789 and 1979, such as Marie Curie and Pierre Curie. They observe:

> In all these cases, the consolidation of the women's independent status as researchers derived both from their great talent and determination and from the husbands' progressive, liberal, or unconventional beliefs and attitudes.[34]

Barbara Reskin[35] pointedly proposes that men yield privilege "only when failing to yield is more costly than yielding". Her central thesis is that that men resist the idea of men and women collaborating together on an equal basis because doing so "undermines differentiation and hence male dominance" (1988, 65).

It is possible that the intense lifestyle commitment required to be successful today as a faculty member at a highly competitive research department is part of how some men have found themselves in a position to forego some of the privileges of patriarchy. In the 1990s, there is more social opprobrium for accepting substantial unacknowledged labor from a spouse, and there are fewer nonworking spouses than there were in the 1970s or before. Some professional men may be in a position where they have more to gain than to lose in terms of the quality of their personal relationship and their career advancement by yielding some of the advantages traditionally bestowed by patriarchal versions of masculinity. The extent that both men and women participants involved in long-term scholarly projects with a partner expressed the sentiment that the work they had produced collaboratively was clearly superior to anything they might have produced individually further supports the argument that the benefits of an egalitarian relationship may be perceived by its members to outweigh its costs.

Peer partnerships are more likely to be viable for dual-career couples as a family form when both members perceive they are mutually beneficial rather than when one member's gain is perceived to come at the expense of the other's career success. This, however, is largely how egalitarianism has been portrayed in contemporary literature that explores its relationship to faculty publishing productivity. It has been assumed that married women's gains in productivity have come at the expense of a husband, just as men's success in earlier generations rested on the shoulders of the invisible labor supplied by an unemployed or underemployed wife.

Implications for Practice
Is Productivity a Matter of Time Devoted to Research and Writing?
An article by Alison Schneider (1998) in an issue of the *Chronicle of Higher Education* featured a discussion of the issue of gender differences in the impact of traditional publishing productivity measures that was the central topic of my 1998 book.[36] One of the comments made by a prolific scholarly writer who was quoted in the article generated a firestorm on his own disciplinary Internet discussion list. He suggested that the simple explanation is that prolific scholars work harder and devote more time to research than do writers who produce less.

If asked if to weigh the truth of this statement based on my research with prolific writers, I would have to reply with a qualified "yes." Prolific writers probably do devote a disproportionate amount of their effort to research and writing. The defining issue, however, is that they manage to sustain that commitment over decades. Prolific scholarly writers are those who, for a variety of personal reasons and environmental conditions, have the drive, stamina, work assignment, resources, and institutional support over 20 or 30 years in the same type of faculty position to sustain a relatively consistent output.[37] They stand in contrast to the average faculty member, whose productivity peaks during the first 10 to 15 years of their career and declines after that.[38]

The impression that the participants presented in the case narratives give of the life of senior faculty at research universities in the late 1990s differs starkly from the romanticized image of "the life of the mind" and the leisurely life conducive to contemplation that it conjures. It is consistent with the metaphor of the "time bind" presented by Arlie Russell Hochschild, best-selling author of a number of books dealing with family and work.[39] The participants seem preoccupied with time. Most of the highly productive faculty I interviewed described a hectic schedule full of travel, publishers' deadlines, proposal writing, grant negotiations, and commitment to graduate students. Among other things, the lifestyle embodied by the three couples presented in the case narratives in Part 1 of the book reveals how strategic these faculty are about organizing their lives in order to preserve regularly scheduled time for research and writing.

Measuring time or effort invested in research is not in itself adequate to explain long-term publication productivity, however. If that were the case, faculty with few obligations outside their work assignment would be expected to be more productive than those with intense time commitment to family, friends, and/or the community. This has not proven to be the case in the past for either men or women.[40] Long-term productivity demands institutional support and a lifestyle that readily accommodates the habit of consistently devoting time to research over the course of decades. Although many books are certainly written this way, this is not the same thing as the person who occasionally sequesters him or herself during a leave or sabbatical to write a book. I think that it is likely that many faculty at research universities step back from the intense commitment to publishing necessary to earn tenure because it requires a lifestyle they find incompatible with other interests and they believe it exacts too high a price on personal relationships or family.

The Question of Balance

People often react to my description of members of my sample by using the expression "workaholic." I interpret this expression to imply that these are people who are obsessively unidimensional; always working and never committing time to their personal well-being and growth or to that of their friends and family. While this may be an apt characterization for some of them, I believe that faculty who achieve the status of prolific are those who have, in one way or another, found a way to craft a lifestyle that is compatible with intense work commitments. Such a lifestyle may be compatible with some family forms, may exclude a family entirely, or may be dependent on a very traditional configuration of family where the breadwinner is essentially absent from daily affairs.

The peer partners I have described in the case narratives have found ways to integrate their personal and professional lives. They manage to spend a good deal of time in each other's company, in part because they are engaged in collaborative projects and accomplish work-related tasks at home. Several of the interview participants, including one presented in a case in Part I, also spoke of involving children in research during travel or fieldwork. Some participants who are now senior faculty mentioned the generativity of publishing with a son or daughter who had also entered a faculty career.

Teaching, Research, and Service

In his reply to one of the case narratives presented in Part I, Peter Magolda raised the issue of balance in terms of the priority awarded by faculty to teaching, research, and service. This introduces a long-standing debate in the literature about faculty research productivity: Are teaching and research compatible and mutually reinforcing or are teaching and research mutually competing enterprises? The mutually reinforcing argument applies mostly to faculty who teach largely in graduate programs where the topic of their teaching and the topic of their research, as well as their work with graduate students, are interrelated. It has less relevance to faculty who teach undergraduate courses and have little access to the resources and support of graduate student assistants.

A similar scenario seems to be played out among the three faculty couples presented in the case narratives in Part I. Because of the ongoing involvement of graduate students in fieldwork, it might be argued that there is some balance between the priority awarded teaching and the priority awarded research in the first case of geographers. In the other two cases, however, it is the research and writing that captures their best energies. While the fact that they are so articulate suggests they might be effective teachers as well as mentors, their schedules are organized in such a way that priority is given to research rather than teaching. Their summers are generally devoted to doing research, fieldwork, and/or writing, for example, and not to teaching. Their teaching schedules are established in ways that fit with a schedule that maximizes their writing productivity. In some cases, that means concentrating on teaching during two or three days of the week, while in others it may mean scheduling late-afternoon or evening classes to accommodate the person who writes best on a regular basis in the uninterrupted hours past midnight. These are forms of support research universities are generally willing to provide to accommodate the needs of senior faculty with a proven track record of research productivity. I am confident that faculty who belong to an even more elite group of high producers than I studied, such as those who have published dozens of books and/or hundreds of articles, are even more likely to be relieved of most routine teaching responsibilities over a substantial portion of their careers.

Impact on Higher Education

One of the most obvious questions presented by bringing attention to ways that partners in the same profession may impact faculty productivity is the question of what impact they might have in the nature of higher education. In the process of conducting the research presented in this book, I must admit that I encountered little evidence that convinced me that the academic workplace is undergoing profound change at the institutional level attributable to the growing presence of dual-career couples. Individual faculty may take a stand to preserve time to interact in meaningful ways with their children, but this is change at the individual rather than institutional level. Few faculty take advantage of formal couples- and families-friendly institutional policies, such as those that stop the tenure clock for childbirth or unusual family crises. Instead, contemporary couples are likely to attempt to adjust their fertility patterns to the academic calendar, such as by delaying childbirth until after tenure or trying to time birth to coincide with research leaves or summer breaks.[41]

It is my perception that other changes occurring in the academic workplace are having a more profound impact on faculty work than the demographic reality of the growing presence of dual-career academic couples. Advances in technology are one of these. Cellular or digital telephones, computers, facsimile machines, and other electronic and digital forms of communication have made it easier for academics to work from home and to collaborate with both a nearby partner and with a colleague in a distant location. The growth of distance education and virtual office hours make it more and more possible for some faculty to conduct a good part of their regular business away from their campus offices. The blurring of the line between work and home that has been made possible for some faculty by technology is what I argue is one of the principal arenas for change in the academic workplace.

The recent technological advances that provide faculty with more freedom to accomplish some of their work at home may have especially significant implications for the scholarly productivity of faculty women, if not necessarily in ways that are anticipated. An increased presence of men in the household accomplishing productive labor may legitimize the labor that women do in that setting and reshape the ideology that has trivialized women's contribution as largely sexual or reproductive. An increased presence of men in the home is likely to signal both an enhanced information exchange as well as a larger-than-traditional role in domestic affairs. When accompanied by mutuality and comparable commitment to both careers, these factors may contribute to equalizing the long-standing differences in career publication productivity of men and women faculty by equalizing differences in the social and material conditions in the household. The social change that is occurring in the family as the result of dual-career commitments may be related to technology that makes it possible to relocate some paid labor to the home and affords the physical proximity for men and women to work together in comparable roles.

Couples-Friendly Hiring Policies and Job-Sharing

A few authors have investigated institutional policies regarding recruiting and hiring academic couples.[42] Evidence of institutionalization of these polices would support the argument that the growing presence of dual-career couples and concern for the family are reshaping the academic workplace. This is a topic that I anticipated would emerge in the participants' descriptions of the various stages of the evolution of both their personal relationship and their careers. Somewhat to my surprise, however, it was not something participants' underscored as being significant to their careers. Even though two of the couples presented in the case narratives are fortunate enough to be working at the same university, an overt policy to recruit couples was a factor in only one of the cases presented in the narratives. Although this may be a surprise, it was consistent with the findings from the larger population of academics whom I interviewed. It is also consistent with research reports[43] and my own conversations with provosts. Even at institutions with reputations for being proactive about hiring couples, they generally described ad hoc programs serving only a small number of faculty couples each year.[44]

Resistance to dual-career-couple recruiting polices is deeply rooted in traditional faculty cultures. As Peter Magolda pointed out in his reply to the second case narrative, it is often faculty rather than administrators who actively oppose spousal hires. Such hires may be perceived to challenge faculty control of a decentralized hiring process. They may also run counter to affirmative action goals set at the university level. It is also possible that such hires may stigmatize faculty in a process similar to the one that is often reported by faculty perceived to be hired because of affirmative action policies.[45] These are all issues that need to be pursued further in the research about dual-career-couple recruiting policies and practices.

My original plan was to include a chapter on spousal hiring policies in this book. Through the course of conducting the research and preparing the manuscript, I grew increasingly reluctant to pursue an in-depth discussion of couples-friendly hiring practices out of a concern for exaggerating the impact of such programs. I do not want to minimize the difficulties dual-career academic couples encounter in finding suitable employment.[46] Many of the largest dual-career-couple hiring programs invest far more resources to assist a "trailing" partner to find employment in an off-campus position than in an on-campus position. Such programs are more likely to be designed with the goal of attracting senior "superstars" to remote, rural locations than with the goal of helping promising young graduates to enter faculty careers. This offers little basis for optimism for young couples where both members are seeking to pursue a career as a faculty member. While these programs may contribute to the morale of faculty who are already secure in the appointments, my strong sense is that there is more rhetoric than significant change occurring on college and university campuses in the United States about couples-friendly hiring policies.

Job-Sharing

I give even less credibility to job-sharing as a satisfactory alternative for academics who have spent a decade or more preparing for a faculty career. This is the practice where two people share a single faculty position and salary, and in some cases each has the option of being reviewed for tenure and promotion. One account of a shared appointment described constant attempts by colleagues to rank each member of the couple relative to the other and to identify one as the better scholar or teacher.[47] Even though bell hooks advocates sharing a high-paying job as a laudatory strategy toward challenging capitalism and redistributing wealth,[48] I interpret it as yet another way that institutions can profit from paying women little or nothing for their labor. A relatively prestigious title and the possibility of tenure is offered to offset the sacrifice of sharing a single salary. I find it a sad commentary on the limited alternatives available that some academics, including members of couples, are grateful for this kind of position as a way to balance the dual demands of family and a career.

Applicability to Couples in Other Professions

An additional question about the implications that academic couples presented in this volume invite is the extent that their experiences are generalizable to dual-career couples in other occupations. There are probably distinct parallels between this population and other affluent, professional couples who have some autonomy over their work and time. Lawyers, engineers, or architects who share a private practice or couples who run a small business or consulting firm from their home would be interesting samples to use to pursue some of these questions. This kind of investigation would provide an opportunity to test further the hypothesis that among more recent cohorts, egalitarianism manifested as mutual support for career goals is more instrumental to career success than the division of household responsibilities. It would also be useful to investigate the lives of academic couples who have collaborated in a full range of faculty roles, including research, teaching, and outreach.

Conclusion

The persistent question that weaves throughout the research reported in this volume is: What are the conditions that explain how some faculty, albeit only a very small and privileged group, are able to sustain research productivity across careers spanning 20 or 30 years? The typical faculty member at a research university generally chooses to replace the early intense commitment to research required to earn tenure by seeking to achieve a greater balance between teaching, outreach, and research. Participants in my research project frequently spoke of the relief upon earning tenure of being able to shift their attention to writing less traditional publications that reached a wider audience.

About half of the academics I interviewed described working collaboratively with a spouse or partner on projects that spanned more than a decade. While couples have the distinct advantage of the access afforded by cohabitation and the opportunity for unusual longevity, this type of collaborative pairing shares many qualities with other types of successful collaborative arrangements. They point to the absolutely critical importance of ongoing access to informal and timely feedback about ideas. As Yvonna Lincoln suggests in her response to the case of the geographers presented in Part 1, successful spousal collaborators may provide a good model for other cross-sex collaborators who do not share such an intense, personal relationship.

A summer 1999 edition of the *Chronicle of Higher Education* ran as a cover story an article about the retirement in their seventies of scions in the faculty world. Included in the edition was a pair of eminent male mathematicians, Louis Nirenberg and Peter Lax.[49] Self-described as "being like brothers," their histories share many parallels with the stories told by couples in the research project reported in this volume. Earning doctorates from the same department in 1949, the two men went on to share amazingly symmetrical careers, working as colleagues for 50 years in the same department at New York University and each earning comparable, exceptionally prestigious awards, honors, and international acclaim. One of the pair, Louis Nirenberg, now in his mid-seventies, says: "it is a wonderful joy to do research. A fantastic pleasure" (A15). He looks forward to retirement as a time when he can continue his research and the "process of discovery."

The lifetime collaboration of these two eminent mathematicians provides a good context for the suggestion for future research Ann Austin posed at the end of her chapter synthesizing the literature about collaboration and its application to spousal collaborators. She asked: What qualities do long-term spousal collaborators share with colleagues who collaborate and have a deep, long-standing personal friendship but do not cohabit or define each other as family? This question underlies what is required to sustain viability as a scholar and what it means to be devoted to the world of ideas or to be committed to the "life of the mind."

Appendix A: The Questionnaire Sample and Respondents

Using a definition of a spouse or partner as someone who shares or has shared a household, I mailed a questionnaire to 750 (375 men; 375 women) senior faculty at research universities in the United States during the summer of 1996. The purpose of the survey was, first, to assess the extent of collaboration among academics who had or ever had a spouse/partner and, second, to identify a population of faculty who had collaborated with a spouse/partner and who would agree to participate in a telephone interview.

Following the line of research I have been engaged in (Creamer, 1994, 1995, 1996, 1998, 1999; Creamer and McGuire, 1998), I developed a sampling method for the questionnaire that reflected the major demographic characteristics of prolific scholarly writers. I identified faculty at the rank of associate and full professor whose first and last names were listed in the graduate catalogs of 22 public and private research universities geographically distributed throughout the United States. This included Research I and Research II universities listed in the 1994 edition of the *Classification of Institutions of Higher Education* published by the Carnegie Foundation. In order to have an equal number of men and women, which is highly unusual for research about publishing productivity, I matched men and women by rank and department. I located each recognizably female name in an alphabetical listing of faculty in select departments in a 1994 to 1995 graduate catalog and matched them with the next recognizably male name with the same rank in the same department, stopping after five matched pairs were identified in any one department. If there were no recognizably female names in a department, I did not sample anyone from the department. If there was no match by rank and department to a female name, I did not include the woman in the population to receive a questionnaire. The response rate was relatively low (n = 263; 35 percent), possibly due to the summer distribution schedule. Because a matched sample was used, respondents did not differ significantly by sex and academic field (see Table A.1.), or sex and academic rank.

Data about the characteristics of the questionnaire respondents are presented in the tables in Appendix A. While not representative of faculty as a whole or of the range of institutional types, respondents are quite similar in most respects to what you would expect to find of prolific scholars, with the exception of the unusually high representation of women. For example, the majority of the respondents (n = 168; 63.9 percent) had the academic rank of full professor. There was little racial diversity among respondents (n = 247; 94.6 percent white). Almost all respondents listed the highest degree completed as a doctorate (n = 254; 96.9 percent) with only a small number of respondents reporting their highest degree as a master's (n = 6; 2.3 percent) or other (n = 2; 0.8 percent). Although significantly more men than women had published fifty or more journal articles over the course of his or her career (Chi-square = 5.954, d.f. = 1, p < 0.05; data not shown), there were no significant differences by gender in the percentage of men and women respondents who had produced 21 or more journal articles and/or three or more books over the course of his or her career (see Table A. 4).

That the sampling technique was effective in reaching an unusually high proportion of prolific scholarly writers can be determined by comparing the faculty responding to the 1995–96 H.E.R.I. Faculty Survey published by the University of California at Los Angeles (*Chronicle of Higher Education*, September 13, 1996, A14).[1] While 21.6 percent of the respondents to the questionnaire had published 50 or more articles in academic or professional journals, only 5.8 percent of faculty responding to the 1995–96 H.E.R.I. Faculty Survey had done so. Across all types of institutions, 15.7 percent of full-time faculty had produced 21 or more articles in academic or professional journals, compared to 54 percent (n = 140) of the respondents to the survey I administered.

The rank, institutional affiliation, terminal degree, and journal article publication level are unusual for the faculty population as a whole and reflect the relatively elite status of most members of the population of prolific scholarly writers. While representative of the largely senior faculty at research universities with unusually high publishing levels, the respondents are likely to differ from the population of faculty as a whole in a number of ways, including having access to graduate students and a work assignment that includes teaching fewer courses and fewer undergraduate courses.

Table A.1.

Questionnaire Respondents by Academic Field and Sex (n = 261)

	Men	Women
	n (%)	n (%)
Field	n = 110	n = 151
Biological Sciences	17 (15.4)	23 (15.2)
Education	10 (9.1)	11 (7.3)
Humanities	39 (35.5)	49 (32.5)
Physical Sciences	8 (7.3)	12 (7.9)
Social Sciences	36 (32.7)	56 (37.1)

Table A.2.

Questionnaire Respondents by Year of Highest Degree and Sex (n = 259)

	Men	Women
Year Earned	n (%)	n (%)
Highest Degree	n = 110	n = 149
1952–1965	22 (20.0)	7 (4.7)
1966–1976	44 (40.0)	59 (39.6)
1977–1986	42 (38.2)	70 (47.0)
1987–	2 (1.8)	13 (8.7)

Chi-square = 19.58, d.f. = 3, p < 0.001.

Table A.3.
Questionnaire Respondents' Journal Article Career-Total Production (n = 259)

	Men	Women
	n (%)	n (%)
Articles Published	n = 111	n = 148
None	0 (0)	4 (2.7)
1–4	3 (2.7)	6 (4.1)
5–10	15 (13.5)	25 (16.9)
11–20	29 (26.1)	37 (25.0)
21–50	32 (28.8)	52 (35.1)
51–	32 (28.8)	24 (16.2)

Table A.4.
Prolific Questionnaire Respondents by Sex (n = 262)

	Men	Women
	n (%)	n (%)
Prolific *	n = 111	n = 151
Yes	74 (66.7)	88 (58.3)
No	37 (33.3)	63 (41.7)

*Prolific is defined as self-reporting a career total of 21 or more articles in academic or professional journals and/or five or more career-total books.

Table A.5. Questionnaire Respondents Producing 21 or More Journal Articles or Three or More Books by Academic Field (n = 261)

	Yes	No	
	n (%)	n (%)	
Field	n = 151	n = 110	
Biological Sciences	36 (23.8)	4 (3.6)	
Education	16 (10.6)	5 (4.5)	
Humanities	41 (27.2)	47 (42.7)	
Physical Sciences	8 (5.3)	12 (10.9)	
Social Sciences	50 (33.1)	42 (38.2)	

Chi-square = 32.802, d.f. = 4, p < 0. 001.

Appendix B: Collaboration with Partner/Spouse among Questionnaire Respondents

One of the major purposes of the survey distributed to a sample of faculty at research universities matched by gender, department, and rank was to provide some measure of the extent of collaboration among senior faculty who had or ever had a spouse or partner. The tables presented in Appendix B provide support for the argument that informal collaboration, such as by providing feedback about draft of publications, as well as formal collaboration, such as coauthoring a scholarly journal article or book, are not uncommon between academics and a spouse/partner in a wide range of academic fields. These data have not been published elsewhere. As shown in Table B.1, 64.1 percent of respondents reported that they had given or received feedback about a draft of a publication from a spouse or partner. Differences by sex were not significant. Twenty-two percent of all respondents including those who had never been married or lived with a partner had coauthored a journal article or book with a spouse/partner (see Table B.2). The differences were not significant by gender (see Table B.2) or by year he or she earned his or her highest degree (see Table B.3). Of those who had coauthored or coedited a scholarly publication with a spouse or partner, the majority (87 percent; n = 73) reported that their spouse or partner held a position in higher education (data not shown). This supports the use of the term "academic partners."

Table B.4 reports findings of no statistically significant difference by academic field in the percentage of respondents reporting they had coauthored a scholarly article or book with a spouse or partner. Coauthorship with a partner was highest among respondents identifying themselves to be in the social sciences and lowest among those in the physical sciences. These findings vary somewhat from what is reported to characterize patterns of collaboration by academic field, where rates of collaboration are higher in the natural and physical sciences than in humanities or social sciences (see chapter 13 by Ann Austin). Differences between the data from questionnaire respondents and the population as a whole may be explained by variation by academic field, as well as by sex, in the proportion of faculty with an academic partner. The especially high rate of coauthorship with a spouse or partner reported by respondents to the questionnaire might be explained by the nature of the research or type of research problem pursued (see chapter 13 by Austin for further discussion of how this impacts rates of collaboration).

Table B.1.
Questionnaire Respondents Reporting They Had Given or Received Feedback from a Spouse/Partner about a Draft of a Publication by Sex

	Men n (%) n = 111	Women n (%) n = 151	Total n (%) n = 262
Yes	71 (64.0)	98 (64.2)	168 (64.1)
No	40 (36.0)	54 (35.8)	94 (35.9)

Table B.2.
Questionnaire Respondents Reporting They Had Published Journal Article(s) or Book(s) with a Spouse/Partner by Sex

	Men n (%) n = 111	Women n (%) n = 151	Total n (%) n = 262
Yes	22 (19.8)	36 (23.8)	58 (22.1)
No	89 (80.2)	115 (76.2)	204 (77.9)

Table B.3.
Questionnaire Respondents Who Had Published Journal Article(s) or Book(s) with a Spouse/Partner by Year of Highest Degree

	Coauthored with Partner	Did Not Coauthor with Partner
Year Earned	n (%)	n (%)
Highest Degree	n = 57	n = 203
1952–1965	4 (13.8)	25 (86.2)
1966–1976	30 (29.1)	73 (70.8)
1977–1986	20 (17.7)	12 (82.3)
1987–	3 (20.0)	12 (80.0)

Table B.4.
Questionnaire Respondents Reporting They Had Published Journal Article(s) or Book(s) with a Spouse/Partner by Academic Field

	Coauthored with Partner	Did Not Coauthor with Partner
	n (%)	n (%)
Field	n = 58	n = 203
Biological Sciences	9 (22.5)	31 (77.5)
Education	6 (28.6)	15 (71.4)
Humanities	10 (11.4)	78 (88.6)
Physical Sciences	5 (25.0)	15 (75.0)
Social Sciences	28 (30.4)	64 (69.6)

Table B.5.
Questionnaire Respondents Who Had Published Journal Article(s) or Book(s) with a Spouse/Partner by Level of Publishing Productivity

	Prolific *	Not Prolific
Coauthored with Partner	n (%)	n (%)
Yes	45 (76.3)	14 (23.7)
No	117 (57.4)	87 (42.7)

Chi-square = 6.76, d.f. = 1, p < 0.01.

*Prolific is defined as self-reporting a career total of 21 or more articles in academic or professional journals and/or five or more books.

Appendix C: Characteristics of the Interview Sample

The tables in Appendix C provide comparisons between the respondents to the questionnaire who had coauthored with a spouse/partner and the members of the interview sample. Some of these data have been published elsewhere but not in the same format (Creamer, 1999).

Of the 263 respondents to the questionnaire distributed to a sample of 750 faculty at 22 research universities matched by gender, rank, and department, 115 (43.7 percent) volunteered to participate in a telephone interview. This question was in the section of the questionnaire reserved for respondents who had coauthored or coedited a scholarly publication with a spouse or partner. Twenty-eight of the respondents who agreed to participate in a telephone interview met two additional criteria: they had published a journal article or book with a spouse/partner and published 21 or more journal articles and/or 5 or more books. This group, consisting of prolific scholars who had coauthored with a spouse/partner, became the initial interview population.

Fourteen (50 percent) of the 28 prolific survey respondents who had coauthored with a spouse participated in a one-on-one, semistructured, hour-long telephone interview and supplied a copy of a complete curriculum vitae. The spouses/partners of seven of the respondents to the original survey were also interviewed by telephone. Two of the three couples presented in the case narratives are from this group. The second member of an academic couple was not interviewed either because he or she was not available or willing to participate in an interview or because the collaborative relationship described by the primary informant was so brief or circumscribed that I was convinced that there was little new information to gain by interviewing the second person. With the permission of the informant, the telephone interviews were recorded and a verbatim transcript completed.

An additional 12 people were added to the interview sample through a snowball sampling technique, for a total of 33 academics (20 women; 13 men). One of the couples presented in the case narrative is from this group. The 33 participants include 12 pairs where both members were interviewed (n = 24) and an additional nine where only one member of the pair was interviewed. The sample consists of 21 collaborative pairs. Not all are heterosexual pairs. There is no racial diversity in the group; no one in the interview sample identified him- or herself as a racial or ethnic minority.

I refer to the first member of the couples I interviewed, which includes all who responded to the mailed questionnaire, as the primary informant. In addition to having coauthored at least one scholarly publication with a spouse or partner, the 21 primary informants meet two additional criteria: first, each is a tenured faculty member at the rank of associate or full professor. Second, each meets the definition of being a prolific scholarly writer by virtue of having published 21 or more journal articles or three or more books over the course of his or her career. Each of the three cases also meet these qualifications. Primary informants are employed at 14 colleges and universities geographically dispersed throughout the United States. Most of primary informants (n = 12; 86 percent) have a spouse/partner who is also a faculty member and whose highest degree is in the same disciplinary group (date not shown; n = 12; 86 percent).

Descriptive information about the primary informants appears in Tables C.1 and C.2. The primary interview informants (n = 21) shared some characteristics with the questionnaire respondents who had collaborated with a spouse/partner and who are central to the focus of this research about prolific scholars. They did not differ by year they earned a doctorate (Table C.1), academic rank, or total-career journal article productivity (Table C.2). Like questionnaire respondents, the majority of primary interview informants had published 21 or more journal articles in academic or professional journals over the course of his or her career to date (75 percent questionnaire respondents, 86 percent of the primary informants). There were no statistically significant differences between questionnaire respondents and primary interview informants in the number of journal articles or chapters coauthored with a partner (see Table C.2), or there were statistically significant differences in the number of books coauthored with spouse/partner (see Table C.2; Chi-square = 1.92, d. f. = 1, p < 0.05). These findings support the argument that in most ways the primary interview informants were representative of the respondents to the questionnaire.

Not surprisingly, the percentage of respondents to the questionnaire coauthoring with a spouse/partner increased between graduate school, before earning tenure, and after earning tenure, with the highest percentage of respondents indicating that they had coauthored a journal article or book with a spouse/partner after earning tenure (data not shown). The majority of primary informants (data not shown; 15 of 21; 71 percent) had coauthored only 10 or fewer journal articles with a spouse/partner, but the majority had published one or more books with a spouse/partner (data not shown; 11 of 21; 52 percent). About 10 percent (n = 26; 9.9 percent) of the questionnaire respondents had collaborated with a partner in scholarly writing projects for 11 to 15 years, which is true for the interview participants and the three couples described in the case narratives as well (data not shown).

Table C.1.

Descriptive Information about Questionnaire Respondents Who Had Coauthored with a Spouse/Partner and Primary Interview Informants

	Questionnaire Respondent	Primary Interview Informant
Year Earned Doctorate	n = 57	n = 21
1952–1965	4 (7.0)	2 (9.5)
1966–1976	30 (52.6)	13 (61.9)
1977–1986	20 (35.1)	6 (28.6)
1987–	3 (5.3)	0 (0.0)
Academic Rank	n = 59	n = 21
Associate	12 (20.3)	2 (9.5)
Full	47 (79.7)	19 (90.5)
Academic Discipline of Doctorate	n = 58	n = 21
Biological Sciences	9 (15.5)	2 (9.5)
Education	6 (10.3)	2 (9.5)
Humanities	10 (17.2)	2 (9.5)
Physical Sciences	5 (8.6)	1 (4.8)
Social Sciences	28 (48.3)	14 (66.7)

Table C.2.
Publishing Productivity of Questionnaire Respondents Who Had Coauthored with a Spouse/Partner and Primary Interview Informants

	Questionnaire Respondent	Primary Interview Informant
Journal Article Productivity	n = 56	n = 21
Less than 21	14 (25.0)	3 (14.3)
21 to 50	23 (41.1)	8 (38.1)
More than 50	19 (33.9)	10 (47.6)
Articles or Chapters Coauthored with Partner	n = 56	n = 21
None	8 (14.3)	4 (19.0)
1–4	32 (57.1)	9 (42.9)
5–10	8 (14.3)	2 (9.5)
11–20	5 (8.9)	2 (9.5)
21 or more	3 (5.4)	4 (19.0)
Books Coauthored with Partner*	n = 57	n = 21
None	37 (64.9)	10 (47.6)
1 or More	20 (35.1)	11 (52.4)

*Chi-square = 1.92, d.f. = 1, $p < .05$

Notes

Notes to Chapter 1

1 Finkelstein, M. J., Seal, R. K., and Schuster, J. H. (1998). *The new academic generation*. Baltimore, MD: Johns Hopkins University Press. Reporting on findings from 1993 NSOPF National Study of Postsecondary Faculty; among senior academics, 83.2 percent of the men and 61.5 percent of the women were married (p. 16).

2 Astin, H. S., and Milem, J. F. (1997). The status of academic couples in U.S. institutions. In M. A. Ferber and J. W. Loeb (Eds.), *Academic couples: Problems and promises* (pp. 128–155). Urbana, IL: University of Illinois Press.

3 Ferber, M. A., and Loeb, J. W. (Eds.). (1997). *Academic couples: Problems and promises*. Urbana, IL: University of Illinois Press.

4 Bowen, H. R., and Schuster, J. H. (1986). *American professors: A national resource imperiled*. New York: Oxford University Press.

5 Ward, K. B., and Grant, L. (1996). Gender and academic publishing. In J. Smart (Ed.), *Higher education: Handbook of theory and research, vol. 12* (pp. 172–212). Edison, NJ: Agathon, p. 202.

6 I first presented a detailed discussion of the role of a domestic partner in the social and material conditions associated with faculty in a scholarly productivity in the following publication: Creamer, E. G. (2001, forthcoming). Intimate partnerships and publication productivity. In J. Smart (Ed.), *Higher education: Handbook of theory and research, vol. 16*. Edison, NJ: Agathon.

7 This topic is also briefly discussed in Wilson, R. (1998, April 17). When officemates are also roommates. *Chronicle of Higher Education, 44*(2), A12.

8 Although I am aware that roles assigned are socially constructed and thus "gender" is the term most authors would select, I have chosen to use the word "sex" rather than "gender" in most cases throughout the text. I have done this to make the point that work roles and roles in the home are usually prescribed with a single consideration in mind, and that is biological sex.

9 I defined "prolific" as self-reporting a career total of 21 or more articles in academic or professional journals and/or five or more career-total books.

10 Long, J. S., and Fox, M. F. (1995). Scientific careers: Universalism and particularism. *Annual Review of Sociology, 21*, 45–71.

11 Ward and Grant, 1996.
12 I explain this argument in detail in my 1998 book, *Assessing faculty publishing productivity: Issues of equity*. ASHE–ERIC Higher Education Report Volume 26, No. 2. Washington, DC: George Washington University, School of Education and Human Development.
13 Schwartz, P. (1994). *Love between equals: How peer marriages really work*. New York: The Free Press.
14 I am aware that the depiction of the home presented in *Working Equal* is a radical departure form the embodiment of the home as a place of confinement for women powerfully presented by some feminist literary scholars, including Sandra M. Gilbert and Susan Gubar in their landmark 1979 book, *The madwoman in the attic: The woman writer and the nineteenth-century literary imagination*. New Haven, CT: Yale University Press. I am not challenging the accuracy of their historical presentation of marriage, family, and home but suggesting that new cohorts of women may experience home in very different ways.
15 Hochschild, A. R. (1997). *Time bind: When work becomes home and home becomes work*. New York: Metropolitan Books. Henry Holt and Company.
16 Dickens, C. S., and Sagaria, M. A. (1997). Feminists at work: Collaborative relationships among women faculty. *Review of Higher Education, 21*(1), 79–101.
17 Dickens and Sagaria, 1997, p. 95.
18 Dickens and Sagaria, 1997, p. 95.
19 Dickens and Sagaria, 1997.
20 Astin, H. S., and Davis, D. E. (1985a). Research productivity across the life and career cycles: Facilitator and barriers for women. Reprinted in J. S. Glazer, E. M. Bensimon, B. K. Townsend (Eds.), (1993), *Women in higher education: A feminist perspective* (pp. 415–423). Needham Heights, MA: ASHE Reader Series, Ginn Press.
21 Chadwick, W., and De Courtivron, I. (Eds.). (1993). *Significant others: Creativity and intimate partnerships*. London: Thames and Hudson.
22 Eisler, B. (1991). *O'Keeffe and Stieglitz*. New York: Penguin Books.
23 Rose, P. (1984). *Parallel lives*. New York: Vintage Books.
24 This is a metaphor utilized by Whitney Chadwick and Isabelle De Courtivron, 1993.
25 The relationship of both of these couples is described by Ruth Perry and Martine Watson Brownley in their 1984 edited volume, *Mothering the mind: Twelve studies of writers and their silent partners*. New York: Holmes and Meier.
26 Abir-Am, P. G., and Outram, D. (Eds.). (1987). *Uneasy careers and intimate lives: Women in science 1789–1979*. New Brunswick, NJ: Rutgers University Press. Pycior, H. M., Slack, N. G., and Abir-Am, P. G. (Eds.). (1996). *Creative couples in the sciences*. New Brunswick, NJ: Rutgers University Press.
27 Cole, J. R., and Zuckerman, H. (1987, February). Marriage, motherhood, and research performance in science. *Scientific American*, 119–125.

28 Abir-Am and Outram (Eds.), 1987, pp. 3–4.

29 Abir-Am and Outram (Eds.), 1987.

30 Pycior, Slack, and Abir-Am (Eds.), 1996.

31 Chadwick and De Courtivron (Eds.), 1993.

32 Chadwick and De Courtivron (Eds.), 1993.

33 hooks, b. (1984). *Feminist theory: From margin to center*. Boston, MA: South End Press, p. 38.

34 Dickens and Sagaria, 1997. Mackie, M. (1977). Professional women's collegial relations and productivity: Female sociologists' journal publications, 1967 and 1973. *Sociology and Social Research, 61*, 277–293.

35 Ward and Grant, 1996.

36 Pycior, Slack, and Abir-Am (Eds.), 1996.

37 Ann Austin and Roger Baldwin used this expression to characterize one type of collaborative relationship in their 1991 publication, *Faculty collaboration: Enhancing the quality of scholarship and teaching*. ASHE–ERIC Higher Education Report No. 7. Washington, DC: George Washington University, School of Education and Human Services.

Notes to Chapter 2

1 An article by Christopher Shea in the *Chronicle of Higher Education* in May 1997 (Vol. 43, A13–A14) discussed several scholars described as "hyperproductive," including one in religious studies who has written a book a week for some years. This is not the population of scholars I am attempting to depict in this book.

2 Stake, R. (1994). Case studies. In N. K. Denzin and Y. S. Lincoln (Eds.), *Handbook of qualitative research* (pp. 236–247). Thousand Oaks, CA. Sage.

3 In their book *Gender Differences in Science Careers: The Project Access Study* (New Brunswick, NJ: Rutgers University Press), Sonnert and Holton (1995) acknowledge some of these stereotypes in their speculation for the reasons why coauthorship with a mentor during graduate school did not have a comparable significant, positive, long-term impact on career publication output for women as it did for men. They note that it was difficult to determine whether women gained fewer skills from these relationships because they assumed lower-order tasks, or if it was just assumed by others that this is what occurred.

4 In their coauthored book, *The art and science of portraiture* (1997, San Francisco: Jossey-Bass), Sara Lawrence-Lightfoot and Jessica Hoffman Davis use the term "portraiture" to describe an interdisciplinary method of presenting biographical materials that incorporate elements of ethnography. Although my intent is not biographical, the narratives presented in this text share a number of similarities with the approach taken by Lawrence-Lightfoot and Hoffman Davis.

5 Career total of 21 or more refereed publications (journal articles and book chapters) or five or more books (self-reported).

6 For further analysis of this distinction, see Creamer, E. G. (1999). Knowl-

edge production, publication productivity, and intimate academic partnerships. *Journal of Higher Education, 70*(3), 261–277.

7 Examples of this type of relationship and the term "enabler" are presented
by Ruth Perry and Martine Brownley in their 1984 edited book, *Mothering
the mind: Twelve studies of writers and their silent partners.* New York: Holmes
and Meier.

8 Creamer, E. G. (2001, forthcoming). Intimate partnerships and publication
productivity. In J. Smart (Ed.), *Higher education: Handbook of theory and
research, vol. 16.* Edison, NJ: Agathon.

9 I discuss how these vary by gender in the publication Creamer, E. G.
(1998). *Assessing faculty publishing productivity: Issues of equity.* ASHE–ERIC
Higher Education Report Volume 26, No. 2. Washington, DC: George
Washington University, School of Education and Human Development.

10 Few participants made more than glancing reference to the role of institutional resources in their publication productivity. Even those who made extensive use of research leave rarely mentioned it in anything more than a cursory
manner. My interpretation is that as successful senior faculty who are secure
in their positions, they take these resources somewhat for granted.

11 Schwartz, P. (1994). *Love between equals: How peer marriages really work.*
New York: The Free Press.

Notes to Chapter 3

1 Ward, K. B., and Grant, L. (1996). Gender and academic publishing. In J.
Smart (Ed.), *Higher education: Handbook of theory and research, vol. 12,* (pp.
172–212). Edison, NJ: Agathon.

2 Being strategic about collaborative enterprises, including with a partner, is a
quality that I found to be characteristic of senior scholars at research universities. While in a few cases I heard of partners who pursued collaborative
projects with a partner for the sheer fun it, most of my participants undertook such projects in ways that scrupulously acknowledged the reward
structure at research universities. This extended to the conventions they utilize to determine the order their names would appear in a list of authors. I
discuss this further in an unpublished ERIC manuscript: Creamer, E. G.
(1998b, November). Coauthorship and recognition among academic couples. Research/scholarly paper presented at the 1998 ASHE National Conference. Miami, FL.

3 Austin, E. A., and Baldwin, R. G. (1991). *Faculty collaboration: Enhancing the
quality of scholarship and teaching.* ASHE–ERIC Higher Education Report
No. 7. Washington, DC: George Washington University, School of Education and Human Services.

4 Reskin, B. F. (1978). Sex differentiation and the social organization of science. *Sociological Inquiry, 48* (winter), 6–37.

Notes to Chapter 5

1 This locution is not original with me. I owe it to a stunning chapter on "self-

Other" relations in qualitative fieldwork and writing, written by Michelle Fine. Many of her ideas about the self and the Other—problems in representation, legitimacy, and authority in postmodern ethnographic fieldwork—are equally critical in scholarly collaboration, even when the "self" and the "other" share racial, economic, and historical social locations. See Fine, M. (1994). Working the hyphens. In N. K. Denzin and Y. S. Lincoln (Eds.), *Handbook of qualitative research, 1st ed.* (pp. 70–82). Thousand Oaks, CA: Sage.

2 Austin, A. E. (1996, November). Relationship, epistemology, and community: Autobio-Graphical reflections on collaboration. Paper presented at the Association for the Study of Higher Education Annual Meeting, Memphis, TN.

3 Lincoln, Y. S. (1996, November). Chair and Organizer, Symposium, The intimate critic: Psychological rewards of academic collaboration. Annual Meeting, Association for the Study of Higher Education, Memphis, TN.

4 I take this term from a symposium that I organized for the annual meeting of the Association for the Study of Higher Education in 1996. It is meant to signal both the critical faculties that a collaborator brings to mutual or joint work, and at the same time, the psychological intimacy that such collaboration often confers. Contributors to this session were Ann E. Austin, Roger Baldwin, Julie Neururer, Robert A. Rhoades, and William G. Tierney. Each of these individuals collaborates widely, and many of them had collaborated with one or more of the others at some point in time.

Notes to Chapter 6

1 In the book *Love between equals* (1994, The Free Press), Pepper Schwartz observed that this kind of negotiation was a characteristic of couples with egalitarian relationships. She views it as a reflection of mutual respect and that neither member of the couple was "pulling rank" on the other.

Notes to Chapter 8

1 Smart, M. S., and Smart, R. C. (1990, January–February). Paired prospects: Dual-career couples on campus. *Academe*, 33–37.

2 Austin, A. E., and Pilat, M. (1990, January–February). Tension, stress, and the tapestry of faculty lives. *Academe*, 38–42.

3 Smart and Smart, 1990, p. 33.

4 Magolda, P., and Baxter Magolda, M. B. (1998). Book review of *Academic couples: Problems and promises. Journal of College Student Development, 39,* 299–302.

5 Wilson, R. (1998, April 17). When officemates are also roommates. *Chronicle of Higher Education,* 44(2), A12.

6 Ferber, M. A., and Loeb, J. W. (Eds.). (1997). *Academic couples: Problems and promises.* Urbana, IL: University of Illinois Press, p. 12.

7 Smart and Smart, 1990, p. 34.

8 Austin and Pilat, 1990.

Notes to Chapter 11

1 Astin, H. S., and Milem, J. F. (1997). The status of academic couples in U.S. institutions. In M. A. Ferber and J. W. Loeb (Eds.), *Academic couples: Problems and promises* (pp. 128–155). Urbana, IL: University of Illinois Press, p. 143.

2 DuBois, W. E. B. (1990). *The souls of black folk.* New York: Vintage Books, p. 9.

3 DuBois, 1990, p. 8.

4 Bourdieu, P. (1991). *Language and symbolic power.* Cambridge: Harvard University Press, p. 122.

5 Bourdieu, 1991, p. 121.

6 DuBois, 1990, p. 9.

7 Cannon, K. (1995). *Katie's canon: Womanism and the soul of the black community.* New York: Continuum.

8 Cannon, 1995, pp. 15, 18.

9 Freire, P. (1981). *Pedagogy of the oppressed.* New York: Continuum, p. 33.

10 hooks, b. (1994). *Teaching to transgress: Education as the practice of freedom.* New York: Routledge, pp. 1–2.

11 hooks, 1994, p. 12.

Notes to Chapter 12

1 Fox, M. F., and Faver, C. A. (July, 1982). The process of collaboration in scholarly research. *Scholarly Publishing, 13,* 327–339.

2 Creamer, E.G. (1999). Knowledge production, publication productivity, and intimate academic partnerships. *Journal of Higher Education, 70*(3), 261–277.

3 This is contrary to most research, which classifies a pair of collaborators with the assumption of a single approach, even when these approaches are recognized as overlapping. For this approach, see, for example, Bayer, A. E., and Smart, J. C. (1991). Career publication patterns and collaborative "styles" in American academic science. *Journal of Higher Education, 62,* 613–636. Dickens, C. S., and Sagaria, M. A. (1997). Feminists at work: Collaborative relationships among women faculty. *Review of Higher Education,* 21(1), 79–101.

Notes to Chapter 13

1 For example: Bayer, A. E., and Smart, J. C. (1988, April). Author collaborative styles in academic scholarship. Paper presented at the annual meeting of the American Educational Research Association, New Orleans, LA. Baum, W. C., Griffiths, G. N., Matthews, R., and Scherruble, D. (1976). American political science before the mirror: What our journals reveal about the profession. *Journal of Politics, 38,* 895–917. Beaver, D. B., and Rosen, R. (1979). Studies in scientific collaboration, part III. *Scientometrics* 1, 213–245. Fox, M. F., and Faver, C. A. (May–June 1984). Independence and cooperation in research: The motivations and costs of collaboration.

Journal of Higher Education 55(3), 347–359. Over, R. (September, 1982). Collaborative research and publication in psychology. *American Psychologist 37*, 996–1001. Patel, N. (1973). Collaboration in the professional growth of American sociology. *Social Science Information, 12*, 77–92.

2 See for example: Austin, E. A., and Baldwin, R. G. (1991). *Faculty collaboration: Enhancing the quality of scholarship and teaching*. ASHE–ERIC Higher Education Report No. 7. Washington, DC: George Washington University, School of Education and Human Services. Baldwin, R. G., and Austin, A. E. (1995). Toward greater understanding of faculty research collaboration. (1995). *Review of Higher Education, 19* (2), 45–70. Creamer, E. G. (1999). Knowledge production, publication productivity, and intimate academic partnerships. *Journal of Higher Education, 70*(3), 261–277. Fox and Faver, 1984.

3 Smart, J. C., and Bayer, A. E. (1986). Author collaboration and impact: A note on citation rates of single-authored and multiple-authored articles. *Scientometrics, 10*, 297–305.

4 Brady, L. A. (1988). *Collaborative literary writing: Issues of authorship and authority*. Unpublished Ph.D. dissertation, University of Minnesota.

5 Patel, 1973.

6 Baldwin and Austin, 1995, p. 54.

7 Baldwin and Austin, 1995, p. 55.

8 Baldwin and Austin, 1995, p. 55.

9 Finkelstein, M. J. (1984). *The academic profession: A synthesis of social scientific inquiry since World War II*. Columbus, Ohio: Ohio State University Press.

10 Bayer and Smart, 1988.

11 Gibson, G. L. (1987). *Multiple authorship in the Journal of Personality and Social Psychology, 1985–1986: Probable causes, possible effects*. Unpublished doctoral dissertation, Brigham Young University.

12 Fox and Faver, 1984. Hargens, L L. (1975). *Patterns of scientific research*. Washington, DC: American Sociological Association.

13 Patel, 1973.

14 Bayer and Smart, 1988.

15 Fox and Faver, 1984; Gibson, 1987.

16 Stone, S. (1982 December). Progress in documentation: Humanities scholars' information needs and uses. *Journal of Documentation 38*, 292–313.

17 Patel, 1973.

18 Gordon, M.D. (1980). A critical assessment of inferred relations between multiple authorship, scientific collaboration, the production of papers, and their acceptance for publication. *Scientometrics 2*, 193–201.

19 Choi, J. M. (1988). An analysis of authorship in anthropology journals, 1963 and 1983. *Behavioral and Social Sciences Librarian 6*, 85–94.

20 Over, 1982.

21 Luttaca, L. (1996). Envisioning interdisciplinarity: Processes, contexts, and outcomes. Unpublished dissertation. Ann Arbor: University of Michigan.

22 Austin and Baldwin, 1991.

23 Creamer, 1999.

24 Bayer and Smart, 1988. Meadows, A. J. (1974). *Communication in science.* London: Butterworths.

25 Austin and Baldwin, 1991.

26 Beaver, D. B., and Rosen, R. (1978). Presser, S. (1980). Collaboration and the quality of research. *Social Studies of Science 10,* 95–101.

27 Smart and Bayer, 1986, p. 303.

28 Astin, H. S., and Milem, J. F. (1997). The status of academic couples in U.S. institutions. In M. A. Ferber and J. W. Loeb (Eds.), *Academic couples: Problems and promises* (pp. 128–155). Urbana, IL: University of Illinois Press, p. 139.

29 Creamer, E. G., 1999, p. 270.

30 Creamer, E. G., 1999, pp. 271–272.

31 Creamer, E. G., 1999, citing, Fox, M. F. (1983). Publication productivity among scientists: A critical review. *Social Studies of Science, 13,* 285–305.

32 Creamer, E. G., 1999, p. 274.

33 Creamer, E. G., 1999.

34 Fox and Faver, 1984.

35 Hagstrom, W. O. (1964). Traditional and modern forms of scientific teamwork. *Administrative Science Quarterly, 9,* 241–263.

36 Baldwin and Austin, 1995.

37 Gray, B. (1989). *Collaborating: Finding common ground for multiparty problems.* San Francisco, CA: Jossey-Bass, p. 227. See also: Day, R., and Day, J. V. (1977). A review of the current state of negotiated order rheory: An appreciation and a critique. *Sociological Quarterly 18,* 126–142. Goffman, E. (1983). The interaction order. *American Sociological Review, 48,* 1–17. Strauss, A., Schatzman, L., Ehrlich, D., Bucher, R., and Sabshin, M. (1963). The hospital and its negotiated order. In E. Freidson (Ed.), *The hospital in modern society.* New York: The Free Press. Strauss, D. (1978). *Negotiations: Varieties, contexts, processes, and social order.* San Francisco, CA: Jossey-Bass.

38 Baldwin and Austin, 1995, p. 59.

39 Fox, M. F., and Faver, C. A. (July, 1982). The process of collaboration in scholarly research. *Scholarly Publishing, 13,* 327–339.

40 Quoted by Baldwin and Austin, 1995, p. 60.

41 Baldwin and Austin, 1995; Fox and Faver, 1982.

42 Baldwin and Austin, 1995; Fox and Faver, 1982.

43 Austin and Baldwin, 1991.

44 Austin and Baldwin, 1991.

Notes to Chapter 14

1 Astin, H. S., and Davis, D. E. (1985). Research productivity across the life and career cycles: Facilitators and barriers for women. In *Scholarly writing and publishing: Issues, problems, and solutions,* Mary F. Fox (Ed.), pp.147–160. Boulder, CO: Westview Press. Astin, H. S., and Milem, J. F. (1997). The sta-

tus of academic couples in U.S. institutions. In M. A. Ferber and J. W. Loeb (Eds.), *Academic couples: Problems and promises* (pp. 128–155). Urbana, IL: University of Illinois Press. Davis, D. E., and Astin, H. S. (1987). Reputational standing in academe. *Journal of Higher Education, 58,* 261–275.

2   Clark, S. M., and Corcoran, M. (1986). Perspectives on the professional socialization of women faculty: A case of accumulative disadvantage? *Journal of Higher Education, 57*(1), 20–43. Crane, D. (1969). Social structure in a group of scientists: A test of the "invisible college" hypothesis. *American Sociological Review, 34,* 335–352. Fox, M. F., and Faver, C. A. (1984). Independence and cooperation in research. *Journal of Higher Education, 55,* 347–359. Hill, S. K., Bahnuik, M. H., and Dobos, J. (1989). The impact of mentoring and collegial support on faculty success: An analysis of support behavior, information adequacy, and communication apprehension. *Communication Education, 38,* 15–33. Price, D. J. (1963). Invisible colleges and the affluent scientific commuter. In *Little science, big science.* New York: Columbia University. Price, D. J., and Beaver, D. B. (1966). Collaboration in an invisible college. *American Psychologist, 21,* 1011–1018. Reskin, B. F. (1978). Sex differentiation and the social organization of science. *Sociological Inquiry, 48* (Winter), 6–37. Rose, S. M. (1985). Professional networks of junior faculty in psychology. *Psychology of Women Quarterly, 9,* 533–547.

3   Fritz, J. M. H. (1997). Men's and women's organizational peer relationships: A comparison. *Journal of Business Communication, 34,* 27–46.

4   Kram, K.E., and Isabella, L.A. (1985). Mentoring alternatives: The role of peer relationships in career development. *Academy of Management Journal, 28,* 110–132.

5   Kirchmeyer, C. (1998). Determinants of managerial career success: evidence of male/female differences. *Journal of Management, 24,* 673–692.

6   Fritz, J. M. H., 1997.

7   Schor, S. M. (1997). Separate and unequal: The nature of women's and men's career-building relationships. *Business Horizons, 40,*(5), 51–58.

8   Brass, D. J. (1985). Men's and women's networks: A study of interaction patterns and influence in organization. *Academy of Management Journal, 28,* 327–343.

9   Price, D. J., 1963.

10 Price, D. J. and Beaver, D. B., 1966.

11 Crane, D. (1969). Social structure in a group of scientists: A test of the "invisible college" hypothesis. *American Sociological Review, 34,* 335–352. Crane, D. (1972). The social organization of research areas. *Invisible colleges: Diffusion of knowledge in scientific communities.* Chicago: University of Chicago Press.

12 Bode, R. K. (1999). Mentoring and collegiality. In R. J. Menges and associates, *Faculty in new jobs: A guide to settling in, becoming established, and building institutional support* (pp.118–144). San Francisco: Jossey-Bass.

13 Hitchcock, M. A., Bland, C. J., Hekelman, F. P., and Blumenthal, M. G. (1995). Professional networks: The influences of colleagues on the aca-

demic success of faculty. *Academic Medicine, 70,* 1108–1117.

14 Bode, R. K., 1999. Sands, R. G., Parson, L. A., and Duane, J. (1991). Faculty mentoring faculty in a public university. *Journal of Higher Education, 62,* 174–193.

15 Williams, R., and Blackburn, R. T. (1988). Mentoring and faculty productivity. *Nursing Education, 5,* 204–209.

16 Bode, 1999.

17 Bode, 1999.

18 Menges, R. J. (1999). Dilemmas of newly hired faculty. In R. J. Menges and associates, *Faculty in new jobs: A guide to settling in, becoming established, and building institutional support* (pp. 19–38). San Francisco: Jossey-Bass.

19 Trautvetter, L. C. (1999). Experiences of women, experiences of men. In *Faculty in new jobs: A guide to settling in, becoming established, and building support.* San Francisco: Jossey-Bass.

20 Finkelstein, M. (1982, March). Faculty colleagueship patterns and research productivity. Paper presented at the annual meeting of the American Educational Research Association, New York, NY. (ERIC Document Reproduction Service No. ED 216 633).

21 Funded by the National Center on Postsecondary Teaching, Learning, and Assessment, the New Faculty Project followed newly hired faculty (persons hired into full-time, tenure-track positions) in five colleges and universities for a period of three years. Utilizing qualitative information from interviews and case studies and quantitative data from surveys, this longitudinal study was designed to "lead to better understanding of faculty experiences and provide a basis for easing faculty transitions into new jobs" (Menges, 1999, 20).

22 Hunter, D. E., and Kuh, G. D. (1985, March). What higher education scholars have to say about their careers. Paper presented at the Annual Meeting of the Association for the Study of Higher Education. Chicago, IL.

23 Hitchcock, et al., 1995.

24 Fox, M. F., and Faver, C. A., 1984.

25 Hill, S. K., Bahnuik, M. H., and Dobos, J., 1989.

26 Rose, 1985.

27 Olsen, D., Maple, S. A., and Stage, F. K. (1995). Women and minority faculty job satisfaction: Professional interests, professional satisfactions, and institutional fit. *Journal of Higher Education, 66,* 267–293.

28 Reskin, B. F., 1978.

29 Kaufman, D. R. (1978). Associational ties in academe: Some male and female differences. *Sex Roles, 4*(1), 9–21.

30 Parson, L. A., Sands, R. G., and Duane, J. (1992). Sources of career support for university faculty. *Research in Higher Education, 33,* 161–176.

31 Blackwell, J. E. (1988). Faculty issues: The impact on minorities. *Review of Higher Education, 11,* 417–434.

32 Alexander-Snow, M., and Johnson, B. J. (1999). Perspectives from faculty of color. In R. J. Menges and associates, *Faculty in new jobs: A guide to settling*

in, becoming established, and building institutional support. San Francisco: Jossey-Bass.

33 Bode, 1999.

34 Alexander-Snow and Johnson, 1999.

35 Tierney, W. G., and Bensimon, E. M. (1996). *Promotion and tenure: Community and socialization in academe.* Albany, NY: State University of New York Press.

Notes to Chapter 15

I would like to thank Marianne Ferber for her helpful suggestions on an earlier version of this chapter.

1 Astin, H. S., and Milem, J. F. (1997). The status of academic couples in U.S. institutions. In M. F. Ferber and J. W. Loeb (Eds.) *Academic couples: Problems and promises* (pp. 128–155). Urbana, IL: University of Illinois Press.

2 Loeb, J. W., Ferber, M. F., and Lowry, H. M. (1978). The effectiveness of affirmative action for women. *Journal of Higher Education, 49*(3), 218–230. Fairweather, J. S. (1993). Faculty reward structures: Toward institutional and professional homogenization. *Research in Higher Education, 34*(5), 603–623. Ferber, M. F., and Hoffman, E. P. (1997). Are academic partners at a disadvantage? In M. F. Ferber and J. W. Loeb (Eds.), *Academic couples: Problems and promises* (pp. 182–207). Urbana, IL: University of Illinois Press.

3 Braxton, J. M., and Bayer, A. E. (1986). *Assessing faculty scholarly performance.* In J. W. Creswell (Ed.), Measuring faculty research performance. New Directions for Institutional Research, No. 50, XIII(2). (pp. 25–42). San Francisco: Jossey-Bass.

4 Long, J. S., Allison, P. D., and McGinnis, R. (1993). Rank advancement in academic careers: Sex differences and the effects of productivity. *American Sociological Review, 58*(October), 703–722.

5 Persell, C. H. (1983). Gender, rewards, and research in education. *Psychology of Women Quarterly, 8*(1), 33–47.

6 Blackburn, R. T., and Lawrence, J. H. (1995). *Faculty at work: Motivation, expectation, satisfaction.* Baltimore, MD: Johns Hopkins University Press. Bentley, R. J., and Blackburn, R. T. (1990). Changes in academic research performance over time: A study of institutional accumulative advantage. *Research in Higher Education, 31*(4), 327–353.

7 Crane, D. (1965). Scientists at major and minor universities: A study of productivity and recognition. *American Sociological Review, 30,* 699–714.

8 Biglan, A. (1973a). The characteristics of subject matter in different academic areas. *Journal of Applied Psychology, 57*(3), 195–203. Biglan, A. (1973b). Relationships between subject matter characteristics and the structure and output of university departments. *Journal of Applied Psychology, 57*(3), 204–213.

9 Ferber, M. F., Loeb, J. W., and Lowry, H. M. (1979). Faculty patterns of publications and rewards. *Atlantic Economic Journal, 7*(2), 46–53.

10 Bentley, R., and Blackburn, R. T. (1992). Two decades of gains for female faculty? *Teachers College Record, 93*, 697–709.

11 Cole, J. R. (1979). *Fair science: Women in the scientific community.* New York: Macmillan.

12 Cole, 1979. Long, Allison, and McGinnis, 1993. Sonnert, G., and Holton, G. (1995). *Gender differences in science careers: The project access study.* New Brunswick, NJ: Rutgers University.

13 Bentley and Blackburn, 1992, p. 701.

14 Astin, H. S., and Bayer, A. E. (1973). Sex discrimination in academe. In A. S. Rossi and A. Calderwood (Eds.), *Academic women on the move* (pp. 333–356). New York: Russell Sage.

15 Loeb, J. W., and Ferber, M. F. (1971). Sex as predictive of salary and status on a university faculty. *Journal of Educational Measurement, 8*(4), 235–244.

16 Barbezat, D. (1988). Gender differences in the academic reward system. In D. W. Breneman and T. I. K. Youn (Eds.), *Academic labor markets and careers* (pp. 138–164). New York: Falmer. Ransom, M. R., and Megdal, S. B. (1993). Sex differences in the academic labor market in the affirmative action era. *Economics of Education Review, 12*(1), 12–43. Toutkoushian, R. K. (1998). Racial and marital status differences in faculty pay. *Journal of Higher Education, 69*(5), 513–541.

17 Lindsey, D. (1982). Further evidence for adjusting for multiple authorships. *Scientometrics, 4*(5), 389–395.

18 Long, J. S., and McGinnis, R. (1982). On adjusting productivity measures for multiple authorship. *Scientometrics, 4*(5), 379–387.

19 Ervin, E., and Fox, D. L. (1994). Collaboration as political action. *Journal of Advanced Composition, 14*, 53–71.

20 Burbules, N. C (1995). From the editor. *Educational theory, 45*(2), 123–4.

21 Anderson, M. S. (1996). The doctoral experience and the departmental environment. *Review of Higher Education, 19*(3), 305–326.

22 Burnett, R. E., and Ewald, J. R. (1994). Rabbit trails, ephemera, and other stories: Feminist methodology and collaborative research. *Journal of Advanced Composition, 14*, 21–51. Hafernik, J. J., Messerschmitt, D. S., and Vandrick, S. (1997). Collaborative research: Why and how? *Educational Researcher, 26*(9), 31–35.

23 Murray, B. (1998). The authorship dilemma: Who gets credit for what? *APA Monitor, 29*(12), 1, 31.

24 Merton, R. K. (1968). The Matthew effect in science. *Science, 159*, 56–63.

25 Dickens, C. S., and Sagaria, M. A. D. (1997). Feminists at work: Collaborative relationships among women faculty. *Review of Higher Education, 21*(1), 79–101.

26 Fox, M. F., and Faver, C. A. (1986). The process of collaboration in scholarly research. In M. F. Fox (Ed.), *Scholarly writing and publishing: Issues, problems, and solutions* (pp. 126–138). Boulder, CO: Westview.

27 Davis, D. E., and Astin, H. S. (1987). Reputational standing in academe. *Journal of Higher Education, 58*(3), 261–275.

28 Bentley and Blackburn, 1992.

29 Ferber, M. F. (1986). Citations: Are they an objective measure of work of men and women? *Signs, 11*, 381–389. Ferber, M. F. (1988). Citations and networking. *Gender and Society, 2*, 82–89.

30 Ward, K. B., Gast, J., and Grant, L. (1992). Visibility and dissemination of women's and men's sociological scholarship. *Social Problems, 39*(3), 291–298.

31 Long, J. S. (1992). Measures of sex differences in scientific productivity. *Social Forces, 71*(1), 159–178.

32 Cole, J. R., and Zuckerman, H. (1984). The productivity puzzle: Persistence and change in patterns of publication of men and women scientists. In M. W. Steinkamp and M. L. Maehr (Eds.), *Advances in motivation and achievement: vol. 2. Women in science* (pp. 217–258). Greenwich, CT: JAI Press.

33 Wenneras, C., and Wold, A. (1997, May 22). Nepotism and sexism in peer review. *Nature, 387*, 341–343.

34 Beaver, D. B., and Rosen, R. (1978). Studies in scientific collaboration, part I: The professional origins of scientific coauthorship. *Scientometrics, 1*(1), 69.

35 Rossiter, M. W. (1993). The Matilda effect in science. *Social Studies of Science, 23*(2), 325–341.

36 Pycior, H. M. (1993). Reaping the benefits of collaboration while avoiding its pitfalls: Marie Curie's rise to scientific prominence. *Social Studies of Science, 23*(2), 301–323.

37 Grant, L., Ward, K. B., and Forshner, C. (1993, April). Mentoring, gender, and careers of academic scientists. Paper presented at the annual meeting of the American Educational Research Association, Atlanta, GA.

38 Long, J. S. (1990). The origins of sex differences in science. *Social Forces, 68*(4), 1297–1315.

39 Clark, S. M., and Corcoran, M. (1986). Perspectives on the professional socialization of women faculty. *Journal of Higher Education, 57*(1), 20–43. Grant, Ward, and Forshner, 1993.

40 Grant, Ward, and Forshner, 1993.

41 Clark and Corcoran, 1986. Sonnert and Holton, 1995.

42 Sonnert and Holton, 1995.

43 Reskin, B. (1978). Sex differentiation and the social organization of science. *Sociological Inquiry, 48*(3–4), 6–37.

44 Dey, E. L., Milem, J. F., and Berger, J. B.(1997). Changing patterns of publication productivity: Accumulative advantage or institutional isomorphism? *Sociology of Education, 70*(4), 308–323. Bentley and Blackburn, 1990.

45 Cole, 1979; Sonnert and Holton, 1995; Astin and Milem 1997.

46 Cole, 1979; Cole and Zuckerman, 1984.

47 Bentley and Blackburn, 1992; Zuckerman, H. (1991). The careers of men and women scientists: A review of current research. In H. Zuckerman, J. R. Cole, and J. T. Bruer (Eds.), *The outer circle* (pp. 27–56). New York: Norton.

48 Bellas, M. (1997). The scholarly productivity of academic couples. In M. F.

Ferber and J. W. Loeb (Eds.), *Academic couples: Problems and promises* (pp. 156–181). Urbana, IL: University of Illinois Press. Sonnert, 1995.

49 Cole, J. R., and Zuckerman, H. (1991). Marriage, motherhood, and research performance in science. In H. Zuckerman, J. R. Cole, and J. T. Bruer (Eds.), *The outer circle* (pp. 157–170). New York: Norton. Fox and Faver, 1986a. Fox, M. F., and Faver, C. A. (1986b). Men, women, and publication productivity: Patterns among social work academics. *Sociological Quarterly, 26*(4), 537–549.

50 Sonnert and Holton, 1995; Long, 1990; Astin, H. S., and Davis, D. C. (1985b). Research productivity across the life and career cycles: facilitators and barriers for women. In M. F. Fox (Ed.), *Scholarly writing and publishing: Issues, problems, and solutions* (pp. 147–160). Boulder, CO: Westview. Cole, 1979.

51 Sonnert and Holton, 1995; Long, 1990.

52 Cole, J. R., and Singer, B. (1991). A theory of limited differences: Explaining the productivity puzzle in science. In H. Zuckerman, J. R. Cole, and J. T. Bruer (Eds.), *The outer circle* (pp. 277–310). New York: Norton.

53 Dey, Milem, and Berger, 1997; Bentley and Blackburn, 1992.

54 Astin and Milem, 1997; Astin and Davis, 1985b; Bentley and Blackburn, 1992; Bellas, 1997.

55 Bellas, 1997.

56 Long, J. S., and McGinnis, R. (1981). Organizational context and scientific productivity. *American Sociological Review, 46*(4), 422–442.

57 Lawrence, J. H., and Blackburn, R. T. (1985). Faculty careers: Maturation, demographic, and historical effects. *Research in Higher Education, 22*(2), 135–154.

58 Creamer, E. G., and McGuire, S. P. (1998). Applying the cumulative advantage perspective to scholarly writers in higher education. *Review of Higher Education, 22*(1), 73–82.

59 Long, J. S., and McGinnis, R. (1985). The effects of the mentor on the academic career. *Scientometrics, 7*(3–6), 255–280.

60 Long and McGinnis, 1985.

61 Long and McGinnis, 1985; Grant, Ward, and Forshner, 1993.

62 Hunter, D. E., and Kuh, G. D. (1987). The "write wing": Characteristics of prolific contributors to the higher education literature. *Journal of Higher Education, 58*(4), 443–462.

63 Sonnert and Holton, 1995, p. 116.

64 Wells, W. P., and Pelz, D. C. (1966). Groups. In D. C. Pelz and F. M. Andrews, *Scientists in organizations* (pp. 240–260). New York: Wiley.

65 Creamer, E. G. (1998b). Co-authorship and recognition among academic couples. Research/scholarly paper presented at the 1998 ASHE National Conference. Miami, FL.

66 Creamer, 1998.

67 Creamer, E. G. (1999). Knowledge production, publication productivity, and intimate partnerships. *Journal of Higher Education, 70*(3), 261–277.

Notes to Chapter 16

1 Hochschild, A. R. (1997). *Time bind: When work becomes home and home becomes work.* New York: Metropolitan Books. Henry Holt and Company.

2 This explanation is referred to as entitlement or equity theory and comes from the work of a dual-career academic couple, Denise Bielby and William Bielby. Bielby, D. D., and Bielby, W. T. (1988). She works hard for the money: Household responsibilities and the allocation of work effort. *American Journal of Sociology, 5,* 1031–1059).

3 Astin, H. S., and Milem, J. F. (1997). The status of academic couples in U.S. institutions. In M. A. Ferber and J. W. Loeb (Eds.), *Academic couples: Problems and promises* (pp. 128–155). Urbana, IL: University of Illinois Press.

4 Creamer, E. G. (2000, forthcoming). Intimate partnerships and publication productivity. In J. Smart (Ed.), *Higher education: Handbook of theory and research, vol. 16.* Edison, NJ: Agathon.

5 Hertz, R. (1986). *More equal than others: Women and men in dual-career marriages.* Berkeley, CA: University of California Press. Risman, B. J. (1998). *Gender vertigo: American families in transition.* New Haven, CT: Yale University Press. Steil, J. M. (1997). *Marital equality: Its relationship to the well-being of husbands and wives.* Thousand Oaks, CA: Sage.

6 Hertz, R., 1986.

7 Hochschild, 1997.

8 Bielby, W. T., and Bielby, D. D. (1992). I will follow him: Family ties, gender role beliefs, and reluctance to relocate for a better job. *American Journal of Sociology, 97*(5), 1241–1267.

9 Schwartz, P. (1994). *Love between equals: How peer marriages really work.* New York: The Free Press.

10 Ferree, M. M. (1991). The gender division of labor in two-earner marriages. *Journal of Family Issues, 12*(2), 158–180.

11 Schwartz, P., 1994.

12 Rosenbluth, S. C., Steil, J. M., and Whitcomb, J. H. (1998). Marital equality: What does it mean? *Journal of Family Issues, 19*(3), 227–244.

13 Scanzoni, L., and Scanzoni, J. (1976). *Men, women, and change: A sociology of marriage and family.* McGraw-Hill.

14 Heilbrun, C. G. (1997). *The last gift of time: Life beyond sixty.* New York: Ballantine Books.

15 Heilbrun, C. G. (1988). *Writing a woman's life.* New York: Balantine Books, p. 81.

16 Heilbrun, 1988, p. 95.

17 Astin and Milem, 1997.

18 Cole, J. R., and Zuckerman, H. (1987, February). Marriage, motherhood, and research performance in science. *Scientific American,* 119–125.

19 Xie, Y., and Shauman, K. A. (1998). Sex differences in research productivity: New evidence about an old puzzle. *American Sociological Review, 63,* 860.

20 Karen Blaisure and Katherine Allen reported that this is one way heterosex-

ual couples publicly demonstrate a commitment to egalitarianism (Blaisure, K. R., and Allen, K. R. (1995). Feminists and the ideology and practice of marital equality. *Journal of Marriage and Family, 57,* 5–19). Barbara Risman and Johnson-Sumerford (1998) interpreted it to reflect an early commitment to egalitarianism. Risman, B. J., and Johnson-Sumerford, D. (1998). Doing it fairly: A study of post-gender families. *Journal of Marriage and Family, 60,* 23–40.

21 Ferree, 1991.

22 Hunt, J. G., and Hunt, L. L. (1982). The dualities of careers and families: New integration or new polarization? *Social Problems, 29*(5), 499–510.

23 Rosenbluth, et al., 1998.

24 In a study that challenges the utility of traditional mentoring models for women, Gerhard Sonnert observed that part of the reason that women received disproportionately fewer long-term benefits in terms of productivity from collaboration with a senior mentor is that they assumed sex-appropriate, lower-order tasks, thus not gaining the skills necessary to enable future research. Sonnert, G., and Holton, G. (1995). *Gender differences in science careers: The Project Access study.* New Brunswick, NJ: Rutgers University Press.

25 Cohen, B. P., Kruse, R. J., and Anbar, M. (1982). The social structure of scientific research teams. *Pacific Sociological Review, 25*(2), 205–232.

26 Schwartz, 1994.

27 Phyllis Rose used the expression "parallel lives" in the title of her 1984 book about the contribution of a spouse or partner to the work of five well-known Victorian writers. Rose, P. (1984). *Parallel lives.* New York: Vintage Books.

28 Reskin, B. F. (1988). Bringing the men back in: Sex differentiation and the devaluation of women's work. *Gender and Society, 2*(1), 58–81.

29 Schwartz, 1994.

30 Creamer, E. G. (1999). Knowledge production, publication productivity, and intimate academic partnerships. *Journal of Higher Education, 70*(3), 261–277.

31 Hertz, 1986.

32 McLaughlin, S. D., Melber, B. D., Billy, J. O. G., Zimmerle, D. M., Winges, L. D., and Johnson, T. R. (1988). *The changing lives of American women.* Chapel Hill, NC: University of North Carolina Press.

33 Risman, B. J., 1998.

34 Abir-Am, P. G., and Outram, D. (Eds.). (1987). *Uneasy careers and intimate lives: Women in science 1789–1979.* New Brunswick, NJ: Rutgers University Press, p. 11.

35 Reskin, B. F., 1988.

36 Schneider, A. (1998, September 11). Why don't women publish as much as men? *Chronicle of Higher Education, XLV*(3), A14–A16.

37 Creamer, E. G. (1998). *Assessing faculty publishing productivity: Issues of equity.* ASHE–ERIC Higher Education Report Volume 26, No. 2. Washington, DC: George Washington University, School of Education and Human Development.

38 Blackburn, R. T., and Lawrence, J. H. (1996). *Faculty at work: Motivation, expectation, satisfaction.* Baltimore, MD: Johns Hopkins University Press.

39 Hochschild, A. R., 1997.

40 In Chapter 15, Jane Loeb summarizes the research that has demonstrated that both married men and women faculty outpublish unmarried faculty.

41 Wilson, R. (1999, June 25). Timing is everything: Academe's annual baby boom. *Chronicle of Higher Education, XLV*(42), A14–A15.

42 For example, Wolf-Wendal, L. E., Twombly, S., and Rice, S. (1998, November). Dual career couples: How institutions are keeping them together. Unpublished paper presented at the annual meeting of the Association for the Study of Higher Education. Miami, FL. Snyder, J. K. (1990). *Comparison of university practices in dual career couple issues.* Virginia Polytechnic Institute and State University Institutional Research and Planning Analysis Document 89–90, 53A.

43 See Snyder, J. K. (1990).

44 This was the conclusion reached by Julie Snyder (1990) after analyzing the results from a survey of institutional policies conducted by the Institutional Research Department at Virginia Polytechnic Institute and State University (VA Tech, Document 89–90, 53A).

45 Noel Collier-Bajczyk of Washington State University raised this point in her presentation of a research paper, The slippery slope: Partner accommodation and retention of dual career couples in academia, at the Association for the Study of Higher Education National Conference in San Antonio, TX, November 1999.

46 Wilson, R. (1996, September 20). Weary of commuter marriages, more couples in academe make career sacrifices to be together. *Chronicle of Higher Education, XLIII*(4), A10–A11.

47 Deis, E., and Frye, L. (1993). Balancing the personal and the professional: A shared appointment, the 50–50 solution. *Written Communication, 10,* 420–437.

48 See bell hooks (1984), Rethinking the nature of work. In *Feminist theory: From margin to center.* Boston, MA: South End Press.

49 Leatherman, C. (1999, July 16). At NYU, the parallel careers of 2 mathematicians. *Chronicle of Higher Education, XLV*(5), A15.

Note to Appendix A

1 Faculty attitudes and characteristics: Results of a 1995–96 survey. (1996, September 13). *The Chronicle of Higher Education,* p. A12–A15.

References

Abir-Am, P. G., and Outram, D. (Eds.). (1987). *Uneasy careers and intimate lives: Women in science 1789–1979.* New Brunswick, NJ: Rutgers University Press.

Alexander-Snow, M., and Johnson, B. J. (1999). Perspectives from faculty of color. In R.J. Menges and associates, *Faculty in new jobs: A guide to settling in, becoming established, and building support.* San Francisco: Jossey-Bass.

Anderson, M. S. (1996). The doctoral experience and the departmental environment. *Review of Higher Education, 19*(3), 305–326.

Astin, H. S., and Bayer, A. E. (1973). Sex discrimination in academe. In A. S. Rossi and A. Calderwood (Eds.), *Academic women on the move* (pp. 333–356). New York: Russell Sage.

Astin, H. S., and Davis, D. E. (1985a). Research productivity across the life and career cycles: Facilitator and barriers for women. Reprinted in J. S. Glazer, E. M. Bensimon, B. K. Townsend (Eds.), (1993), *Women in higher education: A feminist perspective* (pp. 415–423). Needham Heights, MA: ASHE Reader Series, Ginn Press.

Astin, H. S., and Davis, D. E. (1985b). Research productivity across the life and career cycles: Facilitators and barriers for women. In *Scholarly writing and publishing: Issues, problems, and solutions,* Mary F. Fox (Ed.), pp. 147–160. Boulder, CO: Westview.

Astin, H. S., and Milem, J. F. (1997). The status of academic couples in U.S. institutions. In M. A. Ferber and J. W. Loeb (Eds.), *Academic couples: Problems and promises* (pp. 128–155). Urbana, IL: University of Illinois Press.

Austin, A. E. (1996, November). Relationship, epistemology and community: Autobiographical reflections on collaboration. Paper presented at the Association for the Study of Higher Education Annual Meeting, Memphis, TN.

Austin, A. E., and Baldwin, R. G. (1991). *Faculty collaboration: Enhancing the quality of scholarship and teaching.* ASHE-ERIC Higher Education Report No. 7. Washington, DC: George Washington University, School of Education and Human Services.

Austin, A. E., and Pilat, M. (1990, January–February). Tension, stress, and the tapestry of faculty lives. *Academe,* 38–42.

Baldwin, R. G., and Austin, A. E. (1995). Toward greater understanding of faculty research collaboration. (1995). *Review of Higher Education, 19* (2), 45–70.

Barbezat, D. (1988). Gender differences in the academic reward system. In D. W. Breneman and T. I. K. Young (Eds.), *Academic labor markets and careers* (pp. 138–164). New York: Falmer.

Baum, W. C., Griffiths, G. N., Matthews, R., and Scherruble, D. (1976). American political science before the mirror: What our journals reveal about the profession. *Journal of Politics, 38,* 895–917.

Bayer, A. E., and Smart, J. C. (1988, April). Author collaborative styles in academic scholarship. Paper presented at the annual meeting of the American Educational Research Association, New Orleans, LA.

Bayer, A. E., and Smart, J. C. (1991). Career publication patterns and collaborative "styles" in American academic science. *Journal of Higher Education, 62,* 613–636.

Beaver, D. B., and Rosen, R. (1978). Studies in scientific collaboration, part I: The professional origins of scientific coauthorship. *Scientometrics, 1*(1), 69.

Beaver, D. B., and Rosen, R. (1979). Studies in scientific collaboration, part III. *Scientometrics, 1,* 213–245.

Bellas, M. L. (1997). The scholarly productivity of academic couples. In M. A. Ferber and J. W. Loeb (Eds.), *Academic couples: Problems and promises* (pp. 156–181). Urbana, IL: University of Illinois Press.

Bentley, R., and Blackburn, R. T. (1990). Changes in academic research performance over time: A study of institutional accumulative advantage. *Research in Higher Education, 31*(4), 327–345.

Bentley, R., and Blackburn, R. T. (1992). Two decades of gains for female faculty? *Teachers College Record, 93,* 697–709.

Bielby, D. D., and Bielby, W. T. (1988). She works hard for the money: Household responsibilities and the allocation of work effort. *American Journal of Sociology, 5,* 1031–1059.

Bielby, W. T., and Bielby, D. D. (1992). I will follow him: Family ties, gender role beliefs, and reluctance to relocate for a better job. *American Journal of Sociology, 97*(5), 1241–1267.

Biglan, A. (1973a). The characteristics of subject matter in different academic areas. *Journal of Applied Psychology, 57*(3), 195–203.

Biglan, A. (1973b). *Relationships between subject matter characteristics and the structure and output of university departments.* Baltimore, MD: Johns Hopkins University Press.

Blackburn, R. T., and Lawrence, J. H. (1996). *Faculty at work: Motivation, expectation, satisfaction.* Baltimore, MD: The Johns Hopkins University Press.

Blackwell, J. E. (1988). Faculty issues: The impact on minorities. *Review of Higher Education, 11,* 417–434.

Blaisure, K. R., and Allen, K. R. (1995). Feminists and the ideology and practice of marital equality. *Journal of Marriage and Family, 57,* 5–19.

Bode, R. K. (1999). Mentoring and collegiality. In R. J. Menges and associates, *Faculty in new jobs: A guide to settling in, becoming established, and building support* (pp. 118–144). San Francisco: Jossey-Bass.

Bourdieu, P. (1991). *Language and symbolic power.* Cambridge, MA: Harvard University Press.

Bowen, H. R., and Schuster, J. H. (1986). *American professors: A national resource imperiled.* New York: Oxford University Press.

Brady, L. A. (1988). *Collaborative literary writing: Issues of authorship and authority.* unpublished Ph.D. dissertation, University of Minnesota.

Brass, D. J. (1985). Men's and women's networks: A study of interaction patterns and influence in organization. *Academy of Management Journal, 28,* 327–343.

Braxton, J. M., and Bayer, A. E. (1986). Assessing faculty scholarly performance. In J. W. Creswell (Ed.), *Measuring faculty research performance* (pp. 25–42). New Directions for Institutional Research, No. 50. San Francisco: Jossey-Bass.

Burbules, N. C. (1995). From the editor. *Educational Theory, 45*(2), 123–124.

Burnett, R. E., and Ewald, J. R. (1994). Rabbit trails, ephemera, and other stories: Feminist methodology and collaborative research. *Journal of Advanced Composition, 14,* 21–51.

Cannon, K. (1995). *Katie's canon: Womanism and the soul of the black community.* New York: Continuum.

Chadwick, W., and De Courtivron, I. (Eds.). (1993). *Significant others: Creativity and intimate partnerships.* London: Thames and Hudson.

Choi, J. M. (1988). An analysis of authorship in anthropology journals, 1963 and 1983. *Behavioral and Social Sciences Librarian, 6,* 85–94.

Clark, S. M., and Corcoran, M. (1986). Perspectives on the professional socialization of women faculty: A case of accumulative disadvantage? *Journal of Higher Education, 57*(1), 20–43.

Cohen, B. P., Kruse, R. J., and Anbar, M. (1982). The social structure of scientific research teams. *Pacific Sociological Review, 25*(2), 205–232.

Cole, J. R. (1979). *Fair science: Women in the scientific community.* New York: The Free Press.

Cole, J. R., and Singer, B. (1991). A theory of limited differences: Explaining the productivity puzzle in science. In H. Zuckerman, J. R. Cole, and J. T. Bruer (Eds.), *The outer circle: Women in the scientific community* (pp. 277–310). New York: Norton.

Cole, J. R., and Zuckerman, H. (1984). The productivity puzzle: Persistence and change in patterns of publication of men and women scientists. In M. W. Steinkamp and M. L. Maehr (Eds.), *Advances in motivation and achievement: Vol. 2. Women in science* (pp. 217–258). Greenwich, CT: JAI Press.

Cole, J. R., and Zuckerman, H. (1987, February). Marriage, motherhood, and research performance in science. *Scientific American,* 119–125.

Collier-Bajczyk, N. (1999, November). The slippery slope: Partner accommodation and retention of dual career couples in academia. Paper presented at the Association for the Study of Higher Education 1999 national conference in San Antonio, TX.

Crane, D. (1965). Scientists at major universities: A study of productivity and recognition. *American Sociological Review, 30,* 699–714.

Crane, D. (1969). Social structure in a group of scientists: A test of the "invisible college" hypothesis. *American Sociological Review, 34,* 335–352.

Crane, D. (1972). The social organization of research areas. *Invisible colleges: Diffusion of knowledge in scientific communities*. Chicago: University of Chicago Press.

Creamer, E. G. (1994). Gender and publications in core higher education journals. *Journal of College Student Development, 35*, 35–39.

Creamer, E. G. (1995). The scholarly productivity of female academics. *Initiatives (Journal of the National Association of Women in Education), 57*(1), 1–9.

Creamer, E.G. (1996). The perceived contribution of academic partners to women's publishing productivity. ERIC Document: HE 029 768.

Creamer, E. G. (1998a). *Assessing faculty publishing productivity: Issues of equity.* ASHE/ERIC Higher Education Report Volume 26, No. 2. Washington, DC: The George Washington University, School of Education and Human Development.

Creamer, E. G. (1998b, November). Coauthorship and recognition among academic couples. Research/scholarly paper presented at the Association for the Study of Higher Education National Conference. Miami, FL.

Creamer, E.G. (1999). Knowledge production, publication productivity, and intimate academic partnerships. *Journal of Higher Education, 70*(3), 261–277.

Creamer, E. G. (2001, forthcoming). Intimate partnerships and publication productivity. In J. Smart (Ed.), *Higher education: Handbook of theory and research, vol. 16.* Edison, NJ: Agathon.

Creamer, E. G., and McGuire, S. P. (1998). Applying the cumulative advantage perspective to scholarly writers in higher education. *Review of Higher Education, 22*(1), 73–82.

Davis, D. E., and Astin, H. S. (1987). Reputational standing in academe. *Journal of Higher Education, 58*, 261–275.

Day, R., and Day, J. V. (1977). A review of the current state of negotiated order theory: An appreciation and a critique. *Sociological Quarterly, 18*, 126–142.

Deis, E., and Frye, L. (1993). Balancing the personal and the professional: A shared appointment, the 50–50 solution. *Written Communication, 10*, 420–437.

Dey, E. L., Milem, J., and Berger, J. B. (1997). Changing patterns of publication productivity: Accumulative advantage or institutional isomorphism? *Sociology of Education, 70*(4), 308–323.

Dickens, C. S., and Sagaria, M. A. (1997). Feminists at work: Collaborative relationships among women faculty. *Review of Higher Education, 21*(1), 79–101.

DuBois, W. E. B. (1990). *The souls of black folk.* New York: Vintage Books.

Eisler, B. (1991). *O'Keeffe and Stieglitz.* New York: Penguin Books.

Ervin, E., and Fox, D. L. (1994). Collaboration as political action. *Journal of Advanced Composition, 14*, 53–71.

Fairweather, J. S. (1993). Faculty reward structures: Toward institutional and professional homogenization. *Research in Higher Education, 35*(4), 603–623.

Ferber, M. F. (1986). Citations: Are they an objective measure of work of men and women? *Signs, 11*, 381–389.

Ferber, M. F. (1988). Citations and networking. *Gender and Society, 2*, 82–89.

Ferber, M. F., and Hoffman, E. P. (1997). Are academic partners at a disadvantage? In M. F. Ferber and J. W. Loeb (Eds.) *Academic couples: Problems and promises* (pp. 182–207). Urbana, IL: University of Illinois Press.

Ferber, M. A., and Loeb, J. W. (Eds.). (1997). *Academic couples: Problems and promises*. Urbana, IL: University of Illinois Press.

Ferber, M. F., Loeb, J. W., and Lowry, H. M. (1979). Faculty patterns of publications and rewards. *Atlantic Economic Journal, 7*(2), 46–53.

Ferree, M. M. (1991). The gender division of labor in two-earner marriages. *Journal of Family Issues, 12*(2), 158–180.

Fine, M. (1994). Working the hyphens. In N. K. Denzin and Y. S. Lincoln (Eds.), *Handbook of qualitative research*, 1st ed. (pp. 70–82). Thousand Oaks, CA: Sage.

Finkelstein, M. J. (1982, March). Faculty colleagueship patterns and research productivity. Paper presented at the annual meeting of the American Educational Research Association, New York, NY. (ERIC Document Reproduction Service No. ED 216 633).

Finkelstein, M. J. (1984). *The academic profession: A synthesis of social scientific inquiry since World War II*. Columbus, OH: Ohio State University Press.

Finkelstein, M. J., Seal, R. K., and Schuster, J. H. (1998). *The new academic generation*. Baltimore, MD: Johns Hopkins University Press.

Fox, M. F. (1983). Publication productivity among scientists: A critical review. *Social Studies of Science, 13*, 285–305.

Fox, M. F., and Faver, C. A. (1982, July). The process of collaboration in scholarly research. *Scholarly Publishing, 13*, 327–339.

Fox, M. F., and Faver, C. A. (1984). Independence and cooperation in research: The motivations and costs of collaboration. *Journal of Higher Education, 55*(3), 347–359.

Fox, M. F., and Faver, C. A. (1986a). The process of collaboration in scholarly research. In M. F. Fox (Ed.), *Scholarly writing and publishing: Issues, problems, and solutions* (pp. 126–138). Boulder, CO: Westview.

Fox, M. F., and Faver, C. A. (1986b). Men, women, and publication productivity: Patterns among social work academics. *Sociological Quarterly, 26*(4), 537–549.

Friere, P. (1982). *Pedagogy of the oppressed*. New York: Continuum.

Fritz, J. M. H. (1997). Men's and women's organizational peer relationships: A comparison. *Journal of Business Communication, 34*, 27–46.

Gibson, G. L. (1987). *Multiple authorship in the Journal of Personality and Social Psychology, 1985–1986: Probable causes, possible effects*. Unpublished doctoral dissertation, Brigham Young University.

Gilbert, S. M., and Gubar, S. (1979). *The madwoman in the attic: The woman writer and the nineteenth-century literary imagination*. New Haven, CT: Yale University Press.

Goffman, E. (1983). The interaction order. *American Sociological Review, 48*, 1–17.

Gordon, M. D. (1980). A Critical assessment of inferred relations between multiple authorship, scientific collaboration, the production of papers, and their acceptance for publication. *Scientometrics, 2*, 193–201.

Grant, L., Ward, K. B., and Forshner, C. (1993, April). Mentoring, gender, and careers of academic scientists. Paper presented at the annual meeting of the American Educational Research Association, Atlanta, GA.

Gray, B. (1989). *Collaborating: Finding common ground for multiparty problems.* San Francisco, CA: Jossey-Bass.

Hafernik, J. J., Messerschmitt, D. S., and Vandrick, S. (1997). Collaborative research: Why and how? *Educational Researcher, 26*(9), 31–35.

Hagstrom, W. O. (1964). Traditional and modern forms of scientific teamwork. *Administrative Science Quarterly, 9,* 241–263.

Hargens, L. L. (1975). *Patterns of scientific research.* Washington, DC: American Sociological Association.

Heilbrun, C. G. (1988). *Writing a woman's life.* New York: Ballantine Books.

Hertz, R. (1986). *More equal than others: Women and men in dual-career marriages.* Berkeley, CA: University of California Press.

Hill, S. K., Bahnuik, M. H., and Dobos, J. (1989). The impact of mentoring and collegial support on faculty success: An analysis of support behavior, information adequacy, and communication apprehension. *Communication Education, 38,* 15–33.

Hitchcock, M. A., Bland, C. J., Hekelman, F. P., and Blumenthal, M. G. (1995). Professional networks: The influences of colleagues on the academic success of faculty. *Academic Medicine, 70,* 1108–1116.

Hochschild, A. R. (1997). *Time bind: When work becomes home and home becomes work.* New York: Metropolitan Books. Henry Holt and Company.

hooks, b. (1984). *Feminist theory: From margin to center.* Boston, MA: South End Press.

hooks, b. (1994). *Teaching to transgress: Education and the practice of freedom.* New York: Routledge.

Hunt, J. G., and Hunt, L. L. (1982). The dualities of careers and families: New integration or new polarization? *Social Problems, 29*(5), 499–510.

Hunter, D. E., and Kuh, G. D. (1985, March). What higher education scholars have to say about their careers. Paper presented at the Annual Meeting of the Association for the Study of Higher Education. Chicago, IL.

Hunter, D. E., and Kuh, G. D. (1987). The "write wing": Characteristics of prolific contributors to the higher education literature. *Journal of Higher Education, 58,* 443–462.

Kaufman, D. R. (1978). Associational ties in academe: Some male and female differences. *Sex Roles, 4*(1), 9–21.

Kirchmeyer, C. (1998). Determinants of managerial career success: evidence of male/female differences. *Journal of Management, 24,* 673–692.

Kram, K. E., and Isabella, L. A. (1985). Mentoring alternatives: The role of peer relationships in career development. *Academy of Management Journal, 28,* 110–132.

Lawrence, J. H., and Blackburn, R. T. (1985). Faculty careers: Maturation, demographic, and historical effects. *Research in Higher Education, 22* (2), 135–154.

Lawrence-Lightfoot, S., and Davis, J. H. (1997). *The art and science of portraiture.* San Francisco: Jossey-Bass.

Leatherman, C. (1999, July 16). At NYU, the parallel careers of 2 mathematicians. *Chronicle of Higher Education, LXV*(45), A15.

Lincoln, Y. S. (1996, November). Chair and Organizer, Symposium, The intimate critic: Psychological rewards of academic collaboration. Annual Meeting, Association for the Study of Higher Education, Memphis, TN.

Lindsey, D. (1982). Further evidence for adjusting for multiple authorships. *Scientometrics, 4*(5), 389–395.

Loeb, J. W., and Ferber, M. F. (1971). Sex as predictive of salary and status on a university faculty. *Journal of Educational Measurement, 8*(4), 235–244.

Loeb, J. W., Ferber, M. F., and Lowry, H. M. (1978). The effectiveness of affirmative action for women. *Journal of Higher Education, 49*(3), 218–230.

Long, J. S. (1990). The origins of sex differences in science. *Social Forces, 68*(4), 1297–1315.

Long, J. S. (1992). Measures of sex differences in scientific productivity. *Social Forces, 71,* 159–178.

Long, J. S., Allison, P. D., and McGinnis, R. (1993). Rank advancement in academic careers: Sex differences and the effects of productivity. *American Sociological Review, 58*(October), 703–722.

Long, J. S., and Fox, M. F. (1995). Scientific careers: Universalism and particularism. *Annual Review of Sociology, 21,* 45–71.

Long, J. S., and McGinnis, R. (1981). Organizational context and scientific productivity. *American Sociological Review, 46*(4), 422–442.

Long, J. S., and McGinnis, R. (1982). On adjusting productivity measures for multiple authorship. *Scientometrics, 4*(5), 379–387.

Long, J. S., and McGinnis, R. (1985). The effects of the mentor on the academic career. *Scientometrics, 7*(3–6), 255–280.

Luttaca, L. (1996). Envisioning interdisciplinarity: Processes, contexts, and outcomes. Unpublished dissertation. Ann Arbor: University of Michigan.

Mackie, M. (1977). Professional women's collegial relations and productivity: Female sociologists' journal publications, 1967 and 1973. *Sociology and Social Research, 61,* 277–293.

Magolda, P., and Baxter Magolda, M. B. (1998). Book review of academic couples: Problems and promises. *Journal of College Student Development, 39,* 299–302.

Meadows, A. J. 1974. *Communication in science.* London: Butterworths.

Menges, R. J. (1999). Dilemmas of newly hired faculty. In R. J. Menges and associate, *Faculty in new jobs: A guide to settling in, becoming established, and building support.* (pp. 19–38). San Francisco: Jossey-Bass.

Merton, R. K. (1968). The Matthew effect in science. *Science, 159,* 56–63.

McLaughlin, S. D., Melber, B. D., Billy, J. O. G., Zimmerle, D. M., Winges, L. D., and Johnson, T. R. (1988). *The changing lives of American women.* Chapel Hill, NC: University of North Carolina Press.

Murray, B. (1998). The authorship dilemma: Who gets credit for what? *APA Monitor, 29*(12), 1, 31.

Olsen, D., Maple, S. A., and Stage, F. K. (1995). Women and minority faculty job satisfaction: Professional interests, professional satisfactions, and institutional fit. *Journal of Higher Education, 66,* 267–293.

Over, R. (1982, September). Collaborative research and publication in psychology. *American Psychologist 37,* 996–1001.

Parson, L. A., Sands, R. G., and Duane, J. (1992). Sources of career support for university faculty. *Research in Higher Education, 33,* 161–176.

Patel, N. (1973). Collaboration in the professional growth of American sociology. *Social Science Information, 12,* 77–92.

Perry, R., and Brownley, M. W. (Eds.). (1984). *Mothering the mind: Twelve studies of writers and their silent partners.* New York: Holmes and Meier.

Persell, C. H. (1983). Gender, rewards, and research in education. *Psychology of Women Quarterly, 8*(1), 33–47.

Presser, S. (1980). Collaboration and the quality of research. *Social Studies of Science 10,* 95–101.

Price, D. J. (1963). Invisible colleges and the affluent scientific commuter. *Little science, big science.* New York: Columbia University Press.

Price, D. J., and Beaver, D.B. (1966). Collaboration in an invisible college. *American Psychologist, 21,* 1011–1018.

Pycior, H. M. (1993). Reaping the benefits of collaboration while avoiding its pitfalls: Marie Curie's rise to scientific prominence. *Social Studies of Science, 23,* 301–323.

Pycior, H. M., Slack, N. G., and Abir-Am, P. G. (Eds.). (1996). *Creative couples in the sciences.* New Brunswick, NJ: Rutgers University Press.

Ransom, M. R., and Megdal, S. B. (1993). Sex differences in the academic labor market in the affirmative action era. *Economics of Education Review, 12*(1), 12–43.

Reskin, B. F. (1978). Sex differentiation and the social organization of science. *Sociological Inquiry, 48* (winter), 6–37.

Reskin, B. F. (1988). Bringing the men back in: Sex differentiation and the devaluation of women's work. *Gender and Society, 2*(1), 58–81.

Risman, B. J. (1998). *Gender vertigo: American families in transition.* New Haven, CT: Yale University Press.

Risman, B. J., and Johnson-Sumerford, D. (1998). Doing it fairly: A study of post-gender families. *Journal of Marriage and Family, 60,* 23–40.

Rose, P. (1984). *Parallel lives.* New York: Vintage Books.

Rose, S.M. (1985). Professional networks of junior faculty in psychology. *Psychology of Women Quarterly, 9,* 533–547.

Rosenbluth, S. C., Steil, J. M., and Whitcomb, J. H. (1998). Marital equality: What does it mean? *Journal of Family Issues, 19*(3), 227–244.

Rossiter, M. W. (1993). The Matilda effect in science. *Social Studies of Science, 23*(2), 325–341.

Sands, R. G., Parson, L. A, and Duane, J. (1991). Faculty mentoring faculty in a public university. *Journal of Higher Education, 62,* 174–193.

Scanzoni, L., and Scanzoni, J. (1976). *Men, women, and change: A sociology of marriage and family.* New York: McGraw-Hill.

Schneider, A. (1998, September 11). Why don't women publish as much as men? *Chronicle of Higher Education, XLV*(3), A14–A16.

Schor, S. M. (1997). Separate and unequal: The nature of women's and men's career-building relationships. *Business Horizons, 40*(5), 51–58.

Schwartz, P. (1994). *Love between equals: How peer marriages really work.* New York: The Free Press.

Shapiro, E., Haseltine, F., and Rowe, M. (1978). Moving up: Role models, mentors, and the patron system. *Sloan Management Review, 19,* 51–58.

Shea, C. (1997, May 9). For these scholarly authors, more is better. *Chronicle of Higher Education, 43,* A13–A14.

Smart, J. C., and Bayer, A. E. (1986). Author collaboration and impact: A note on citation rates of single-authored and multiple-authored articles. *Scientometrics, 10,* 297–305.

Smart, M. S., and Smart, R. C. (1990, January-February). Paired prospects: Dual-career couples on campus. *Academe,* 33–37.

Snyder, J. K. (1990). *Comparison of university practices in dual career couple issues.* Virginia Polytechnic Institute and State University Institutional Research and Planning Analysis Document 89–90. (53a).

Sonnert, G., and Holton, G. (1995). *Gender differences in science careers: The Project Access Study.* New Brunswick, NJ: Rutgers University Press.

Stake, R. (1994). Case studies. In N. K. Denzin and Y. S. Lincoln (Eds.), *Handbook of qualitative research* (pp. 236–247). Thousand Oaks, CA: Sage.

Steil, J. M. (1997). *Marital equality: Its relationship to the well-being of husbands and wives.* Thousand Oaks, CA: Sage.

Stone, S. (1982, December). Progress in documentation: Humanities scholars' information needs and uses. *Journal of Documentation 38,* 292–313.

Strauss, A., Schatzman, L., Ehrlich, D., Bucher, R., and Sabshin, M. (1963). The hospital and its negotiated order. In E. Freidson (Ed.), *The hospital in modern society.* New York: The Free Press.

Strauss, D. (1978). *Negotiations: Varieties, contexts, processes, and social order.* San Francisco, CA: Jossey-Bass.

Tierney, W. G., and Bensimon, E. M. (1996). *Promotion and tenure: Community and socialization in academe.* Albany, NY: State University of New York Press.

Toutkoushian, R. K. (1998). Racial and marital status differences in faculty pay. *Journal of Higher Education, 69*(5), 513–541.

Trautvetter, L. C. (1999). Experiences of women, experiences of men. In R.J. Menges and associates, *Faculty in new jobs: A guide to settling in, becoming established, and building support.* San Francisco: Jossey-Bass.

Ward, K. B., Gast, J., and Grant, L. (1992). Visibility and dissemination of women's and men's sociological scholarship. *Social Problems, 39*(3), 291–298.

Ward, K. B., and Grant, L. (1996). Gender and academic publishing. In J. Smart (Ed.), *Higher education: Handbook of theory and research, vol. 12* (pp. 172–212). Edison, NJ: Agathon.

Wells, W. P., and Pelz, D. C. (1966). Groups. In D. C. Pelz and F. M. Andrews *Scientists in organizations* (pp. 240–260). New York: Wiley.

Wenneras, C., and Wold, A. (1997, May 22). Nepotism and sexism in peer review. *Nature, 387*, 341–343.

Williams, R., and Blackburn, R. T. (1988). Mentoring and faculty productivity. *Nursing Education, 5*, 204–209.

Wilson, R. (1996, September 20). Weary of commuter marriages, more couples in academe make career sacrifices to be together. *Chronicle of Higher Education, XLIII*(4), A10–A11.

Wilson, R. (1998, April 17). When officemates are also roommates. *Chronicle of Higher Education, 44*(2), A–12.

Wilson, R. (1999, June 25). Timing is everything: Academe's annual baby boom. *Chronicle of Higher Education, XLV*(42), A14–A15.

Wolf-Wendal, L. E., Twombly, S., and Rice, S. (1998, November). Dual career couples: How institutions are keeping them together. Unpublished paper presented at the annual meeting of the Association for the Study of Higher Education. Miami, FL.

Xie, Y., and Shauman, K. A. (1998). Sex differences in research productivity: New evidence about an old puzzle. *American Sociological Review, 63*, 847–870.

Zuckerman, H. (1991). The careers of men and women scientists: A review of current research. In H. Zuckerman, J. R. Cole, and J. T. Bruer (Eds.), *The outer circle* (pp. 27–56). New York: Norton.

Contributors

Ann E. Austin is an Associate Professor in the Higher, Adult, and Lifelong Education (HALE) program in the Department of Educational Administration at Michigan State University. During 1998 she was a Fulbright Fellow in South Africa, where she studied transformation in higher education in postapartheid South Africa. Professor Austin's research interests concern faculty careers, roles, and professional development; organizational change and transformation in higher education; the improvement of teaching and learning processes; and issues concerning work and workplaces in academe. Dr. Austin has authored and coauthored numerous chapters and articles, as well as several books and monographs, including *Faculty Collaboration: Enhancing the Quality of Scholarship and Teaching* (coauthored with Roger Baldwin, 1991).

Elizabeth G. Creamer is an Associate Professor in Women's Studies and an adjunct in Higher Education and Student Affairs at Virginia Polytechnic and State University in Blacksburg, Virginia. Creamer spent the first 15 years of her career as an administrator, working first in financial aid and later in academic advising administration. She is the author of more than 30 book chapters and refereed journal articles, as well as the 1998 book *Assessing Faculty Publishing Productivity: Issues of Equity*. Her research interests are on the topics of gender differences in the correlates of faculty publishing productivity, diversity in higher education, and scholarly collaboration.

Stacey Floyd-Thomas is an Assistant Professor of Religion and Interdisciplinary Studies in the Center for Interdisciplinary Studies at Virginia Polytechnic Institute and State University. She is the cofounder of the Black Religious Scholars Group, a national organization of black scholars in religion that focuses on reconciling black academics' work to the task of empowering the black church and community. As a Christian/social/womanist ethicist, Professor Floyd-Thomas's research interests concern developing metaethnography and other social scientific methods for liberating the victims of race, class, and gender oppression. She is presently working on a manuscript tentatively entitled *Racial Bodies and Foresaken Souls: Race, Sex, and the War between Religion and Education*.

Laura Irwin is a doctoral student in counseling and personnel services at the University of Maryland, College Park, where she serves as the coordinator for career development courses sponsored by the Career Center at the University of Maryland. Her research interests include the career development of women, women's studies, and issues affecting Latinas at predominantly white institutions. She received her B.A. and M.Ed. from Frostburg State University. She is an active member of ACPA and NASPA and the proud mother of a two-year-old daughter.

Yvonna S. Lincoln is Professor of Higher Education and head of the Department of Education at Texas A&M University. Her research interests are in the topics of higher education research, organizational analysis, and program evaluation. She is the author of numerous publications, including groundbreaking work on alternative research paradigms. She has authored or coauthored numerous books, including a coedited book with Norman Denzin, *Handbook of Qualitative Research*, that is a widely used textbook in research classes. Lincoln has served as president of both the American Educational Research Association and the Association for the Study of Higher Education. She is the recipient of a number of prestigious research awards.

Jane W. Loeb, a psychologist, is a professor of educational psychology at the University of Illinois at Urbana-Champaign, where she also served for many years as an administrator. Her administrative positions have included Vice Chancellor for Undergraduate Education and Director of Admissions and Records. Her research focuses on equity issues in higher education, including equitable admission practices, access and success of minority students, and the role and status of women on the faculty, and reflects a concern for policy implications. Her coedited book with Marianne A. Ferber, *Academic Couples: Problems and Promises* (1997), addresses both individual professional outcomes and institutional policy issues concerning the hiring of academic couples in higher education. Her monograph, *Academic Standards in Higher Education* (1992), examines the interplay of student preparation for postsecondary education with curriculum, standards, and outcomes of college.

Peter Magolda is an Associate Professor in Miami University's Department of Educational Leadership. He teaches inquiry and educational anthropology courses in the College Student Personnel program. His research interests include college students' rites of passage and qualitative program evaluation.

Jeffrey F. Milem joined the faculty of the College of Education at the University of Maryland in the fall of 1998 after spending five years in the Department of Educational Leadership at Peabody College of Vanderbilt University. He has an extensive background in higher education, having spent the past 20 years working as an administrator, researcher, and teacher. Jeff received his B.A. from Michigan State University, his M.Ed. from the University of Vermont, and his Ph.D. from UCLA. His research interests focus on the impact of college on students, racial dynamics in higher education, the educational outcomes of diversity, and the condition and status of the professorate. He is the author of many book chapters and manuscripts that appear in the *Journal of Higher Education, Sociology of Education, Research in Higher Education,* the *Review of Higher Education, Higher Education: Handbook of Theory and Research, ASHE-ERIC Higher Education Report Series,* and the *Journal of College Student Development.*

Joe Sherlin is a doctoral candidate in college student personnel administration at the University of Maryland, College Park. He serves as an assistant organizational development specialist in the Office for Continuous Quality Improvement at the University of Maryland. His major research interests focus on student retention and first-generation college students. Joe received his B.S. in English Education from the University of Tennessee at Knoxville and his M.A. in higher education and student affairs from Ohio State University. Prior to enrolling at the University of Maryland, Joe worked in residence life at Xavier University in Cincinnati, Ohio.

Index

www.ingramcontent.com/pod-product-compliance
Ingram Content Group UK Ltd.
Pitfield, Milton Keynes, MK11 3LW, UK
UKHW041839280225
455677UK00005B/34